JOHN FORD AND THE TRADITIONAL MORAL ORDER

MARK STAVIG, currently Assistant
Professor of English at the University of Wisconsin, is the editor of the
Crofts Classics *'Tis Pity She's a
Whore*. He holds graduate degrees
from Oxford and Princeton and has
done post-doctoral work at Harvard.

MARK STAVIG

JOHN FORD

and the

Traditional Moral Order

1968

THE UNIVERSITY OF WISCONSIN PRESS

MADISON, MILWAUKEE, AND LONDON

Published by the University of Wisconsin Press
Madison, Milwaukee, and London
U.S.A.: Box 1379, Madison, Wisconsin, 53701
U.K.: 27–29 Whitfield Street, London W.1
Copyright © 1968 by the Regents of the University of Wisconsin
All rights reserved
Printed in the United States of America by
Kingsport Press, Inc., Kingsport, Tennessee
Library of Congress Catalog Card Number 68–14030

For my parents
Lawrence M. and Cora Hjertaas Stavig

PREFACE

No sound modern collected edition of either Ford's plays or his non-dramatic work exists. A recent flurry of editorial activity suggests, however, that we may not have to wait too long for this deficiency to be remedied. Recent editions of individual Ford plays include *'Tis Pity She's a Whore*, ed. N. W. Bawcutt (1966), and *Perkin Warbeck*, ed. Donald Anderson (1965), in the Regents Renaissance Drama Series; *The Broken Heart*, ed. Brian Morris (1965), in The New Mermaids; and this writer's *'Tis Pity She's a Whore* (1966), in Crofts Classics. Recent unpublished dissertations include editions of *Love's Sacrifice*, ed. Herbert Wilson Hoskins, Jr. (Columbia University, 1963); *Love's Sacrifice*, *The Lady's Trial*, and *The Queen*, ed. Joe Andrews Sutfin (Vanderbilt University, 1964); and *The Nondramatic Works of John Ford*, ed. Frederick M. Burelbach, Jr. (Harvard University, 1965).

My references to Ford's early prose and poetry are to the original editions, which I have consulted in xerographic reproductions. For Ford's plays, I have used the microcard reproductions of the quartos in *Three Centuries of Drama: English*. Since the edition of the plays by Bang and De Vocht (Louvain, 1908, 1927) is a facsimile reprint edition, this procedure should be convenient for most readers. As an aid to readers using modern editions, I have included act and scene references for my quotations. These references, together with the signature numbers from the original published versions, follow the quotations parenthetically.

I have adhered faithfully to the punctuation and spelling of the original editions, with the following exceptions: the long ſ has been replaced by the modern letter s, and the letters u and v and i and j, which are often used interchangeably in seventeenth-century texts, have been made to conform to modern usage. In addition, the spelling of the titles of Ford's plays and of the names of some characters has been modernized in accordance with established practice.

Parenthetical references, in Chapter IV and subsequently, to Burton's *The Anatomy of Melancholy* are by volume and page number to the edition of A. R. Shilleto, listed in the bibliography. For the convenience of readers using other editions I include references to partition, section, member, and subsection.

A bibliography has been included primarily to facilitate short references in my notes. I have listed there only the editions of Ford's works to which I refer for quotations and scholarly works which are cited in more than one chapter. All other works are cited in full at the first reference to them. The following abbreviations have been adopted for certain titles cited in text and notes:

Works by Ford
BH	*The Broken Heart*
CBS	*Christ's Bloody Sweat*
FM	*Fame's Memorial*
GM	*The Golden Mean*
HT	*Honor Triumphant*
LL	*A Line of Life*
LM	*The Lover's Melancholy*
LS	*Love's Sacrifice*
TP	*'Tis Pity She's a Whore*

Other
AM	Robert Burton, *The Anatomy of Melancholy*

My debts to others are many and great. The Danforth Foundation financed my graduate education and provided me with a year at Harvard in 1963–64 that enriched my understanding of the theological, philosophical, and cultural background of the period. Donald Fryxell of Augustana College (S.D.) and W. W. Robson of Lincoln College, Oxford University, introduced me to this period and are responsible for my initial interest in the subject of this book. Gerald Eades Bentley of Princeton University supervised this study in its dissertation form and has been a mine of scholarly wisdom and general good counsel through all of its stages. The late Edward Hubler also provided a helpful reading of the dissertation. D. W. Robertson, Jr., and Alan Downer of Princeton answered specific queries; more important they contributed to the intellectual atmosphere which gave this study its original impetus. The late Helen White, Madeleine Doran, Mark Eccles, A. B. Chambers, Standish Henning, Robert Kimbrough, and Eric Rothstein, all of the University of Wisconsin, have read the manuscript at one stage or another and offered useful advice. I am particularly indebted to Miss Doran and Mr. Rothstein for their detailed and extensive criticisms. Longer standing debts need not be explained here. One is expressed in the dedication. Another is to my wife Donna, who was formerly my typist and continues to be my best critic.

M. S.

Madison, Wisconsin
April, 1967

CONTENTS

INTRODUCTION

There is little chance of ever constructing more than a bare
outline of John Ford's life.[1] He was the second son of a
well-established and fairly wealthy Devonshire country
gentleman, was baptized on April 17, 1586, was admitted
to the Middle Temple, with which many Fords were associated, on November 16, 1602, was expelled for not paying
his buttery bill in 1605/6, was readmitted on June 10,
1608, was involved in a dispute about wearing hats in hall
in 1617, and was bequeathed ten pounds when his father died
in 1610 and twenty pounds a year in exchange for some prop-
erty when his elder brother died in 1616. There the record
stops. Whether he was married, whether he had a profession besides his writing, when he died are all unknown.
About all that can be said with any assurance about his life
is that there is very likely some connection between the solid
family background and the assured, aristocratic manner
which is so evident throughout Ford's work. We probably
will never know to what extent Ford was dependent on
writing for his livelihood, but younger sons of the gentry
usually had to make their own way, and the terms of the
two wills do not suggest great affluence. Since Ford did not
write at all regularly before the 1620's, it is reasonable to
assume that he must have had some other source of income

during this period. If the long association with the Middle Temple means anything, it may be that he did legal work of some kind; but speculation is fruitless.

Ford's literary career can be conveniently divided into three periods—non-dramatic writing (1606–1620), dramatic writing in collaboration (c1620–c1625), and independent dramatic writing (c1625–c1639).[2] The non-dramatic work—three prose pamphlets, two long poems, and a number of shorter poems—has little intrinsic merit but provides some knowledge of the young Ford's interests and concerns. The extent of Ford's collaborative work cannot be finally determined, but we know that he had a part in *The Witch of Edmonton* (with Dekker and Rowley) and *The Sun's Darling* (with Dekker) and in three works no longer extant, *A Late Murder of the Son upon the Mother* (with Webster, Dekker, and Rowley), *The Bristowe Merchant* (with Dekker), and *The Fairy Knight* (with Dekker). In his independent period Ford wrote three tragedies, *'Tis Pity She's a Whore, Love's Sacrifice,* and *The Broken Heart;* a history play, *Perkin Warbeck;* and three tragicomedies, *The Lover's Melancholy, The Lady's Trial,* and *The Fancies, Chaste and Noble.* Another tragicomedy, *The Queen,* is also generally attributed to him, and there is some evidence of other plays no longer extant. *The Lover's Melancholy* and *The Broken Heart* were written for the King's Men at the Blackfriars and the other five plays certainly by Ford were for Beeston's companies at the Phoenix.

Ford's seventeenth-century reputation is obscure. Allusions to him are few and, with a couple of exceptions, inconsequential; the only evidence of his literary contacts is found in the prefatory verses which he wrote and which were written for him. They suggest what would be expected—associations with the professional playwrights Webster, Shirley, Massinger, Brome, and Jonson. Ford's dedications are either to great figures of the realm or to now obscure personal friends and suggest little concerning his contemporary stature except that he wanted to be regarded as a detached and honorable scholar rather than as a working dramatist.

The history of Ford criticism has been controversial because of the perhaps inevitable variety of reactions to Ford's best-known works, his tragedies. Nineteenth-century impressionistic criticism of Ford divided into two streams, which may be characterized as the Lamb school and the Hazlitt school. Hazlitt and his followers think of Ford as a decadent romantic who delighted in melodramatic plots, licentious scenes, and revolt against the established moral order. The Lamb group agrees that Ford is at times confused in his moral views but argues that at his best he is a profound and objective analyst of human behavior who portrays a higher morality that stresses the elevating effect of love and the nobility of endurance in time of adversity.[3] Both Lamb and Hazlitt have had numerous supporters in the succeeding years. Among those who follow the general lines of Hazlitt's view have been Gifford, Hartley Coleridge, Saintsbury, Ward, Lowell, Schelling, Thorndike, Neilson, and Tucker Brooke.[4] At their best these studies represent what might be called a common-sense reaction to the behavior of Ford's characters, but too often they are merely expressions of the writers' puritanical opposition to what they regard as sympathy for immorality. Noteworthy among the nineteenth-century followers of Lamb are Swinburne and Havelock Ellis.[5] Both express great admiration for Ford's incisive psychological analyses and contend that Ford is quite different from the other dramatists of his time. Havelock Ellis argues that Ford is closer in spirit to Stendhal and Flaubert than to his contemporaries.[6]

The first attempt to provide a systematic statement of Ford's ethical thought was made by S. P. Sherman.[7] Sherman agrees with Hazlitt that the plays deal with daring subject matter in an unnatural way, but he seizes on Ford's alleged obliquity and attempts to make a consistent system out of it. Sherman's study is valuable in that it indicates the conclusions which logically follow from the interpretations of the tragedies as expressions of Ford's sympathy for his sinful heroes and heroines, but he ignores the evidence both in the drama and in the non-dramatic works that Ford was not an opponent of traditional morality. Most later Ford scholars have been critical of Sherman's attempt to make a rebel out of Ford, but his analysis of Ford's

Platonic bias and of his sympathy for the victims of passion is still widely influential in a modified form.[8]

Partly in reaction against Sherman's doctrinaire study, many have attempted to clarify the vague and impressionistic terms in which Lamb, Swinburne, and Havelock Ellis admired Ford's modernity and fine psychological insight. Generally speaking these scholars, realizing that Sherman's interpretation cannot be applied to all of Ford's work, have argued that Ford was interested in creating effective theater, that he was more concerned about the aesthetic than the moral effect of the plays, and that he avoided moral judgment while making objective analyses of human passions. In so far as they consider the morality of Ford's plays they arrive at a position similar to that of Lamb over a century earlier. M. Joan Sargeaunt in her influential and in many ways excellent book on Ford falls back upon Lamb in summarizing the reasons for admiring Ford:

What is it then that seems to Ford's admirers to give his plays their real and permanent value? For what reward may one look among that welter of melodrama and tomfoolery, of murder and rape and incest? The answer was given more than a century ago by Charles Lamb, and it is simple enough. It lies in Ford's extraordinary power to make us acutely aware even in the midst of depravity and horror of the greatness of the spirit of man. It is this theme and this alone that has absorbed all his creative energy; if this solitary jewel is lost amongst the shoddy assortment of rubbish that surrounds it, there is nothing further to seek.[9]

The books by Miss Bradbrook, Miss Ellis-Fermor, H. J. Oliver, and Clifford Leech should be considered along with the Sargeaunt study because they all agree with Miss Sargeaunt that Ford was a sensitive analyst of psychological problems who was somewhat confined by his need to write for an audience that wanted excitement.[10] In her short section on Ford, Miss Bradbrook makes few claims for his drama. Despite an approving reference to Lamb and Swinburne [11] and admiration for portions of *'Tis Pity, The Broken Heart,* and *Perkin Warbeck,* she feels that Ford's drama is decadent and that much of his work is seriously flawed. In her chapter on Ford, Miss Ellis-Fermor is much more enthusiastic. She contends that Ford's leading characters transcend conventional divisions into good and evil and dismisses the weaknesses in the plays as inevitable, since Ford

whether in his exploration of the abnormal or of the less well understood roots of normal experience, prefers generally to walk where few or none have walked before him; if his judgement staggers for a moment or his inspiration flags, the result is confusion and contradiction; he cannot fall back upon a tried convention or upon deductions from recorded experience. Small wonder if in these little known territories an explorer, in the absence of previous records, is now and again for a time bewildered.[12]

This view of Ford's place in dramatic history is shared by H. J. Oliver, although he is more specific in his criticism of individual plays than Miss Ellis-Fermor. Oliver thinks that Ford's interest was in the analysis of subtle and unusual aspects of human behavior but that he was not independent enough to establish a new tradition of psychological drama and consequently compromised with results that are satisfactory for no one.[13] Although Oliver begins with the Lamb school's assumptions about what Ford was attempting, he avoids the usual vague appreciations of the fineness of sentiments of the Fordian heroes and heroines and is actually much closer to Hazlitt in his criticisms of what he regards as the melodramatic excesses of *The Broken Heart* and *Love's Sacrifice*.[14] Clifford Leech's book is largely a restatement and extension of the positions developed by the earlier critics in the Lamb tradition, although he does include a section on the debt of *'Tis Pity* to Jacobean tragedy. Leech argues that the Ford of *'Tis Pity* "is sharply aware of sin and by no means an active unbeliever in the Christian cosmology." [15] But his evaluations of the major characters of the three tragedies are largely the same as those of Oliver, Miss Sargeaunt, and Miss Ellis-Fermor:

For Ford there is no protestation to be made: the march of events is of course irresistible, it is not to be regretted: the characters who win his praise are those who do not attempt resistance but step grandly on to the scaffold. In *'Tis Pity* he could be in two minds about Giovanni. He is not in two minds about Bianca or Calantha or Warbeck or the other leading characters of these plays: they are all securely among his 'elect.' [16]

Another study which sees Ford as a modern before his time
is a brilliant recent article by R. J. Kaufmann on "Ford's
Tragic Perspective." [17] Kaufmann argues that Ford's habit
of mind was more like that of Henry James or the existen-
tialists than like that of his fellow dramatists or the ethical thinkers of his own time. A tendency present in all of
these studies in the Lamb tradition is to suggest that Ford,
while able to provide profound insights into the sources
of human behavior, was too often unable to unite the pieces
into coherent works of art. Miss Sargeaunt states the argument clearly:

If a deep insight into the human mind and a representation of the
diverse qualities which men and women share by reason of their common humanity can give a play some measure of success, it is achieved
by even the worst of Ford's; but if the Aristotelian canon that plot
is the most important element of drama is accepted without compromise, much of his work must be regarded as a failure.[18]

In recent years many scholars, mostly Americans, have
attempted to establish the nature of Ford's indebtedness to
the ideas of his time and particularly to Burtonian psychology. Mary Cochnower, Lawrence Babb, S. Blaine Ewing,
G. F. Sensabaugh, and Robert Davril have all tried to illuminate Ford's drama by seeing it in relation to contemporary attitudes.[19] Miss Cochnower's book, a description of
Ford's ideas on various subjects from love to religion, suffers from a rather mechanical method which prevents her
from drawing many conclusions from her material. Babb's
study of melancholy, based on his unpublished dissertation
on Ford, is an excellent description of love-melancholy as
disease, but he makes no thoroughgoing attempt even in his
thesis to apply his material to a critical revaluation of the
plays. Ewing's book is an attempt to indicate the specific
nature of the melancholy of the characters, and the critical
comments are largely derivative. Sensabaugh has read
widely in the period, but his conclusion that Ford was both
a scientific determinist and an outspoken advocate of individual rights is, I think, no longer tenable.[20] Davril attempts
to define the importance of melancholy in the Elizabethan
drama and more particularly in Ford's plays and provides

a detailed discussion of various aspects of Ford's characterization, themes, and technique, but he does not utilize the
background material for a systematic analysis of the plays.
Despite the absence of much detailed criticism in any of
these studies, they have provided much valuable information about Ford and his time and some illuminating critical
comments.

A new and, I think, promising direction in Ford criticism
is suggested by the chapters on Ford in the recent studies of
Jacobean tragedy by Irving Ribner and Robert Ornstein.[21]
Both stress the traditional vision of Jacobean dramatists:
their age was still dominated by Christian rather than secular philosophy; their techniques were more symbolic than
realistic, and their interests were more thematic than psychological. Suggestions of this approach may be found in
Clifford Leech's book, particularly in his discussion of *'Tis
Pity,* as well as in Fredson Bowers' treatment of the revenge elements in the plays in his *Elizabethan Revenge
Tragedy.*[22] There are significant differences in the approaches of each of these scholars: Ornstein, for example,
would see these Jacobean dramatists as less pessimistic, less
philosophical, and less medieval than would Ribner. But
they all share a belief in the need for scholarship that is
historical in its awareness that the Jacobean period differs
from our own in certain fundamental respects and still critical in its close attention to the plays themselves. When
judged from this perspective, it can be seen that critics have
been too little aware of the revised estimates of Ford's debt
to contemporary thought while scholars in most cases have
not applied the results of their research to the plays except
in a superficial way.[23]

The intention of the present study is to provide a historical but critical evaluation of all of Ford's work in the hope
that some of the still much disputed questions about his
contribution may be clarified. Ford's early non-dramatic
work is filled with the same themes—love, honor, resolution, ambition—that pervade his plays. In the first two
chapters, I suggest what we can learn from these early
works about Ford's philosophical assumptions and literary
techniques. When Ford turned to the theater, he wrote in

collaboration with the established professional playwrights Dekker, Rowley, and Webster. In Chapter III, I consider Ford's work with them and his debt to the Jacobean theater as well as the significance of the changing theatrical and intellectual atmosphere in Caroline England. In the remainder of the study, I analyze Ford's independent plays in the hope that the techniques of historical criticism can elucidate their structure and meaning. We can never experience the plays in the same way that Ford's Caroline audience did; but the more we can learn about the methods of Ford's theater and the attitudes of Ford and his audience, the closer we will be to the plays themselves.

JOHN FORD AND THE TRADITIONAL MORAL ORDER

I

Attitudes toward Love
in Ford's Early Work

In 1606, when Ford was just twenty years old, he published two works that provide us with a glimpse of his already characteristic interests and methods as a writer. Both works are topical: *Fame's Memorial* eulogizes a recently dead earl, and *Honor Triumphant* deals with a challenge for a tournament set up for the visit of the King of Denmark to England. The topicality of the subjects and the somewhat naive tone of unrestrained excitement in both works suggest that Ford was eagerly trying to establish himself as a professional writer; it may be that there is some connection between this new career and his expulsion from the Middle Temple in 1605/6. No matter what the impetus, Ford succeeded in finding subjects that were congenial to his aristocratic and ambitious temperament. Even though the works are not particularly distinguished, they do show how the young Ford handled many of the themes that were to concern him throughout his career.

Fame's Memorial is an elegiac poem in memory of the Earl of Devonshire and his love for Penelope Rich.[1] It contains eleven hundred and sixty-nine lines, mostly in seven-line stanzas, and is of very uneven quality, as we might expect since Ford was so young at the time. Devon-

3

shire and Penelope are praised for every conceivable virtue, and their detractors are severely criticized for not having recognized the couple's selfless and dedicated devotion to each other and to morality. Since there was considerable controversy over the morality and legality of the Earl's marriage to Penelope, the subject of the poem has been of much interest to scholars studying Ford's views of love. The usual explanation has been that Ford's sympathy for the lovers is an indication of his lack of respect for traditional morality,[2] but I believe that a closer investigation of the poem and of the attitude of society toward the marriage shows that far too much has been made of the matter.

Charles Blount, after 1594 Lord Mountjoy and after 1604 the Earl of Devonshire, became Penelope's lover sometime in the late 1580's while she was still married to Lord Rich.[3] Penelope had four children by Lord Rich after their marriage in 1581; then she had one by Blount in 1589, another by Lord Rich in 1590, and finally four more by Blount after 1590. Although Penelope's new life and family with Blount were common knowledge, Lord Rich accepted the situation, perhaps in part because the influential Earl of Essex was Penelope's brother. At about the time of the triumphant return of Mountjoy from his victories in Ireland in 1603, Lord and Lady Rich initiated a divorce action. They obtained a divorce in the ecclesiastical courts, with the final decree, granted on November 14, 1605, stating specifically that neither party should remarry while the other lived. Mountjoy and Penelope were married on December 26, 1605, with William Laud, later Archbishop, performing the ceremony even though the legality of the marriage was highly questionable. Inevitably there was a controversy. Mountjoy wrote a tract defending the marriage by both theological and legal arguments.[4] Laud, on the other hand, repented of his action and became an active critic of the marriage.

In his book on Mountjoy, Cyril Falls concludes that there was some opposition to the marriage but that it has been exaggerated: although much of the evidence is unreliable "the combination deserves some respect. It is reinforced by Devonshire's tract, and by references to criticism in the obituary tributes of the poets Daniel and Ford. The conclusion must be that the King was in fact offended, that Charles and Penelope were blamed and perhaps by some treated coldly, but that the suggestion of their being sent to Coventry is almost certainly exaggerated." [5] Falls has collected evidence which suggests that they were not ostracized politically or socially before or after their marriage. Before the marriage they were frequently together in society; after the marriage Devonshire continued to be appointed to various committees of the House of Lords, one of them "to consider laws for the preservation of religion." [6] On March 10, 1606, he was excused from attendance at the House of Lords because he was with the king; as Falls says, this "would seem to reduce the weight of the royal displeasure and the social obloquy to relatively small proportions." [7] After Devonshire's death Penelope was "daily visited by the greatest in the land." [8] With our incomplete information a final evaluation of Penelope and Mountjoy is impossible, but it does seem clear that they should be seen less as daring illicit lovers than as two basically moral people trying to live with outmoded divorce laws. At least we can be more sympathetic when we remember the unhappiness of Penelope's first marriage, the difficulty of obtaining a divorce that would permit their remarriage, and the success of their relationship over a period of some fifteen years. When they finally did decide to marry, they undoubtedly realized that there would be a furor but seem to have thought that legitimatizing their five children was worth some unpleasantness. The quality of Mountjoy's mind and the seriousness with which he approached moral questions is suggested by his "Apology" for his marriage, "a notable piece of casuistical argument, forcible and pregnant." [9] That Ford eulogizes Mountjoy and Penelope certainly should not be taken as indicating his instinctive sympathy for passionate lovers and rebels against the moral order.

Perhaps the best evidence for the morality of Ford's attitude is the poem itself. Ford stresses that the Earl was a model of virtuous behavior and contrasts Mountjoy's high moral standards with the lax morality of the rest of the court. No doubt much of this praise is conventional, but the form that it takes is significant. Mountjoy is portrayed as an ideal gentleman who is successful both in the gallantries of court life and in the active life outside the court:

> *Mountjoy* (the mounting joy of heavens perfection)
> Was all a man should be in such an age,
> Not voyd of lov's sence, nor yoakt in subjection
> [O]f servile passion, theame for every stage. (B4)

Ford says that "daliance in chambers, / Becomes a perfect courtier" (B4), and that Mountjoy knew "How Ladyes shold be lov'd, serv'd, wood and woon" (B4); but he also says that Mountjoy was "not wholy bent / To wanton, sicke, lascivious, amours ease" (B4). Later idle passion is explicitly condemned and reason praised:

> Let smooth-chind Amorists be cloyde in play,
> And surfet on the bane of hatefull leisure,
> Let idle howres follies youth betray,
> Unto the idle shame of boundlesse pleasure,
>   Great *Mountjoy* saw such loosnes of the witty
>   Which seing did not more disdain then pity. (B4ᵛ)

The conventionality in the praise of rational love in these passages is a refutation of those who see the poem as glorifying passionate love.

The poem is of greatest interest when Ford deals with subjects that he considers again in his later works. He criticizes courtiers whose smooth words do not reflect an underlying virtue:

> Double toung-oyled courtiers whose neat phrases,
> Do modell foorth your wittes maturity,
> In honied speeches and slick-thoughted graces,
> Cloking our soules in sins obscurity,
> Yet fan your lightnesse in security. (C2)

Ford scorns the ambitions of "parasites and fawning sycophaunts" (D3), and he insists that he himself is above the common concern for advancement and praise (E1). He sees death as the destroyer of all the things of this world: "Ambition, Empire, glory, hopes and joy / For ever dye, for death will all destroye" (G3). But he also mentions a life beyond the grave (G3).

If we attribute any significance to Ford's choice of subject, we might speculate that he was genuinely interested in the plight of two moral people in conflict with society's narrow concept of marriage. If we judge by this poem, Ford's view of the institution of marriage was liberal in that he did not condemn Mountjoy and Penelope's various evasions of the traditional regulations on marriage. It may be, however, that Ford wrote the poem simply because he wanted to flatter Penelope for some reason, perhaps to get patronage for himself; or perhaps he saw the recent death and controversy as providing a topic for a poem that might sell. But no matter how we explain his choice of subject, there is no basis for claiming that the poem is a glorification of romantic passion.

In *Honor Triumphant,* a prose pamphlet on love, Ford presents a series of seemingly outrageous propositions and then proceeds to prove them by arguments that are unlikely if not preposterous. The tone of the title accurately reflects the tone of the pamphlet as a whole: "Honor Triumphant. Or The Peeres Challenge, by Armes defensible, at Tilt, *Turney, and Barriers.* In Honor of all faire Ladies, and in defence of these foure positions following. 1. *Knights in Ladies service have no free-will.* 2. *Beauty is the mainteiner of valour.* 3. *Faire Lady was never false.* 4. *Perfect Lovers are onely wise.* Mainteined by Arguments" (A2). Reactions to the work have been varied. S. P. Sherman took it quite seriously and contended that "The ardor and earnestness of Ford's style suggest that the leading propositions of this pamphlet were to him not merely a set of pretty paradoxes, but a religion." [10] Although most later scholars have seen that Sherman takes the pamphlet too seriously, no one has questioned Ford's sympathy for the praise of women.[11] No one has proposed what seems to me the most plausible interpretation, that Ford was being ironic and was poking fun at the arguments that he seems to be praising.

Much of the confusion has arisen because the work has not been examined carefully in its historical context. James I's brother-in-law, Christian IV, the King of Denmark, was to visit England in July and August of 1606, and a jousting tournament was planned for his entertainment. On June 1, 1606, about a month and a half before the king's arrival, four earls issued a challenge designed to create a chivalric atmosphere for the tournament. Two copies of the challenge are extant.[12] I quote from a letter sent to William Drummond of Hawthornden:

> Knowing the delight your Lordship was wont to take in the sports of Court, whether as Beholder or Actor; I thought I should not importune your Honour in sending you the Challenge of the Errant Knights, proclaimed with sound of trumpet before the Palace-gate of Greenwich.

The challenge itself follows:

> To all honourable Men of Arms and Knights Adventurers of hereditary note and exemplary nobleness, that for most maintainable actions do weild their swords or lances in the quest of glory.
>
> Right, brave, and chevalrous; wheresoever through the world we Four Knights Errant, denominated of the *Fortunate Island,* servants of the Destinies, awaken your sleeping courages with *Mavortial* greetings: Know ye that our Sovereign Lady and Mistriss, Mother of the Fates and Empress of high achievements, revolving of late the Adamantine leafs of her eternal volumes, and finding in them that the triumphal times were now at hand, wherein the marvellous adventures of the *Lucent Pillar* should be revealed to the wonder of times and men, (as *Merlin,* Secretary to the most inward designs, did long since prophecy,) hath therefore (most deeply weighing with herself how necessary it is that sound opinions should prepare the way to so unheard of a marvel) been pleased to command us her voluntary, but ever most humble votaries, solemnly to publish and maintain, by all the allowed ways of knightly arguing, these four indisputable propositions following: 1. That in service of Ladies no Knight hath free-will. 2. That it is Beauty maintaineth the world in Valour. 3. That no fair Lady was ever false. 4. That none can be perfectly wise but Lovers. Against which, or any of which, if any of you shall dare to argue at point of launce and sword in honorable lists before rarest beauty and best judgments: then again know you, that we the said Four Champions shall, by the high sufferance of Heaven and virtue of our knightly valour, be ready, at the valley of Mirefleure, constantly to answer and make perfect our imposed undertakings against all such of you as shall within fourty days after the first publick intimation of our universal challenge, arrive to attend the glorious issue of the thrice famous adventure of the *Lucent Pillar,* in which prizes are reserved

and ordained (by the happy fate of our Country and Crown) for three several succeeding days of trial at Tilt, Tourney, and at Barriers. The Maintainers of the four positions are,

> The Earl of Lenox the first.
> The Earl of Arundel the second.
> The Earl of Pembroke the third.
> The Earl of Montgomery the fourth.

The letter continues:

> The King of Denmark is expected here daily, for whose entertainment this challenge appeareth to be given forth; who, if his courage answer his fame, will not be an idle onlooker to such pastimes, which I would wish your Lordship to see, at least *in speculo constellato*.[13]

It should be apparent that the tone of the challenge is frivolous. There is no indication that the earls or the ladies took the propositions at all seriously or that they wanted to do more than establish a chivalric atmosphere which would provide a framework for the tournament and an opportunity for elaborate compliments to the ladies of the court.[14]

   Ford's pamphlet, listed in the Stationers' Register for July 25, 1606, [15] was apparently an attempt to take advantage of the publicity that the challenge must have been receiving. One would naturally expect that the pamphlet would be in the playful vein of the challenge itself; and in fact it is. Ford composes an elaborate dedication to the Countess of Pembroke and the Countess of Montgomery that parallels the challenge of the earls in its tone of exaggerated compliment: "To whom, (noble Countesses) should I dedicate the ornaments of love, and beauty? but to the beautifullest ornaments, worthy to be beloved" (A3–A3ᵛ). The humor of the pamphlet itself comes in poking fun at the Platonic doctrines that the earls have used for their challenge. No one would have been offended by the jibes at the challenge since no one would have taken them seriously in the first place. Ford adopts the persona of a completely serious advocate of the sovereignty of woman and then undercuts him by having him argue in ways that make his case ridiculous. The result is a humorous exposure of a position that no one has seriously proposed.
   Ford develops the first position, that *"Knights in Ladies*

service have no free-will," as a theological exposition of the
doctrines of the religion of love. In proving that the wise
knight will submit to his lady in all things, Ford's persona
misuses traditional religious beliefs so systematically that by
substituting 'God' for 'lady' in his arguments, one gets a
statement of orthodox Christian beliefs. Man was not
created to satisfy his own selfish desires but to glorify God
(his lady) in all that he does. The man who denies God (his
lady) lives in selfish misery, while the man who willingly
serves God (his lady) finds freedom both in the joy of
service and in being loosed from the bondage of selfishness.
All meaning in life comes from doing God's (his lady's)
will, and the true believer merits God's (his lady's) love by
doing battle in His (her) service. Man need not fear putting absolute trust in God (his lady) for God (his lady) is
good and will do nothing that is not in man's ultimate best
interests. The folly of substituting one's lady for God is
made even more obvious by carefully inserting in inappropriate places traditional religious diction and imagery
and ironic Biblical and mythological references and by using
throughout the argument a mock-serious style that gives the
entire work an air of humorous exaggeration. The point and
much of the humor come from the ironic contrast between
the persona's worship of woman and the traditional views
that woman is lower than man on the chain of being and
that only God should be worshiped. According to the Christian Platonism that even Ford's persona seems to support in
position four, adoration of a woman becomes idolatry unless
one realizes that her beauty is only a reflection of God's
beauty and loves her in the proper spirit of reason and
virtue.

Ford undercuts the elaborate pretensions of the persona
by having him use language that implies that love is physical
and sinful rather than spiritual. For example, in arguing
that man should do homage to woman, the persona claims
that if "the sensible touch of passion toucht them with the
feeling of a passionate sence" (B1), men would recognize
their obligation; later he states that "the lustre of her eyes,
and the glorie of her worth are of such unresistable a force,
as the weaknesse of his manhood, or the aptnesse of his

frailtie, are neither able to endure the ones reflection, or withstand the others temptation" (B1ᵛ). The use of punning references to sense and passion and of diction stressing "weaknesse," "frailtie," and "temptation" would be unlikely in even a half-serious advocacy of woman's sovereignty. Examples could be multiplied. To serve a woman is to partake of the "captived happinesse of love" (B1ᵛ) ; but Ford's readers would be expected to see that bondage to a woman is not likely to free one in the way that bondage to God does.

Ironic Biblical references also help to unmask the persona's virtuous pose. After his eloquent claim that *"to bee captived to beautie, is to bee free to virtue,"* the persona continues : "who would not put of an armour of hard steele and turne from his enemies, to be enchained in pleasure, and turne to a lady in a bed of soft downe?" (B2). This revelation of the decidedly physical basis of love is reinforced by the inverted echo of the arming of the Christian hero in Eph. 6:11–17. Later there is a parallel to the familiar Biblical passage about serving God or Mammon (Matt. 6:24) : "who can serve two Masters? who can be a master of himselfe, when he is a servant to his ladie? but either he scornes the humilitie due to her, or affects a singularitie to himselfe, if the one, he is no servant; if the other, an unfit lover" (B3 ᵛ). In another place the persona counters the traditional argument that a woman was responsible for Adam's fall by claiming that the fall was fortunate, not because it led to Christ, but because it led to glorified earthly love : "alas sillie betrayers of your owne follie? wretched blasphemers against the perfection of nature? can ye not or will yee not understand that the blessing of this fall, is salvation? assurance of heaven? certainty of joyes?" (B2ᵛ). To place woman in the role of Christ as the savior of mankind is obviously ironic, and Ford's reader might be expected to see that man's choice of the earthly "heaven" that woman offers is a repetition of Adam's sin in following Eve rather than God.

Ironic mythological references add to the humor. In submitting to woman, man gives up all "domination over his owne affections. . . . *Mars* throwes downe his weapons, and

Venus leads him captive" (B1ᵛ). The submission of Mars to Venus was a familiar Renaissance icon representing the loss of manliness through passion.[16] Later the persona quotes a ludicrous three-stanza poem on the love of Cupid for Psyche. Until the last stanza the poem seems suitably romantic, but then the crude physical basis for love is revealed: *"Alas, what is it then that men in bed/ Will not vow, urge, to gaine a maiden head"* (B2). In retrospect it becomes clear that the Cupid referred to is the blind Cupid who was often used as a symbol of lust.[17] Later the persona catalogues lovers who have fought for their ladies (a kind of parody of the listings of saints and others who have fought for the Lord). Among those listed are Paris, Troilus, and Pelops. Paris won Helen in the first place because of what many in the Renaissance regarded as his incorrect choice of Venus over Pallas Athene. The Trojan War was a direct result, and Paris' martial feats and his subsequent loss of life were viewed as necessary only because of his immoderate affection for Helen. Troilus also was a familiar image of the folly of love. He would "fight for *Cresseida*" (B4), but the reader of *Honor Triumphant* would have been quite certain that Cressida was not worth fighting for. The reference to Pelops' hazarding his life for Hippodamia is even more obviously ironic. Hippodamia was to be Pelops' bride if he could defeat her father, the king, in a chariot race. Rather than risk losing, Pelops bribed the king's driver to substitute an axle of wax for the regular axle. At the climax of the race the king's axle melted, and Pelops won the race and Hippodamia. This is the kind of noble feat that love provokes! [18]

Ford manages to get the opposite point of view directly stated by having the persona mention what opponents of woman say:

Then what man of reason is he, who would be so unreasonable in his owne desires, to wish himselfe obstinatly foolish; or thinke himselfe foolishlie wise: by containing his owne dissolute infranchisment, in the boundlesse limitts of his owne frantick wilfulnesse? such and of such nature are they, who in the rancorous spleenes of an unprevailing rancour, durst not onelie in the mallice of their tongues to speake, but in the venome of their hearts, to copy out whole pamphlets against the dignitie of the female sex. (B2–B2ᵛ)

The use of the appellation, "man of reason," and the exaggerated language that the persona employs to vilify his opponents should suggest to the reader that the attackers may be closer to the truth. But it would be wrong to conclude that Ford agrees with all that the opponents of love say. The persona's outspoken opposition to pamphlets attacking the role of the woman in society serves to dramatize his own strongly partisan views. The fun of both Ford's pamphlet and the challenge itself is better understood when viewed in the context of the pamphlet war,[19] but neither Ford nor the noblemen can be said to take sides. Rather they are all exploiting the debate for their own particular purposes.

In proving the second position, that *"Beautie is the Maintainer of Valour,"* Ford's persona cites examples which show quite convincingly that women cause men to fight. The question is how we are to regard the valor that results. The answer is easily found, for the argument is a *reductio ad absurdum* of the view that love of woman can lead to valor in men. The persona shows that men are by nature so frail and fearful that some "incitement to livelyhood of manhood" (C2) is necessary. Such "provocation" is provided by "Beautie: upon whose al-perfection, the greedy eye of desire (even in spirits of clay and mud) being fixt, hath stir'd up such a ravishment of possession, as they now esteeme all dangers weake; nay, all impossibilities facilities, to possesse it" (C2–C2 ᵛ). In one sentence ostensibly praising beauty Ford has managed to imply that it appeals only to "the greedy eye of desire" in creatures "of clay and mud," and that it leads to a state of "ravishment" in which a reasonable assessment of dangers is forgotten in unthinking passion.

The valorous actions that men carry out under the influence of beauty hardly support an elevated view of love. The first proof is that the seizure of the Sabine women by the Romans was accomplished and justified by violence, "insomuch as ever after betwixt these warlike Nations began both increase of hatred, and defiance of hostilitie" (C2). Obviously valor which leads to "increase of hatred, and defiance of hostilitie" is not good, and one might also question whether the seizure itself is an example of the noble valor that beauty should maintain.

Ford continues to associate love with ignoble passions. Men are very much deceived "who vainly imagine, that souldiers fight for spoile only; Generals hazard their persons for greedines; Sea-men traffique for avarice: Knights wander for prey, or that any jeopards his life, chiefely for lucre" (C2ᵛ). No! All of this evil is carried out so that the lady at home may be pleased: "and all spoyle that the souldier bleedes for, all the greedinesse that commaunders sweat for, all the avarice that the Marchant trades for, all the prey that the Knight adventures for, all the benefite that everie one and all of these hope, wish, pray, contend for, is the fruition of Beautie" (C3). When man is in love nothing will stop him:

Men in kindnesse are mutually lambs, but in corrivall-shipp of love, Lyons. Should I fight for my friend, I might be appeazed in my choller, but for my lady, I am inexorable.

Chalibs mihi circa pectus.

The teares of widows, the cries of babes, the condolement of Parents, the intreaties of Children, the wounds of the maimed, the wracke of the oppressed, cannot move pity in a steeled hart, which fights for report in the honor of his lady. (C4–C4ᵛ)

Unless these results are regarded as good, Ford's satiric intention must be granted. More ironic proof follows. The Turks' cruelty is explained as their desire to please their women, and Tamburlaine, the "savadgest monster of his time" (C4ᵛ), is said to have been motivated by his desire to please Zenocrate, who "infus'd strength into his armes" (C4ᵛ).

Once again, as in the first position, the views of the opponents of love are mentioned but opposed:

Beauty is the spur to *Honor; Honor* the serviceable attendant on Beauty, yet will some home-bred poring Academicke say, it is the only means to make a warrior a flat coward: for *Beauty* allures to delights,

delights to ease, ease consequently the fosterer to discouraged pusilla-nimity: but let such an unexperienced plodder knowe, it is as difficult for him to censure of courage, as it is easy for the couragious to scorne his censure, or indeed rather pittie his ridiculous folly in censuring. (D1)

By this time the reader should have no difficulty in seeing that Ford sympathizes with the common sense of the "home-bred poring Academicke."

In attempting to defend the third position, that *"Faire Ladie was never false,"* the persona begins by boldly main-taining that all beautiful women are virtuous. To support this view he quotes Aristotle: *"The temperature of the mind follows the temperature of the bodie.* Which certaine axiom (sayes that sage Prince of Philosophers *Aristotle*) is ever more infallible" (D1ᵛ). His argument depends entirely upon the literal application of Aristotle's statement to mat-ters of beauty: "For if *the temperature of the mind, follow the temperature of the bodie?* (text it is) then without controversie, as the outward shape is more singular, so the inward vertues must be most exquisite" (D1ᵛ). Falseness cannot conceivably be hidden under fairness; indeed, de-formity is an indication of "foulest enormities" (D2).[20] In response to the opposition's argument "that *Beauty* of it-selfe is a great *good:* but the abuse most wretched & com-mon" (D2), the persona argues that this "abuse proceeds not from *perfect beautie,* but from the adulterate counter-feit of *beautie, art"* (D2). Unfortunately there are "those that being intemperately wanton, strive with artificiall cun-ning, to cover the defects of *nature"* (D2). But true beauty can never be "tempted to loosnesse" (D2). At this point in his argument, the persona has still not admitted that any exceptions exist.

Later, however, fearing that he will "be gravel'd in the ouze, and quicksand of my own intention" (D3ᵛ), the per-sona makes a reluctant "confession" that negates most of what he has been saying: "I confesse (& blush that occasion should be ministred of confession) that many there are, whose bewitching lookes, drawe youth into folly, and age into dotage, rather madness; too many there are, whose smooth *counterfeit,* in the indiscretion of virility may passe for *Beauty*" (D4). The use of the word *"counterfeit"* recalls the earlier passage, cited above, in which counterfeit referred to artificial devices intended to cover up defects. Here, however, counterfeit seems to refer to ladies whose beautiful exterior covers up a vicious inner nature. In recognizing the existence of this group, the persona admits, in contradiction to the "infallible" "text" from Aristotle, that in some "the *temperature of the body, follows the temperature of the mind,* not the *temperature of the mind, the temperature of the body*" (D4). As a result their once beautiful bodies quickly decay because of the corruption in their minds. It should be apparent that in making this concession, the persona has given up his original point. What has happened is that the meaning of "fair" has shifted completely. If the persona is permitted to define fair as the combination of inner and outer beauty, his case is irrefutable since a lovely lady who becomes immoral proves thereby that she never was fair. Thus "Every *faire* lady is *lovely,* but every *lovely* ladye is not *faire:* so then the *lovely* may be *fickle,* but the *faire* cannot be *inconstant*" (D4 ˇ). In this position, as in none of the others, the persona ends up supporting an argument defensible according to traditional morality. But an observant reader, remembering the "ouze" and "quicksand" and the shifting definitions, would probably be more amused by the inconsistencies in the persona's procedure than impressed by the soundness of his doctrine.

In proving position four, that *"Perfect lovers are onely wise,"* Ford's persona presents the doctrine of a fully developed Platonic theory of love. The irony comes from the disparity between this elevated theory and the actual practice of the lovers discussed in the section. The natural state for lovers is said to be idleness. The *"Wise seeming* Censors" who *"count that labour vaine, / Which is devoted to the hopes of love"* fail to remember

> the wiles which made them tremble,
> *In heat of youth, when youth their bloods did move,*
> *What wit they use'd, what teares they did dissemble.*
> . . . .
> *How provident they were to fawne, to flatter,*
> *To sweare, vow, urge their griefe and to lament it:*
> *Alas who would not doo't in such a matter.* (E1)

The *"Wise seeming"* are condemned, but the persona reveals that love strikes during youth when the blood is hot and leads men to use wit to obtain their ends, to dissemble tears, to fawn, to flatter, etc. Clearly what is being discussed is the love of earthly woman, and the end is still physical conquest.

Once again the opposition is permitted a rebuttal: "a curious surveior will . . . approve, that lovers have beene witty, yet disallow any wisedom in this witt, by distinguishing a different discrepancie betwixt witt and wisdome, since the one tendeth onely to folly of humanity, the other to consideration of divinity" (E1ᵛ). In refuting this sensible argument, the advocate turns to Platonism. His argument is the conventional Platonic one that admiration of the beauty of woman is the first step in the progression to the love of God. The question is whether the progression here is a real one or only a perverted use of Platonic doctrine to justify lust. In establishing his point the persona compares lovers with theologians: "men devoted to contemplation of Theologie, are withdrawne from the absolute, & due reverence (somtime) of him to whome they chiefly owe all due reverence, by humane affaires[;] when *Lovers* have evermore the *Idea* of *Beauty* in their imaginations, and therefore hourely do adore their makers Architecture. *Perfect Lovers are onely wise*" (E2). That theologians have to be concerned at times with earthly affairs is a transparently ludicrous reason for elevating lovers above them. That lovers adore the Maker's architecture is clear, but do they adore the Maker? No; their concern is only how they can win and keep the physical love of their mistresses. The lover will "study any slieght, any device for setting a period to his desires. Insomuch, as no time shall ever present any oportunity of study, but all invention is used, all conceiptes imployed, for the fruition of his beloved: who beeing injoyed, yet his wittes are never idle, but industrious for conservation of what hee injoyes, as loath to impart from that which with so much vigilancie he not easily obtained" (E2–E2ᵛ). God is forgotten; the lover's interest is in winning and keeping his beloved by whatever means are available.

Classical allusions are again used satirically. Although the Greeks desperately needed Ulysses' counsel in the Trojan war, he was unwilling to go because of his love for Penelope. The Greeks

> stood not in more need of *Achilles* for his courage, then of *Ulisses* for his counsaile: who being then newly married, to his perfectly faire Penelope, was upon good cause (moved in the tendernesse of his love) unwilling to that action: but excuse could not prevaile, except pollicie could finde excuse: he feares much, but loves more, which love even at an instant ripens his invention: *Love* ripeneth his *invention,* he faines madnesse, and for *madnesse to advise in sober actions, would prove but a mad advise, an unadvised madnesse.* but he was discovered and went. (E2ᵛ)

His trick in feigning madness does illustrate a kind of wisdom, but it reveals primarily that love causes him to neglect his patriotic duties. The reference to Achilles inevitably recalls that he too tried to avoid the war when his mother disguised him as a girl; readers might also be reminded of the time when Achilles sulked in his tent after Briseis was taken from him.

Ford's persona also mentions the charge: "how can *Lovers* be *wise,* when *Love* it selfe is both *vaine, idle,* and *foolish?* a toye? a meere conceit of fancie?" (E2ᵛ). His answer is once again an elevated Platonic one stressing that love unites the universe and condemning poets who picture love as "sensuall lust" (E2ᵛ). But the persona himself proceeds to quote poetry, and it is poetry which unmasks the high intention of the preceding passage. Once again love is shown to be motivated by desire. The mood of the poem is that of dalliance, not of aspiration:

> Love *is that tickling blood, which softly creepes*
> *Into the pleasures of a quiet brest:*
> *Presenting pretty dreames in slumbring sleepes,*
> *And in a Ladies boosome takes his rest.*
> > *Love bath's him in the channell of delight,*
> > *Which lovers sigh for, and wish they also might.*
>
> . . . .
>
> *Love is that harmlesse* prick, *in pleasant brier,*
> *Which doth most please the sent, and breed desire.* (E3)

One should not be too quick in attaching significance to *Honor Triumphant* as an example of Ford's ideas since it is obvious that his main intention was to write a witty *jeu d'esprit* on a topical subject. But the pamphlet is of importance because it suggests that the young Ford was already developing the ironic tone and the satiric techniques that become distinguishing characteristics of much of his mature work. The picture of a sardonic, analytic, mocking Ford in *Honor Triumphant* complements our impression of an earnest, independent, strong-minded Ford in *Fame's Memorial*. Together these early works suggest a high-spirited, brash, aristocratic young man, somewhat naively eager to unmask the superficial and the stuffy and to champion greatness wherever it might be found. The young Ford seems to have prided himself on being able to cut through the fuzziness of conventional formulas to reveal the truly noble and honorable. But to understand exactly what Ford meant by honor and nobility we must turn to the more systematic statements of his other early writings.

II

FORD'S EARLY ETHICAL THOUGHT

We are fortunate in having three works by Ford which provide a clear outline of his early thinking on many of the ethical questions that he considers later in his plays. They are a long religious poem, *Christ's Bloody Sweat, or the Son of God in his Agony* (1613), and two prose pamphlets, *The Golden Mean* (1613) and *A Line of Life* (1620).[1] Ford's authorship of *Christ's Bloody Sweat* and *The Golden Mean* is not certain, but the internal evidence is so strong that all recent Ford scholars think that Ford probably wrote both. The attributions were first made by Joseph Hunter in *Chorus Vatum*, and M. Joan Sargeaunt's important article has demonstrated, conclusively to my mind, that Hunter was correct.[2] Miss Sargeaunt summarizes the evidence for Ford's authorship of *Christ's Bloody Sweat*:

The dedication, written to one of his known patrons, in the style of his other dedications, is signed 'I.F.' There is one striking parallel (a passage of some length) to a passage in *'Tis Pity*. The central idea of the poem is the one religious idea that occurs with great frequency in Ford's plays. The word 'pearl,' as always in Ford's verse, is dissyllabic. The poem is written in the same manner and style as *Fame's Memorial*. It is, I think, fair to say that there is a strong probability that *Christ's Bloody Sweat* was written by John Ford.[3]

20

H. J. Oliver is perhaps the most skeptical of the later scholars, and even he concludes that the poem is "probably but not certainly by Ford." [4] *The Golden Mean* is accepted as Ford's by all post-Sargeaunt Ford scholars. The evidence is impressive. Ford in *A Line of Life* makes an unmistakable reference to his earlier work: "In all things, no one thing can more requisitely bee observed to be practised, then *The Golden Meane*: the exemplification whereof, however heretofore attributed, I dare not so poorly under-value my selfe and labours, as not to call mine" (*LL*, A5). Also, as Miss Sargeaunt points out: "In manner, form, and style *The Golden Mean* resembles very closely the *Line of Life*." [5] In the rest of my discussion I shall assume that both *Christ's Bloody Sweat* and *The Golden Mean* are by Ford.

Partly because of these uncertainties about authorship and partly because all three works are conventional in subject and form, scholars have been reluctant to use them as serious evidence of Ford's views. It is true that traditional subjects usually receive a traditional treatment, and it is even possible that Ford picked these subjects primarily because he suspected that they would prove popular. But it seems unlikely that his only intention was to make money. Rather, his preoccupation with a few basic themes, frequently and forcefully repeated, suggests his deep involvement with his material. To a modern reader his treatment of these themes may appear both pedestrian and monotonous, but Ford seems to have taken himself quite seriously as a neo-Stoic but Christian moral philosopher. The ideas in the works are not original, but Ford probably would have regarded that as an asset rather than a liability. Like so many other moral works of the Renaissance, *The Golden Mean* and *A Line of Life* are filled with the stock concepts of Christian humanism. Ford refers again and again to the great classical moralists—Aristotle, Cicero, Plutarch, and Seneca—as he illustrates the rational course for any man's life.[6] In *The Golden Mean* Ford shows how to overcome adversity by relying on virtue rather than on the gifts of Fortune; in *A Line of Life* he takes a more positive approach as he outlines the way of life that will lead to "the *Immortalitie* of a Vertuous NAME" (*LL*, A1). He suggests that to fulfill his obligations to himself, his country, and his fellow citizens, man must resolve to persevere in noble actions without expectation of reward.

At first glance *Christ's Bloody Sweat* seems quite different from the two prose works. Its subject—man's salvation through repentance and restorative purgation by the bloody sweat of Christ—seems far removed from the rational ethical formulas of the two pamphlets. But the explanation is not that Ford was a hack writer able to grind out something on any subject with little concern for consistency. The answer is found rather in the confidence with which Renaissance moralists, following a long tradition in Christian thought, distinguished between the realm of faith and the realm of reason. The subject dictated the method of the analysis. Classical moral thought would be out of place in a meditative poem about Christian redemption since the subject is understood through revelation and only secondarily through human reason. In the prose pamphlets revelation would be out of place since the whole point is to see how far man can get through reason alone. Underlying this separation of faith and reason is a typically Anglican suspicion of subtle theologizing about faith. Anglicans in the tradition of Hooker thought that the basic truths of Christianity are simple and self-evident to all men. If man will recognize the need for a decision by the will to reform one's life and participate in the wonder of Christ's sacrifice, he need do no more systematic intellectualizing about faith. But that does not mean that faith has the answers to all of life's problems. In these other areas, however, reason can and should operate; and the discussion can be free and undogmatic because the questions involved are not questions of faith.[7] If we are to understand Ford's thought, we must resist the temptation to see the casual references in the prose works to a Christian framework as mere lip service to religious orthodoxy; we must also resist the temptation to read the poem as proof of narrowly religious attitudes. When the three works are read together, Ford can be seen as an enlightened, thinking Anglican with solid roots in both Christian and classical thought.

There has been some question as to the relationship of

Christ's Bloody Sweat to *Honor Triumphant* and *Fame's Memorial.* In an introductory statement to *Christ's Bloody Sweat,* Ford is critical of poetry's preoccupation with "uncleane" (*CBS*, A4) subjects and mentions his own improper attitudes when he was younger: *"I confesse, I have, touching my perticular, beene long carried with the doubts of* folly, youth, *and* opinion, *and as long miscaried in the darknesse of unhappinesse, both in* invention *and* action. *This was not the path that led to a contented rest, or a respected name"* (*CBS*, A4). In the poem itself, Christ criticizes Ford's early poetry directly:

> Thou (quoth it) that hast spent thy best of dayes
> In thriftlesse rimes (sweet baytes to poyson Youth)
> Led with the wanton hopes of laude and praise,
> Vaine shadowes of delight, seales of untruth. (*CBS,* B1ʳ)

Miss Sargeaunt thinks that Ford "has undergone a definite religious conversion," [8] but I do not believe that either passage justifies such an extreme interpretation. A lamentation for one's private life and writing and for secular writing in general would probably have been taken as a conventional device for assuring the reader of the author's sincerity. Although it may be true that Ford was becoming more serious as he grew older, there is no need to postulate a complete change in his approach to life.

Since the primary interest of these works is what they can tell us about Ford's thought, I have organized my discussion by topics instead of treating each work individually. This procedure is convenient because the same topics—passion and reason, love, resolution, death, and ambition—recur in each of the works. Ford's approach to each of these subjects is consistent with the Christian neo-Stoic stance of his overall philosophy. If any theme may be said to be the dominant one, it is the need for the control of the passions by reason.[9] The Stoics believed that all passions were bad, but the Peripatetics and later the Christians argued that passions are not bad if controlled by reason. Ford, as well as most Renaissance moralists, accepted this Christian view, probably in large part because they needed more justification for an active life than the Stoic view could provide. From this common Renaissance point of view a passion is justified if its expression is evoked by a suitable object at a suitable time and is directed by the reason. But each person, to insure that he is not rationalizing an improper act, must scrutinize the moral implications of his action. It is hard to exaggerate the importance that this context of moral evaluation assumed in almost all discussions of passion in the period. As Miss Campbell comments: "there was always an insistent moral note in the discussion of passion and a determined habit of applying moral judgment to all matters." [10]

Ford's work is no exception. In *Christ's Bloody Sweat* passion is specifically associated with sin, and reason with the Christian life. The error of the man that lives in pleasure is his refusal to give up sinful extremes to follow a reasonable mean:

> A man that lives in pleasures, as his dayes
> Increase, the dayes past over seeme a dreame:
> Stil newer joy, more hope of joy bewrayes,
> And as he lives, he lives still in extreame. (*CBS*, F4ᵛ)

Frequently when Ford speaks of the temptations of sin he mentions them as aberrations of reason. People who follow only pleasure are

> of Reason and of Sence depriv'd:
> Not fearing God, or loving man, giv'n ore
> To Lust and Will, as beasts could doe no more. (*CBS*, I2)

Earlier Ford has spoken of the sin that corrupts man while reason sleeps (*CBS*, H4ᵛ). In another place Ford describes the wooing of the soul, "that Queene of Reason" (*CBS*, G1ᵛ), by Christ. The decision to follow Christ should be the result of a choice dictated by reason; in the same way staying constant in the faith requires reason and fortitude.[11] Christ is not mentioned in the prose works, but the emphasis on the temptation of passion and the need for reason is similar. Since man is the only living creature who is in "possession of a *reasonable soule*" (*LL*, B10ᵛ), he can achieve mastery over his passions, but the task is difficult. "In short, to be a *man*, the first branch of resolution is to know, feele, and moderate affections, which like traitors, and disturbers of peace, rise up to alter & quite change the Lawes of reason, by working in the feeble, and oftentimes the sounder parts, an innovation of folly" (*LL,* C1–C1ᵛ).

One of the most difficult passions to master is love. Ford thought that the attraction that beauty held for men was one of the gravest dangers to the life of reason. The "temptation of a reputed beautie" (*LL,* C5–C5ᵛ) is listed as one of the "inticers" (C5) which destroy the life of reason and "are (if not wisely made use of) but glorious snares, dangerous baites, golden poysons, dreaming distructions, snares to intrappe the mightinesse of constancie; Baites to deceive the constancie of manhood, poysons to corrupt the manhood of Resolution; destruction to quite cast away the Resolution of a just desert" (*LL,* C5ᵛ–C6). The greatness of Epaminondas was a result of his choosing "not with his Countreymen to give Lust, Dalliance, Effeminate softnes a Regiment in the Kingdome of his thoughts" (*LL,* C10–C10ᵛ). Later in the pamphlet Ford explicitly mentions the apostles of the religion of love whose flattery covers their immoral purposes: "Is such a MIGHTIE MAN inticed to overrule his Reason, nay over-beare it, by giving scope to his licentious eye, first to see, then to delight in, lastly, to covet a chaste beauty? Alasse, how many swarms of dependants, being creatures to his greatnesse, will not onely tell him, mocke him, and harden him in a readie and pregnant deceipt, that love is courtly, and women were in their creation ordained to be wooed, and to be won" (*LL,* D10–D10ᵛ). In *Christ's Bloody Sweat* Ford is even more explicit about the error which the worshipers of love make:

> Others there are, who smooth the front of sin,
> And maske his ugly fore-head with the coulour
> Of lust, ingendred novelties; to win
> Grace to their arts by making art seeme fuller:
> And they their foolish wits with pride to prove,
> Will strive forsooth to make a God of love.

> They are the divels secretaries right,
> Whose rules have drawne whole troopes of soules to hell
> That might have else bene sav'd; they day and night
> Toyle out their braines, that mischiefe might excell,

> They feele the whips whiles as they kisse the rod,
> By making lust the divell, and the god.
>
> Love is no god, as some of wicked times
> (Led with the dreaming dotage of their folly)
> Have set him foorth in their lascivious rimes,
> Bewitch'd with errors, and conceits unholy:
>   It is a raging blood[,] affections blind,
>   Which boiles both in the body and the mind. (*CBS*, F3)

Here are all of Ford's objections to love neatly compressed
into three short stanzas. Love is viewed as a physical dis-
turbance which rages in the blood and leads men to foolish
actions. But the initial cause is not physical; Ford is no
determinist. The cause is the sinful nature of men who allow
themselves to become "the divels secretaries." Their
method should be familiar to the readers of *Honor Triumphant*. Like the poets who glorify sinful actions in beautiful
rhymes, these people justify their lust by speaking of it in
elevated terms; but all the fine phrasing cannot hide the sin
which lies underneath. They make a god of love and worship it.

Ford goes on in the next stanzas to present the worthier
kind of love:

> But such whose lawfull thoughts, and honest heat,
> Doth temperately move with chast desires,
> To choose an equall partner, and beget
> Like comforts by a like inkindled fires:
>   Such find no doubt in union made so even,
>   Sweet fruits of succors, and on earth a heaven.
>
> Such find the pastures of their soules and hearts,
> Refreshed by the soft distilling dew,
> Of *Christs deare bloody sweate,* which still imparts
> Plenty of life and joyes so surely trew,
>   As like a barren ground they drinke the pleasure,
>   Of that inestimable showre of treasure. (*CBS*, F3)

There is only the faintest hint of the Platonic background of
this attitude; the lovers will find "on earth a heaven." But
the passage is a characteristic Christian version of the celestial love in Platonic theory.

Later in the poem Ford describes the wooing of the soul by Christ (*CBS*, G1ʳ–G2). The use of erotic imagery to express divine love follows a long Christian tradition stemming from allegorical interpretations of The Song of Songs [12] and is a good indication of the clarity of the Renaissance division between proper and improper love. Ford is critical of the use of elevated language to disguise physical passion, but he is not opposed to using erotic language to describe Christ's relationship to man. The wooing of the soul by Christ is made an image of the right kind of love.

Ford illustrates the wrong kind of love in his description of the wooing of Simplicitie by Young Lust, aided by Old Sinne. The arguments used are a good example of the smooth talking that Ford has warned against. The passage also exhibits Ford's early skill in developing a convincing dramatic tone despite his opposition to the points being made. Old Sinne is speaking:

> Unhealthie, old, forsaken, and despis'd,
> I lead a life, who was adored then;
> Beautie amidst the croppe is only priz'd,
> Faire soules, in youth, are chiefly lik'd of men:
>   But when my time did court me I for-went it,
>   And lost my daies, and now I doe repent it.
>
> Daughter wilt thou alone live unpossest,
> Of youths best ornaments and natures joyes?
> Wilt thou deny to be a mother blest,
> In pretty daughters, and more pretty boyes?
>   O no, had not our mothers tooke their lot,
>   Wee had bene yet unborne and unbegot.
>
> Heaven hath ordained thee to be sweet on earth,
> Both love and youth do homage to thine eyes,
> And wilt thou curbe thy selfe of pleasures mirth?
> By vainely striving how to be precise?
>   She that hath fairenesse were as good have none,
>   If foolishly she keepe it all for one. (*CBS*, G2–G2ʳ)

The speech goes on in this manner, describing the folly of hoping "to marry with the Sonne of God" (*CBS*, G2ʳ) and urging Simplicitie to revel now and repent later. Through such arguments "Sins sweet temptation" (*CBS*, G3) conquers the lady.

The discussion of beauty in *Christ's Bloody Sweat* is of particular interest because Ford's attitude is revealed as the exact opposite of the persona's view in *Honor Triumphant*. In *Christ's Bloody Sweat* Ford stresses the fleeting quality of beauty. Man is described as no more than "dust made up in forme" (*CBS*, F1ᵛ); his beauty passes away quickly: "Mans beautie but a frame made up in snow, / Immixt with waxe, which melts with every Sun" (*CBS*, F1ᵛ). Woman's beauty, far from being always an image of the divine, is frequently a lure to sin:

> here saw he Creatures
> In face as sweete as Angels, dy'd in grayne,
> Of nature's Art, fayre Miracle of features,
> Wonder of beauty, loves delicious trayne,
>   Adorn'd with seeming graces that did shine
>   So glorious, as they were esteem'd devine.
>
> Women they were, Saintes to behold, in view
> Chast Matrons, but (O frailtyes curst) in triall
> More vaine then vanitie, and more untrue
> Then falshood :[ ] only cunning in deniall :
>   In whose deniall vertue was so scant,
>   As when they [most] deni'd, they most will graunt.
>
> Wordes, wit, and fayrnesse, [are] the smiling ginnes
> Wherewith they catch insnard men : whereto heaven
> Bestow'd for blessings, are but bands to sinnes
> Abus'd ; whom God made straight, those make even :
>   Of whom the most are worst, the fewer good,
>   The good not free, for all he sweated bloud. (*CBS*, C3ᵛ–C4)

If one were to set out to look for passages that would refute the third position of *Honor Triumphant*, that *"Faire Ladie was never false,"* he could find nothing better than these lines from Ford's own poem published only seven years later.

Ford is also critical of poets who write of wanton love :

This did the lov-sicke musicke-straining wanton,
Who leades his life in sonnetting some *Ay-mees:*

Ponder, he'd cease, and then there would be scant one
En-amourd on so many lisping *Shees:*
> But changing better notes, they would take pittie
> On their owne soules, and sing a sweeter dittie. (*CBS*, D1ᵛ)

Later Ford describes the punishments the love poets will
receive in hell:

> he who wrote
> *Soule-killing rimes,* shall living be consum'd
> By such a gnawing worme, that never dies,
> And heare in stead of musicke hellish cries. (*CBS*, E2)

The Ford of this passage could not be more unsympathetic
to defenses of romantic passion.

In dealing with any passion that threatens the rational
life, resolution is the key. The problem is less in knowing
what is right than in having the resolution to do what is
right. To Ford resolution involves both the idea of free
will—that man can do what he resolves to do—and the idea
of stoical resignation—that man can accept what he resolves
to accept. If man has a proper sense of values he can be at
once above the petty concerns of this world and active in
making the world a better place. The greater part of *The
Golden Mean* is concerned with how man can by resolution
elevate himself above the miseries that any person is bound
to encounter. In proving the wisdom of this stoical course,
Ford invokes the familiar classical and Christian concept of
Fortune.[13] Man should never allow the happiness of his life
to depend on the things of this world, for they are governed
by a fickle Fortune that is beyond man's control. As Ford
says: "He is onely miserable that knowes not to be content
with his Fortune" (*GM*, F4ᵛ). Man's security in his own
virtue should be sufficient to enable him to disregard completely his station in life and to treat the adversities that
inevitably will come as a test of that virtue: "A sure Pilot is
proved in a doubtfull storme, and a wise noble minde is truly
tried in the storme of adversitie, not in the calme of felicitie.
Fortune envies nothing more then a setled and well governed resolution" (*GM*, B6–B6 ᵛ). Most of *The Golden
Mean* deals with how to face six specific miseries that can
befall man: disfavor, neglect, forfeit of estate, banishment,

imprisonment, and death. Ford distinguishes between the adversities that men bring on themselves and the inevitable adversities that are a part of life. If a man has lived virtuously, any of these eventualities must have resulted from forces beyond the individual's control. Man can then only accept his misery, secure in the knowledge that he has done no wrong and that fortune in this world is unimportant. If a man has been responsible for his plight through some fault of his own, he should immediately repent and reform. In *The Golden Mean,* Ford emphasizes the efficacy of repentance: "It appertaines not to any man what he hath beene, if he be throughly reformed; since a new life gives another birth: the leaving of evill, being but a buriall of eville, and the imbracing of worthinesse, a christning of reputation" (*GM,* D7). The actual restoration of reputation of position is less important than the knowledge that one is again worthy of being honored. No matter what happens man can face adversity if he has made a wise appraisal of the human condition and of the essential values in life.

Although recommending resignation to inevitable adversities, Ford does not think that a passive acquiescence in whatever happens is the proper course for the wise man. Man has a great deal to say about what happens to him; consequently passivity is a sign of weakness: "Most men subject to those unhappinesses, like things floating on the water, doe not goe, but are carried" (*GM,* C6ᵛ). The emphasis here is still negative, however, with the stress being on the avoidance of adversity. In *A Line of Life* Ford states a more positive philosophy—that the virtuous person is obligated to act because he has responsibilities to himself, his society, and his fellow men. Ford stresses "that *Action* is the Crowne of Vertue. . . . For to be vertuous without the testimonie of imployment, is as a rich Minerall in the heart of the Earth, un-useful because unknowne" (*LL,* B3–B3ᵛ). But the action must be virtuous, for tranquility in the individual's mind is more important than any worldly accomplishment. A noble man trying to decide whether to take part in a questionable activity will decide "that the toyle in common affaires, is but trash and bondage, compared to the sweet repose of the minde, and the goodly Contemplation of mans peace with Himself. All glory whether it consist of profits or preferments, is WITHOUT, and therefore makes nothing to the essence of true happinesse; but the feeling of a resolved constancie is WITHIN, and ever keepes a Feast in a mans soundest content" (*LL,* Gɪʳ–G2). Ford seems to have two kinds of ambition in mind: the ambitious person either strives through worthy deeds to accomplish virtuous ends or seeks power or money or self-glory in some form. The idea of two kinds of ambition is of course a commonplace. The French moralist Charron in *Of Wisdom* describes the difference clearly: "The *one* aspires after Glory and Honour, a Good Reputation, a Great and Immortal Name; and this is of great Use and publick Benefit: It is not only allowable, but in some Sense, and under certain Qualifications and Restraints, highly commendable: The *other* sort affects Greatness and Power; and this is generally not only vicious but destructive, and of most fatal Consequence to the World." [14] To modern readers it may seem naive to make such a clearcut distinction between good and evil; but the complex modern psychology which tends to reduce all behavior to relativism and is able to find a questionable motive for almost any action did not exist. Ford, like most Renaissance thinkers, still thought it was possible to have absolute good unqualified by reservations as to motivation. Although Ford recognizes man's essential depravity, he believes that through an effort of the will man can overcome evil and choose to do good. Man should recognize both his merits and his weaknesses and have confidence without excessive pride: "*Let no man bee too confident of his owne merit, The best doe erre: Let no man relye too much on his owne Judgment, the wisest are deceived: yet let every man so conceive of himselfe,* that he may indevour to bee such a one, as distrust shal not make him carelesse, or confidence secure" (*LL,* C9). This dual view is a characteristic Renaissance fusion of belief in man's depravity with confidence in man's ability to choose to make good use of the talents that he has.

Accompanying this positive view of man's ambition is the belief that fame that comes to man for doing worthy deeds is not at all tainted. In *A Line of Life* Ford speaks of "the truest honour *A deserved fame,* which is one (if worthie) of the best and highest rewards of virtue" (*LL,* B10). But the mention of *"deserved"* makes the standard of reference once again the individual himself, who is after all the only one (except God) who can judge whether the praise is deserved. No matter how good the cause, the individual's motivation must be the desire to do good, not the desire for fame as an end in itself.

If one is to discover true virtue, honor, and wisdom and avoid their false varieties, he must become adept at judging both himself and other people. In judging others the appearance of virtue is no guarantee of the reality because everyone strives to appear good: "hypocrisie is reputed the surest & the safest ground of pollicie" (*LL,* C3ᵛ). In Ford's view such disguise is all too easy and all too common: "How easie it is to guild a rotten post, to paint a Sepulcher, to varnish an ill meaning, is soone resolved: Many men can *speake well,* few men will *doe well*" (*LL,* C2ᵛ–C3). The result is a waste that is tragic both for the individual, who does not realize his potential for good, and for society, which suffers instead of profiting from his life. As an example Ford cites Caius Curio, "a man most *wittily wicked,* and most *singularly eloquent* in mischiefe against the Commonwealth. . . . How much better had it been for him, to have had a *duller braine,* if better imployed, and a *slower tongue,* if availeable for the publique good?" (*LL,* C2). If this situation is to be changed, each person must take responsibility for the quality of his own contribution to society. Perhaps because of this insistence upon individual moral values, Ford is obsessed with the idea of proving his own personal integrity. So that no one will claim that he is using flattery for his own advancement, he dedicates *A Line of Life* to all readers and protests, almost too vigorously, that "I never fawned upon any mans Fortunes, whose person and merit I preferred not. Neither hath any court-ship of applause, set me in a higher straine, a higher pinnacle of opinion, then severest Approbation might make warrantable" (*LL,* A3ᵛ–A4). Such a statement may make Ford seem unrealistic in his pursuit of this almost unattainable ideal of conduct;

but whether or not he lived up to his ideals, it is clear that his moral earnestness is sincere.

Throughout his life Ford was particularly attracted to great figures who had the potential both in status and in personal qualities to achieve his ideal of noble wisdom but who failed to do so because of some personal fault. Because of the important role that great but flawed men play in the Jacobean drama and in Ford's own plays, his comments on the subject are of particular interest and significance. A common view has been that the drama of the time expresses admiration for men who assert their individuality with little or no regard for the consequences to others. The tendency has been to think that greatness even without virtue would win an audience's instinctive admiration. After becoming acquainted with Ford's overall Christian neo-Stoic approach, it should come as no surprise that Ford insists that greatness without goodness is a curse. The idea can be documented at length in all three works. In *A Line of Life* Ford states that if a public leader is not good, "his Honours are a burthen, his Height a Curse, his Favours a Destruction, his Life a Death, and his Death a Misery" (*LL*, D3ᵛ). Elsewhere in *A Line of Life* Ford says that "to be truly good is to be great" (*LL*, A5ᵛ) and that *"A good Man* is the man, that even the greatest or lowest should *bee*, and resolve *to be"* (*LL*, G3–G3ᵛ). In the dedication to *Christ's Bloody Sweat* Ford says that "most usually to bee Great, and to bee Good, is required a double person" (*CBS*, A3). In *The Golden Mean* he says that a wise noble should learn "the difference betweene a great and a good man, the one preferring vertue only for greatnesse the other preferring greatnesse for the greatnesse of vertue onely" (*GM*, D8). Ford's view that grandeur must be accompanied by virtue is typical of both classical and Christian stoicism. While it is perhaps possible that an assertion of the individual's superiority to any moral code might be justified by reference to the tradition of the mythical hero who is above conventional moral judgment,[15] it would be hard to establish it from the philosophical or moral works of the time. If we are to judge by Ford's comments on heroic, although admittedly not mythical, figures like Essex, Byron, and Barnevelt, he himself did not recognize such a double standard. All three are criticized for failing to maintain a standard of personal morality consonant with their high position (*LL*, E2ᵛ–E5).[16] Ford does, however, sympathize with the problems such great men have in staying virtuous. Because of their positions they are subjected to many more pressures than ordinary men. One group that hopes to win the great man's favor minimizes or even justifies vice with flattering words that disguise ambition, lust, or callousness. And there are always others who can turn the smallest fault or even suspicion of a fault into a charge of scandal or corruption that may result in the great man's fall. Ford is perceptive enough to see the tragedy of the small error with huge consequences; but his recommendation is that the great man should realize the danger and be even more resolute in remaining above reproach. If he should fall he should, of course, be stoical in accepting what he cannot change, but Ford sees nothing very admirable in posturing grandly about a disaster that one has brought on himself: "In example, as a man who hath committed some wicked act, as the murther of his Prince, or other subject, being prompted hereto by no other reason, then his owne private ambition and revenge, and afterwards applaudes impenitently his cursed assassination or villanie. This man is indeede come into a fulnesse of miserie" (*GM*, C10ᵛ–C11). Only the innocent victim of circumstances beyond his control is justified in asserting his superiority to his fate.

Ford's attitude toward death reflects the same distinction between the just and the unjust. If a person's values are temporal then death is an unmitigated evil forcing him from his possessions to an eternity in hell. In several places Ford speaks of the fear of death which should accompany evildoing in this world. In *A Line of Life* he says: "Life desired for the only benefit of living, feares to dye; for such men that so live, when they dye, both dye finally & dye all" (*LL*, B1ᵛ). In *The Golden Mean* the reference to hell is more explicit: "It is to be confessed that if the weight of our misdeeds torture us when we are to leave the world, and that we have not set the household of our soules and bodies in order, then the cause is otherwise, for he is not to be blamed who is willing to shunne an ending misery for a miserie that hath none end; and this is not the feare of Death, but the feare of being for ever a dying, which torments the conscience" (*GM*, H2). But the wise and virtuous man is able to approach death with no misgivings because he sees in it a release from the cares of this world and the assurance of a better life to come: "*Death* to a wise man cannot come unlooked for, nor to a good man unwisht for: since the wise, knowing that they must die, know likewise that *resolution* is the best comfort to welcome *death*, and the good being confident of their owne innocencies, desire the change of a better life" (*GM*, G12). Life itself is no more than a running toward death. Those who vainly seek pleasure or power in this world are always thinking of what they will be getting in the future. If they were wise, they would realize that the desired passage of time only brings them closer to what they should dread, the grave: "They that enjoy what their owne hearts can crave / Crave onely time, which brings them to the grave" (*CBS*, F4ᵛ). But to the virtuous, death is the goal toward which all life has pointed: "The end of all sorrowes is *Death*, if the partie to die be truly reconciled to his God and to his conscience" (*GM*, H1).¹⁷

We may conclude from these early works that Ford was a traditional and quite orthodox Christian who was deeply influenced by classical ethics. Ford believed that man, through reason, resolution, and perseverance, could steer between the extremes of passion and achieve the golden mean of a well-ordered life. The passions are not bad if they are organized by the reason for virtuous purposes. Ambition, fame, and pride are worthy if they are associated with honorable actions. The same ideals can be expressed in Christian terms: reason forces man to see the sin of his passionate life and to repent. Through reason man can achieve both the immortality of a worthy name and the immortality of heaven.

III

FORD AND THE
DRAMA OF HIS TIME

In order to understand the form and the themes of Ford's plays, it is essential to see the influence both of the new court or Cavalier drama of the Caroline period and of the more traditional drama of the professional playwrights of the Jacobean period. Ford's natural ties—his experience as a writer, his collaborative work in the early 1620's—were with the professional playwrights; but the theatrical situation was changing significantly at the very time when Ford was beginning to write plays independently. Shortly after Charles I became king in 1625, he married the young French princess, Henrietta Maria. Ford seems to have had no close associations with the court, but the Platonic love cult that developed around the queen considerably influenced his independent plays, all of which were produced during the Caroline period and almost all of which have love as their major theme. Since there has been much misunderstanding about the connection between Ford and the love cult, an examination of the nature of the cult and the drama it inspired is necessary.

In 1615 the Marquise de Rambouillet had formed a salon which attempted to refine the manners and morals of the French court. The intention was to elevate the status of women so that their influence could raise the tone of the society. The ideals of Platonic love were perfectly suited to the new group, and Honoré D'Urfé's romantic novel, *L'Astrée,* illustrating types of love and praising refined and innocent Platonism, became its code.[1] Faced with the gross behavior which had become all too characteristic of the English court under James I, Henrietta Maria took upon herself the task of similarly refining the manners of her new subjects. Scattered non-dramatic evidence for the existence of the Platonic love cult exists, among which is a letter written by James Howell:

The Court affords little News at present, but that there is a Love call'd Platonick Love, which much sways there of late; it is a Love abstracted from all corporeal gross Impressions and sensual Appetite, but consists in Contemplations and Ideas in the Mind, not in any carnal Fruition. This Love sets the Wits of the Town on work and they say there will be a Mask shortly of it, whereof her Majesty and her Maids of Honour will be part.[2]

Establishing the period when the love cult was at its height is difficult. We know that Platonic love was being talked about as early as 1629, for Jonson's *The New Inn* includes extended satire of it. We also know that Henrietta Maria gained more influence in the years after Buckingham's death in 1628, and it may be that the love cult began to flourish at the same time.[3]

To understand the English reaction requires some knowledge of the roots of the new fashion. The resurgence of Platonism in late fifteenth- and sixteenth-century Italy under Ficino, Pico, Castiglione, and others gave a refined and courtly twist to the Platonism that had pervaded Christianity since Augustine. According to the Christian tradition, love was the great link which held all of God's creation together, with the motivation for love in the individual being his desire for beauty. The highest beauty and the greatest good were, of course, to be found in God, but the choice of the object of love rested with man. He could either through reason raise his sights, often through the worship of the Blessed Virgin, to the love of God (*caritas*) or lower them to love the material things of this world (*cupiditas*).

The creatures of this world should also be loved, not for themselves but for the image of God that appeared in them.[4] The stress of Ficino and his followers that earthly beauty is the incarnation of divine beauty was partly the cause and partly the effect of a more refined atmosphere in aristocratic circles as courtly compliment of noble ladies became fashionable. The mainstream of the new theories came to England through Italian and French literature and quickly assumed a dominant place in the art, literature, drama, and culture of sixteenth-century England, particularly after Elizabeth became queen.[5] Perhaps the strongest influence of the new love doctrines was on poetry. An important point that can hardly be overstressed is that most of this Platonic poetry did not glorify the passions; rather it idealized love and showed man possibilities that were above the merely physical level. One of the main results of the new trend was a higher status for the gentlewoman and a refinement of manners as women, with Elizabeth showing the way, played a larger social role.

Queen Henrietta Maria's brand of Platonism differed in significant respects from that of Elizabeth's time. In the first place, Henrietta Maria was actively supporting a code of beliefs about love whereas in Elizabeth's time the refined atmosphere had developed gradually and never became controversial. Perhaps the most important difference is that Henrietta Maria's cult emphasized that rationality and spirituality were essential if love were to escape contamination. Although praise of virginity and spiritual love had been common under the virgin Queen Elizabeth and the importance of marriage and procreation was never slighted by the happily married and frequently pregnant Henrietta Maria, there was more stress on marriage in Elizabeth's reign and more on rational, non-physical love in Henrietta Maria's time. The difference is mainly one of emphasis since both views are rooted in the Renaissance Platonism typified by Ficino. Ficino had argued that God acts both through the celestial Venus and the earthly Venus: "there is a Love in each case: in the former, it is the desire of contemplating beauty; and in the latter, the desire of propagating it; both loves are honorable and praiseworthy, each is concerned with the divine image." [6] Since Ficino stresses that physical love must be guided by reason and morality and not by passion, there is no conflict between the two views even though the emphasis differs. One explanation of the increased stress on virginity in the code of Henrietta Maria is the great veneration accorded to the Virgin Mary during the period. In Protestant Elizabethan England, there was much more stress on marriage. [7]

For various reasons it is difficult to evaluate the impact of Henrietta Maria's cult upon English society. Most of the direct attacks upon the cult came from the Puritans, who were of course quick to attribute all sorts of bad intentions to the queen because they were so violently opposed to her political and religious activities, particularly her attempts at Catholicizing England. Since the Puritans had these reasons for wanting to discredit the court, it is hard to tell how much in the attacks on the cult is Puritan propaganda, how much is the usual Puritan moralistic attack on all sin, and how much represents a justified reaction to a bad situation. If you believe the Puritans, the court was dominated by a decadent group that glorified love and beauty and minimized the importance of chastity and marriage. [8] But to believe the extreme charges requires one to adopt a Puritan outlook and to ignore or minimize the evidence of the virtuous goals of the love coterie, the innocence of the queen's interest in the theater, and the sincerity of her dedication to Catholicism. The queen's behavior may have been immature and perhaps frivolous, but there is no good evidence that she was guilty of anything more serious.

An alternative interpretation is that the queen's intentions were good but that the court society around her transformed her cult into something quite different. Again the evidence is inconclusive, but Harbage, who has made the most thorough study of the reactions to the cult, concludes both that the coterie was innocent and moral and that its

success was not spectacular, for most Englishmen, even at court, were apt to be unimpressed by involved pretense—especially by the unpointed ardors of platonic courtship, which seemed to them a species of grouse-shooting with the grouse omitted. Henrietta herself, though refined and virtuous, was of a more robust type than the typical *précieuse.* Nevertheless the ideals of D'Urfé occasioned volumes of talk, and even won some lip service—devout murmurings disturbed on occasion by the unharmonious birth of a child by one of the Queen's unwedded maids of honor.[9]

One useful way to evaluate the reaction of the court society as a whole is to study the plays that they enjoyed. As the queen's influence rose, young courtiers began imitating her beliefs about Platonic love and taking an interest in writing for the theater. Before long the court became a center of interest in drama, and most of the plays that resulted are filled with the Platonized theories of the queen. In his book on Ford, G. F. Sensabaugh examines all of the plays and masques presented at court during the Caroline period in an effort to determine the nature of the love coterie and its influence on Ford. All of the plays Sensabaugh considers are also studied in Harbage's *Cavalier Drama.* Their conclusions are opposite: Sensabaugh thinks that the plays reveal libertine tendencies and form the background for the similarly libertine drama of Ford, while Harbage regards them as innocent and moral and sees little connection between the plays and Ford.[10] My own study of the plays leads me to conclude that Harbage is right about the innocence of the plays' themes but that Sensabaugh is right in arguing that the cult influenced Ford. I think, however, that Sensabaugh misunderstands the nature of the influence. In his attempt to establish the immorality of the coterie's views, he quotes libertine speeches out of context and implies that they represent the total view of the plays and hence of the coterie. Such a method is dangerously misleading because the characters who use Platonic arguments to mask immoral intentions are consistently satirized. Although Sensabaugh sometimes grants the satire, he argues that such passages nevertheless prove the existence of a libertine love cult. We can no doubt assume that the frequency of such satire indicates that there was much hypocritical rationalization of immorality during the period; it may even be true that the popularity of the Platonic doctrines led to an increased use of perversions of Platonic arguments. But the point at issue is the theory of the cult and not the actual practice of people at court. If it is true, as

seems likely, that plays written to entertain supporters of
the cult would reflect their views, then the morality of these
plays is of crucial importance. If the playwrights always
criticize immorality and praise virtue, Sensabaugh's case
collapses.

I can think of four possible treatments of Platonic love in
the drama: 1) praise of innocent and pure Platonism; 2)
satire of innocent and pure Platonism; 3) praise of Platonism which condones physical love outside the moral code; 4)
satire of perverted Platonism. My study of all of the plays
that Sensabaugh uses as evidence reveals that not a single
play falls into category three. Play after play praises innocent Platonism. Carlell's plays, *The Passionate Lovers*
(1638),[11] *Arviragus and Philicia* (1635–1635/6), and *The
Deserving Favourite* (c. 1622)⟨1629⟩), Davenant's plays,
The Fair Favourite (1638) and *The Unfortunate Lovers*
(1638) and his masque *The Temple of Love* (1634/5),
Cartwright's *The Royal Slave* (1636), Montagu's *The
Shepherd's Paradise* (1632/3), Randolph's *The Jealous
Lovers* (1631/2), Berkeley's *The Lost Lady* (1637–38),
Townshend's *Albion's Triumph* (1631/2) and *Tempe Restored* (1631/2), Habington's *The Queen of Arragon*
(1640), Rutter's *The Shepherds' Holiday* (1633–34?),
and Goffe's *The Careless Shepherdess* (1618–29 and c.
1638), all mentioned by Sensabaugh, are plays which upon
close analysis definitely fall into category one. The list could
be extended considerably because many plays which tried to
please Henrietta Maria naturally used these arguments.
The plots of all of these plays and masques are from the
world of romance. Virtuous young lovers, lustful villains,
the mix-up of children at birth, shepherds who turn out to be
princes, disguises, mistaken identities, separations of lovers
through villainy—all of the standard devices of romance are
present. The artificially refined language of Platonism is
ideally suited for these improbable plots, and the virtuous
characters are the perfect exemplification of the doctrines of
the love coterie. I agree that the plays are a reflection of the
beliefs of Henrietta Maria and her group, but I can find
only a naive innocence and a refined courtliness reflected.

Various plays, some of which belong to category one,

satirize this pure and innocent Platonism. Among them are Carlell's *The Passionate Lovers* (1638) and *Arviragus and Philicia* (1635–1635/6), Habington's *The Queen of Arragon* (1640), and Davenant's *The Platonic Lovers* (1635). The criticism is very mild; for example in Carlell's *The Passionate Lovers* a mildly anti-Platonic character exclaims to his love:

> O fear not Lady, I am not so much taken yet
> To trouble you with lamentable verses,
> Or blow the candle out with sighs: breaking my buttons
> After a full meal's the highest I can reach to: I assure you,
> Methinks that Princely pattern is scarce worth
> The following.[12]

Perhaps such a speech is intended as criticism of the excesses of the doctrines, but it may be that the audience would have been laughing at the speaker for not being able to rise to their elevated level. Considering the possibilities for criticism that the doctrines seem to invite, the absence of more satire is significant. Apparently no playwright needed to be told that satire of innocent Platonic love was not the way to win favor from the court.

Category four, satire of perverted Platonism, is also well represented in these plays. Davenant's *The Platonic Lovers* (1635) and *The Unfortunate Lovers* (1638), Randolph's *The Jealous Lovers* (1631/2), Carlell's *The Passionate Lovers* (1638) and *The Deserving Favourite* (c. 1622)⟨1629⟩, Marmion's *A Fine Companion* (1632–3), Habington's *The Queen of Arragon* (1640), Suckling's *Aglaura* (1637), and the anonymous *Lady Alimony* (c. 1640?) all include satiric attacks on those who use Platonic doctrine as a mask to cover up licentious intentions. The fact that this category is so frequently represented is solid evidence of the coterie's attitudes, since obviously satire of perverted Platonism would not find much favor with the queen or a courtly audience if they were supporters of the arguments presented. The villains or rakes in the plays of the fourth category invariably use Platonic arguments in their attempted seductions. Asotus in *The Jealous Lovers* (1631/2), Cleon in *The Passionate Lovers* (1638), Hilde-

brand in *The Unfortunate Lovers* (1638), Sanmartino in
The Queen of Arragon (1640), and Spruse in *A Fine Companion* (1632–33) are all criticized for their immoral intentions. An excellent example of the response true Platonic
characters should make to invitations to illicit love comes in
Carlell's *The Deserving Favourite*. Lysander, the noble
hero, wants to convince his love, Clarinda, that she should
despise him so that she will marry another without regrets.
To accomplish this end he utilizes the usual arguments for
illicit love since he knows that Clarinda will hate him for
suggesting such things. His arguments sound plausible and
might even sound sympathetic to a modern reader:

> now every time
> That we shall meete in secret, will farre passe
> A wedding-night in joy, stolne pleasures give
> An appetite, secure delights but cloy.[13]

Clarinda's response is the expected rebuke:

> either *Lysander*
> Is chang'd from what he was; or else he never
> Was what I esteem'd him either of which
> Makes me most miserable.[14]

Later, of course, the truth comes out, and the couple is
eventually reunited. The scene is a good illustration of the
ethics of these plays and, by reflection, of the ethics of the
audience. Apparently no hero could propose extramarital
relations without automatically becoming a villain in the
eyes of a virtuous lady. The surest way for Carlell to change
Lysander's character in the mind of Clarinda is to make him
argue in this way.

If we take these plays seriously, we must conclude that
the Cavalier audience was traditional in most of its views.
There has perhaps been too strong a tendency to divide the
English people into Puritan and Cavalier and to think about
austere Puritans and libertine courtiers. Undoubtedly there
were Cavalier libertines, but in their religious, social, political, economic, and ethical views, the bulk of the Cavalier
audience would be staunchly traditional. Tradition for them
would mean the ideals of Tudor humanism, and nostalgia

for past values was greater because of increasing tension resulting from the diverse pressures associated with the rise of the Puritan revolution. It may be that the escapist unreality of the plays is a measure of the extent to which the English upper classes were finding it necessary to avoid the real problems of the time. In the heroes and heroines of Cavalier drama can be seen the highest ideals of Caroline society. In making these traditional abstractions the basis for action, the Cavalier dramatists suggested that the individual is strongest when his personal standards depend upon a whole culture's carefully defined social and ethical ideals.

Although the plays of the Caroline professional playwrights were better constructed and more theatrical, they too can be characterized as conventional in style and traditional in thought. Except in the drama of Ford, little of the excitement or controversy of the Jacobean theater remained. The Jonsonians, notably Richard Brome, wrote satiric plays that exposed corruption and called implicitly for a return to the ideals of traditional England, while the Fletcherians, notably Massinger and Shirley, presented fairly innocuous imitations of their more provocative predecessors. Massinger can be counted on to moralize whether or not it is relevant to the situation; Shirley on the other hand is apt to settle for skillfully told stories that suggest little larger significance. Davenant managed more successfully than the others to fuse the new Cavalier interests with the older methods, but he seldom seems very deeply involved in his subjects. At any rate the old charge that the drama of the period reflects a decadent society is not borne out by these plays. Parrott and Ball, after considering Ford with the Jacobeans, discuss the conventionality of the plays of Massinger, Shirley, and Davenant. They summarize: "It is wrong to label this period, as has often been done, with the stigma of moral degeneracy. The tone of courtly society was probably purer in the days of Charles than in those of his father." [15]

Even though the Caroline drama as a whole remained artificial and unimpressive, the topics raised by the love cult provided Ford with material that he was able to transform into effective theater. Shunning the unrealities of the Cavalier drama, Ford creates characters and situations calculated to attract the attention of an audience that was aware of the subtleties of the Platonic theories and of the influence they were having on society. It could even be postulated that Ford was trying to take advantage of the popularity of the topic of love at the time. Not only was the Platonic code of Henrietta Maria the new fashion, but the writings of Robert Burton on melancholy were also at the peak of their popularity.[16] Since Ford himself had written extensively about love in his early works, he was a natural person to capitalize on the topic.

Unfortunately we cannot be sure of the exact make-up of Ford's audiences at the Blackfriars and the Phoenix.[17] They no doubt included many who also went to the Cavalier plays, particularly those that were presented in the private theaters; but the Caroline plays of the professional playwrights obviously appealed to a broader audience than the Cavalier drama. It is commonly assumed that the orientation of the private theaters of the time was aristocratic or at least upper class, but generalizations about their views are dangerous. It would be helpful if we could assume that they were homogeneous groups whose views on any subject might be accurately predicted. When I began this study I was more ready to assert how they would think and respond, but I have come increasingly to the view that their reactions would be quite diverse and that no generalization about their specific views can be made. In their attitudes toward love, for example, they probably represented quite different viewpoints. Some would be enthusiastic supporters of Henrietta Maria's love cult; judging by the popularity of the Cavalier plays, this group may have been quite large. Others perhaps went along with the new code but not too enthusiastically. Even more theater-goers perhaps remained aloof, being aware of the new trends but not wanting or needing to commit themselves. Among those who were critical of the new code, there were probably many differences in motivation. Some would question the French influence, some the Catholic influence, some the feminine influence; others would be suspicious of the code's naive idealism, or its romanticization of love, or its glorification of the woman.

Others were probably opposed on principle to anything connected with the increasingly unpopular King Charles. About all that can be said with any assurance is that the audience, while representing more diverse attitudes than the audience of the Cavalier drama, would still be quite conservative in that most at least of the upper classes could be expected to support established institutions and traditions.

In writing drama that would appeal to this audience Ford was able to turn to already existing dramatic traditions which were both congenial to him and familiar to his audience. In his own collaborations during the early 1620's, Ford had been introduced to the techniques of structuring a play and holding an audience's interest by such masters of popular stagecraft as Dekker, Rowley, and Webster. It is significant that, despite the somewhat condescending aloofness from his profession that Ford expresses in some of his prefaces, his first writing for the theater was for productions obviously though skillfully designed to appeal to conventional tastes. Although Ford may later have wanted to dissociate himself from the working theater, he never forgot what he learned from such productions as *The Witch of Edmonton.*

What prompted Ford to turn to the theater when he was thirty-five years old is unclear. Perhaps he needed the money, or perhaps a friendship with Dekker or Rowley or simply their need for another writer led to their collaboration on Ford's first known play, *The Witch of Edmonton.* After this play in 1621 there is no clear evidence of Ford's collaboration on anything until 1624. Then there is a flurry of activity with *The Sun's Darling, The Fairy Knight, A Late Murder of the Son Upon the Mother,* and *The Bristowe Merchant* (the last three are lost), all licensed in 1624. Ford collaborated with Dekker on all four works, with Webster and Rowley helping out on the hastily written *A Late Murder.*[18] Although scholars have attempted to find Ford's hand in other plays of the time,[19] the evidence is exasperatingly meager and is insufficient to prove that, except for *The Witch of Edmonton,* Ford had any part in any plays before 1624.

The Witch of Edmonton is a fairly successful domestic

tragedy combined with some elements of topical comedy. Although the evidence for authorship is entirely internal, most scholars have assumed that Ford was responsible for the Frank-Winnifred plot and Dekker for most of the witch scenes and the characterization of Susan, a Patient Griselda type common in his plays. That would leave the sometimes amusing but inconsequential Cuddy Banks scenes for Rowley.[20] The division is plausible and probably generally accurate, but it would seem possible that the older dramatists helped the inexperienced Ford with his parts. Certainly under these circumstances too-confident attribution of scenes and speeches would be unwise.

There is evidence in the play of many of the dramatic techniques used by Ford in his independent plays. First, like all of Ford's plays, it is immensely theatrical. In their use of an English witch, a devil that takes the form of a dog, bigamy, illicit love, murder, a realistic English middle-class setting, and lively dialogue, the dramatists have made an obvious attempt to write exciting theater that would hold the interest of their audience. Any analysis of the play's themes must be prefaced by the recognition that the authors' primary intention was to entertain. In doing so, however, they make use of the usual traditional methods that give Elizabethan and Jacobean plays deeper meaning. Despite their surface reality the characters are largely two-dimensional, with their characterizations determined by their functions in the plot. The plots themselves are interconnected thematically so that each segment of the play contributes to an overall structure and meaning. The authors are constantly shaping the play to suggest a generalized commentary on the human situation.

Frank Thorney is the most fully developed character, but even he is a combination of the qualities required by his role in the play rather than a rounded psychological portrait. He is passionate enough to get involved with Sir Arthur's maid and mistress, Winnifred, innocent enough to be duped into marrying her because he thinks that he is responsible for her pregnancy, impulsive enough to marry the virtuous Susan too even though he has no good plan for concealing his bigamy, villainous enough to murder her on a sudden whim, and finally noble enough to be shocked at his own actions even as he carries them out and to be sincerely repentant when he is finally caught. Modern readers are apt to see the shrewd study of Frank's vacillations as indications of a sensitive psychologist at work. But, as is pointed out in Chapter II, psychology and ethics were more closely connected in the seventeenth century than today. Appreciation of the accuracy of the analysis of Frank's motivations should not disguise the moral outline of that analysis. Frank, like so many of Ford's later characters, is given so much surface vitality that we can be fooled into taking him primarily as a psychological study instead of seeing his more important functional role in the development of the play's themes.

The other characters appear less rounded primarily because their functions in the plot are less complex. Sir Arthur is villainous; Susan is faithful and virtuous; Winnifred at first is scheming and corrupt; later, impressed by Frank's nobility, she is repentant and becomes a symbol of the moral values that Frank himself can never quite carry through. Throughout the play the development of the characters is determined by the controlling theme—that people, though basically good, are easily corrupted but can through sincere repentance be reconciled with God and man. Frank, Winnifred, and the witch of the title all repent, and even the dog-devil becomes the vehicle for a sermon to Cuddy Banks on moral responsibility and the nature of evil.

When the play is read in this symbolic way, the totally unrealistic use of the devil in the form of a dog can be seen as consistent with the play's overall form. The handling of the dog is in fact an instructive illustration of the ways in which symbolism, realism, psychology, and morality are often linked in seventeenth-century plays. The dog-devil has no control over the characters until they want his help. Dekker, with his usual eye for social commentary and moral analysis, shows that the witch was originally innocent of the charges of witchcraft made by the townsmen. As long as she remains innocent, the devil cannot harm her. But when the old woman wishes for revenge on her accusers, she is corrupted by the dog-devil and actually turned into a witch.

Frank too is brushed by the·dog-devil and thereby tempted into murder only after he has realized, subconsciously at least, that he needs to be rid of Susan. It should be seen that these symbolic techniques are directed toward clarifying the subtleties of moral responsibility. The portraits of the witch, Frank, and the townspeople, as well as of the other characters in the play, are convincing in terms of seventeenth-century ethics and psychology and are never intended to become more fully rounded psychological analyses. Unless we take them on their own terms, we are in danger of misunderstanding the play's form and consequently its meaning as well.

The only other extant work from Ford's collaborative period with Dekker is the moral masque, *The Sun's Darling* (licensed, 1624). The masque was not published until 1656, and the printed version seems to be that of a revival in the late 1630's.[21] Speculation as to Ford's share in the collaboration has not been fruitful since the style differs so radically from any of Ford's other work. What is obvious is that the work was marred, possibly during a revision, because of an attempt to include a compliment to the king. When Raybright is suddenly transformed from an everyman into a prince who discourses on the need for order in the kingdom, the effect is jarring. To suggest to the prince (King Charles?) that he should be identified with the changeable Raybright seems insulting.

Despite these problems the version that we have is clear enough to permit an analysis of the masque's structure. The allegory is not difficult: Raybright's progress through the seasons parallels man's progress through life. At the beginning the youthful Raybright, rather than face the harsh realities of earthly existence, prefers to live in a world of fantasy where all his desires are satisfied. Because of his preoccupation with mutability, he is convinced that all ambition and glory are sterile. The priest of the Sun reprimands him for his "fond indulgence"[22] in seeking a dream world instead of trying to make the pilgrimage of his life worthwhile. When Raybright argues that the Sun scorns him, the priest rebukes him and tells him that, despite his attitude, the Sun has agreed "to gratifie/ All your wilde longings"

(p. 21). Reading allegorically we see that Raybright represents mankind, upon whom God (the Sun) pours his bounties, requesting only that man do what he can to use those bounties wisely. After Raybright is given a vision of the Sun, he wisely decides that "that dutie which invites / My filial pietie" (p. 25) must be placed before his own greedy preference of an "Eternitie of earths delights" (p. 25). The Sun commends him since "The reason breeds the appetite" (p. 25), but once the Sun is gone Raybright quickly falls under the influence of Folly and Lady Humour. Raybright is never able to escape Folly and Lady Humour, just as man can never be rid of his disordered imagination and mutable body.

The natural life offered to Raybright by the beautiful lady, Spring, is unable to compete with the artificial world of Lady Humour. Youth, Health, and Delight hold little attraction for Raybright when compared with Lady Humour's promise to teach him to dress well, dance well, eat well, and fight well through the help of her fashionable entourage. Raybright's choice is the choice, frequently presented in pastoral literature, between the virtue and honor of the country life and the vice and dishonor of the court. He must choose nature or art, virtue or vice, reality or fantasy, reason or passion, contemplation or rash action, permanence or change. Spring can offer only a chaste world of delight in nature, virtue, poetry, and knowledge, while Folly and Humour can offer a world much more glamorous at first but ultimately illusory. Apparently Ford and Dekker were concerned that some in the audience might take this anti-court theme too literally and think Spring's world excessively Puritan, for they find it necessary to include a speech by Health that stresses that extensive travel and courtly pleasures will be a part of this world too. But even this description fails to win Raybright, who is much more impressed by a fairyland castle that Lady Humour will create for him "by art" (p. 35). Only too late does he recognize that he has given up the true world for an empty illusion; even then he is unable to assert himself and quickly falls back under the influence of Folly and Lady Humour.

By repudiating Spring, Raybright antagonizes Summer

too, for with his innocence gone and with his lack of interest in a reformed life, there is little chance for a romance with a chaste lady. The Sun intervenes and gets Summer to try to win him back to virtue, but Raybright is little interested and goes off again with Humour. Having failed in her mission, Summer is afraid of death, but the Sun assures her that she will be cured in nine months; reading allegorically we see that nature shares none of the blame for Man's Fall and that the progression of nature toward yearly death is a natural cycle in which there is permanence despite mutability.

Autumn is much more friendly. Despite Raybright's companions, the Sun puts Fortune and Cupid at his disposal, and Raybright is offered the full harvest of Autumn's bounty— that is, pleasure and reward in this world despite his human weaknesses. The scene is made into an extended glorification of the richness and fullness of the material blessings that are man's because of God's boundless generosity. Raybright is gloriously happy for a time but once again Humour and Folly are able to convince him that change is desirable. They persuade him to leave the country and go to the city to the court of Winter, where Folly assures him *"Plenties* horne is alwaies full"* (p. 55). The appeal is primarily to his gluttony: rich banquets are promised, significantly including what Lady Humour suggests will be art added to nature:

> Mistery there, like to another nature,
> Confects the substance of the choisest fruits,
> In a rich candy, with such imitation
> Of forme and colour, 'twill deceive the eye:
> Untill the taste be ravished. (pp. 55–56)

Raybright is easily persuaded again, but he has begun to resign himself to failure:

> Now if I fail, let man's experience read me;
> 'Twas *Humor,* join'd with *Follie,* did mislead me. (p. 56)

Act V is marred by the sudden transformation of Raybright from an erring everyman to a faultless prince, but very likely something resembling the present version was originally intended. If Raybright were not so perfect, the section would fit well with the rest of the masque. Having Winter represented by the court after having the other three seasons in the country is an ingenious way of adding color to a lifeless season while at the same time establishing the necessary courtly context for the end of the masque. The setting at court also provides another dimension to the microcosm-macrocosm theme. When some rebellious clowns resist sharing their harvest with Raybright, Winter tells them that they are unreasonable not to perceive that the ordered state that Raybright will govern will provide for everyone. Just as reason should lead each man to order his own life according to God's eternal law, so reason should lead all men to order their society through the temporal law established by God's representative, the prince.

In the dances that follow all nature is in harmony. The four elements and the four humours are made to dance together without discord as an image of man's potential perfection. Later the four seasons also join in, and we are made to perceive the possibility of concord between man and his entire universe. Unfortunately, since the world is fallen, such a vision can exist only as an abstract ideal toward which we can strive. Evidence of the world's continuing discord is quickly forthcoming. Detraction scorns the dance as a meaningless show, and Lady Humour begins imploring Raybright to think again of change and of a Spring that is clearly meant to represent earthly rather than heavenly delights. Now Raybright has reached the winter of his life, but age has not brought wisdom. In the cycle of nature, as Winter explains to Raybright,

> my sharper breath
> Doe's purge grosse exhalations from the earth;
> My frosts and snows do purifie the air
> From choking foggs, makes the skie clear and fair. (p. 65)

If Raybright could treat his old age as such a time of purgation, he might through Winter's "grave and sage advice" (p. 65) be brought to an eternal rebirth in the "happy shades of Paradice" (p. 65). But he is still the servant of his changeable nature and quickly decides that he should follow Humour to her illusory Spring.

At this point the Sun intervenes and draws the obvious moral: even at the end of life, when old age should serve as a forceful reminder of approaching death,

> a humor of som novel fancie
> Untasted, or untry'd, puts off the minute
> Of resolution, which should bid farewel
> To a vain world of wearinesse and sorrow. (p. 66)

If man could avoid the disruption of his humours by Lady Humour and the seduction of his reason by Folly, he could participate in the harmonious dance of life. But man remains imperfect: Folly and Humour will never leave him. His only hope is to recognize his weakness and follow the Sun's advice to "worship with amazement" (p. 66). At the end of the masque, Raybright finally does capitulate with a simple "Yes! gracious Lord" (p. 66). During the Sun's final long speech calling for moral reformation, Raybright is before us in worship. We are left with this visual image of his restored faith and with a statement of the power of God's grace when man is truly repentant:

> Man hath a double guard, if time can win him;
> Heavens power above him, his own peace within him. (p. 67)

Such an analysis as the above makes the masque seem much more sober than it would have to a Jacobean audience, who would have assimilated the highly conventional ideas without difficulty and could thus enjoy the byplay, the poetry, and the spectacle. Realization of the serious message that the masque contains would certainly not have prevented an audience from enjoying the antics of Raybright, Folly, and Lady Humour. If in addition we try to visualize what probably was an elaborate scenic display, we begin to get an idea of the fun and spectacle of the masque. But we should also remember that much of the pleasure must have come from the intellectual comprehension of the masque's structure and meaning.

The Sun's Darling at first seems completely different from Ford's other work, and it is so in the sense that it is a masque while all of Ford's other dramatic works are plays. But the techniques of the masque are not completely foreign to the techniques of Ford's plays. Here the symbolic, representational, moral approach is obvious; in Ford's plays the technique is disguised by the apparently realistic surface qualities that a play usually has. Raybright, the everyman-type hero of *The Sun's Darling,* has many qualities in common with Frank in *The Witch of Edmonton.* Both are troubled, indecisive, passionate, but basically good men who are forced to make decisions as to the lives they will lead. Both choose badly at first and fall into sin, but both are redeemed at the end through traditional moral and religious formulas. The main difference is that in *The Witch* the choices are given a realistic setting whereas in *The Sun's Darling* all is presented in an allegorical mode.

In his later plays too Ford made use of techniques that are at least analogous to the clearly symbolic technique of the masque. Many of Ford's characters are little more than types. He never uses tag names in the manner of Jonson or allegorical abstractions in the manner of the masque but he often uses names which clearly reveal the character's nature. In *The Broken Heart* Ford helps the reader by translating the names for him; in the other plays he does not, but the educated members of the audience would have no trouble in recognizing the derivations of such names as Putana in *'Tis Pity She's a Whore* and D'Avolos in *Love's Sacrifice* and perhaps little more with Eroclea (honorable love) and Parthenophil (devoted to virginity) in *The Lover's Melancholy.* More important than the clues to meaning is the method of characterization that Ford's use of such names suggests. He seems to think of his characters as having distinct and recognizable characteristics rather than as being fully developed psychological entities. It should suggest to us that his characters need to be understood in relation to what they represent instead of being psychoanalyzed as if they have some independent being outside the play. Ford was fascinated by psychology, but his interest never leads him beyond the conventional humours-and-passions psychology of the seventeenth century. It could indeed be argued that the fact of his academic interest in the subject makes it even less appropriate to talk in modern terms about his characters.

When Ford began to write independent plays some time after 1625, he made good use of his training in works like *The Witch of Edmonton* and *The Sun's Darling*. When he wrote tragedy he turned to the Italianate tragedy of intrigue, introduced in England by Kyd's *The Spanish Tragedy* and made popular by Marlowe, Shakespeare, Chapman, Tourneur, Webster, Fletcher, Middleton, and others. Ford's tragedies, *'Tis Pity She's a Whore, Love's Sacrifice,* and *The Broken Heart,* were clearly influenced by such plays as Chapman's *Bussy D'Ambois,* Webster's *The White Devil* and *The Duchess of Malfi,* and Middleton's *Women Beware Women* and *The Changeling.* Sensational and complicated plots emphasizing illicit love, violence, and intrigue, southern European settings, theatrical protagonists glorying in their heroic or pseudo-heroic actions, and ingeniously depicted ethical problems are characteristic of both Ford's tragedies and the earlier tragedy. Evaluation of the intention and tone of such drama is difficult since the plays combine elaborate theatricality with sophisticated thematic and psychological analysis.

That the Jacobean theory of tragedy was moral is unquestionable, but the trouble with most theories of tragedy, then as now, is that they often do not fit the plays being considered. Since the Elizabethans were never strong on theory, we are apt to find that any abstract theory of what they were doing is not likely to fit exactly. With the Elizabethans one suspects that the form came first and then the theory. Since the theory itself was drawn forth partly in refutation of Puritan attacks on the stage, even more caution is necessary. But even with these qualifications it must be granted that the acceptance of the moral basis of tragedy was more than defensive.[23] Among the formative influences on Elizabethan tragedy were the classical and medieval principle that all poetry should be moral and the medieval tradition of teaching the good by illustrating in *exempla* the results of evil actions. The hope was that men would be pleased by the imitation of varied actions and instructed by the moral lessons drawn from the stories.[24] Nevertheless Elizabethan drama is too protean to be contained in any such neat formula. No doubt almost all of the dramatists would approve the theory, and most would be influenced at least to the extent that the superstructure of their plots would permit a moral explanation of their purpose. But no one needed to be told that much of the popularity of the theater comes from the fascination and excitement of evil and not from sober admonitions to do good. Particularly in the private theaters, where the audiences were more sophisticated and less interested in moral exhortation, explicit didacticism became less prominent.

Many who have noted this change have charged that in Jacobean tragedy the dramatists are much more interested in telling sensational stories than in serious analysis.[25] Even if this charge is true, we are probably not justified in concluding, as many have, that the theater was entering a period of moral decadence. It is not surprising that audiences were interested in exciting stories of lust, intrigue, and revenge; nor is it surprising that playwrights wrote plays which satisfied this demand. If some drama designed for entertainment is acceptable, as most would agree, how are we to decide when it becomes unhealthy? When does funloving bawdiness become indecent? When does delight in the machinations of villains become condonement? When does sympathy for illicit lovers go too far? To claim to rule on these matters presupposes a clearer definition of goodness and healthy sexuality than is available to us or was to the Elizabethans. It is no doubt true that the dramatists took advantage of these ambiguities in presenting some themes and scenes in questionable taste. But since the answers to these questions are so subjective, serious discussion of moral decadence is almost impossible. It seems better to consider the question on the aesthetic level. Do the plays become more than mere entertainment? In the more serious dramatists the escape from didacticism did not mean an escape from seriousness, and the extent to which the best dramatists continued to concern themselves with important social, political, and ethical issues has been too often underestimated. Instead of being merely excited or amused by the plays we should ask whether the themes are sensational for sensation's sake or are necessary for the analysis that is being attempted. That a plot contains lurid elements is not proof that the intention is merely to entertain, since utilizing exaggerated situations may be a graphic means of emphasizing a conflict of ideals or a conflict within an individual. Thematic or psychological studies are most easily carried on when the analysis is of people who are boldly simplified so as to become types or who have departed in some way from normal patterns of living. An extraordinary situation which states a conflict forcefully is not only highly dramatic but can also provide a framework for intensive thematic or psychological analysis. The use of such situations is an indication of dramatic technique but in itself says little about a playwright's seriousness. Then as now, sensational stories could be used for serious purposes.

Some playwrights such as Fletcher are no doubt primarily concerned with entertaining; others such as Chapman seem to take their plays quite seriously as philosophical analyses. But most of the playwrights—Chapman and Fletcher included—probably saw themselves as practical dramatists trying to write successful plays in traditional forms. To view them as mere entertainers without recognizing their deeper intention is to underestimate the seriousness of the form; but the opposite danger—to regard them as subtle and profound thinkers who present their philosophical conclusions in dramatic form—must, I think, also be avoided.[26] There are several reasons for being suspicious of such attempts, whether applied to Shakespearean or to Jacobean tragedy. The most important perhaps is that the theater was a competitive commercial venture, and the playwrights were professionals who had to be more concerned about pleasing audiences than about presenting an even mildly original philosophy of life. Audiences probably regarded tragedy as one of the traditional dramatic forms and would have expected the tragedies that they saw to fit the general pattern. Many people today think of the tragic view of life as an independent philosophy of life that is beyond the religious and of tragedy as an analysis of what man's condition is in a world with no solid foundations. To read these modernist assumptions into all seventeenth-century plays that are not explicitly religious is to distort them out of their traditional form. The error can creep in in subtle ways. Thus Robert

Ornstein, who is admirably historical in most of his readings of Jacobean tragedy, can still claim that the best tragedy was in some way a universal form that called forth the best in the writers of the time. He speaks of "the need to distinguish between Jacobean drama as popular entertainment and as serious and inspired art" [27] and argues against interpreting "the inspired fraction" of plays by the standards of the whole. In so far as this concern leads to respect for the form and close attention to the text, it is commendable; but the danger is that we appeal to modern values under the mistaken notion that they are universal values. No doubt we should not judge seventeenth-century plays by the platitudes of the age, but we should judge them by the best thought of their age, not our own; and we should beware of concluding that anything that now seems outdated was platitude then. It is at least more likely that their tragedies would reflect the prevailing intellectual atmosphere rather than express a new or original approach to life.

Ultimately the disagreement concerns the definition of the religious and philosophical atmosphere during the Jacobean period, for many modern scholars would claim that the impact of more modern ways of thinking in the writings of Machiavelli, Montaigne, and others was already changing the atmosphere significantly. There are several potential dangers in this approach. One is that we exaggerate the modernism of a writer like Montaigne by calling attention to his stress on individual values without noting how closely his views parallel those of a conservative like Hooker on such matters as the need for an ordered society, the suspicion of system-building theologians and philosophers, the importance of tolerance and common sense, and the need to base all values on religious faith. Another danger is the vicious circle we get into when we show the age's intellectual context by reference to its literature and then in turn interpret this same literature by that context. This tendency has perhaps been most prevalent in the interpretation of Jacobean tragedy.

In her influential book, *The Jacobean Drama,* Una Ellis-Fermor argues that the Jacobean drama reflects "the loss of a spiritual significance" [28] as society increasingly fails to find any connection between the spiritual world of the first cause and the material world of second causes. Accompanying this loss of assurance in an ordered hierarchical society is an obsessive preoccupation with death and a realization that man's only remaining nobility comes in accepting suffering stoically and reasserting his essential dignity. No longer do the characters find hope and dignity through the education that suffering brings, as Lear had; now there is only the "sense of the lateness of time, the weariness of the spirit, the burden of fruitless experience." [29] Sensing the failure of their religious tradition, they fall back upon Seneca's pessimistic repudiation of the glories of the world and reassertion of noble fortitude in the face of decay and corruption. According to this view the Jacobean tragedians were profound thinkers who saw more deeply into the malaise of the age than anyone else. Irving Ribner, following Miss Ellis-Fermor, maintains that these dramatists were aware of the breakdown of the values of Christian humanism and saw their plays as a "philosophical exploration," [30] a quest for a new basis for moral order. Although Ornstein does not claim a philosophical content, he believes that the pessimism is a reflection of their sensitive response to the changing situation.[31]

That the Jacobeans felt the sense of rising tensions is unquestionable, although even that feeling may be exaggerated. As F. P. Wilson said: "Perhaps the insistence on Jacobean 'pessimism' is due to a too exclusive attention to Jacobean tragedy and the poetry of Donne." [32] The Jacobeans saw changes, changes that in retrospect we can see as the beginning of the modern world—a new science, a new empirical method, a rising middle class, a new individualism; but it would be wrong to attribute too much awareness of the causes or the significance of the new trends to the Jacobeans themselves. In so far as they were pessimistic their pessimism was solidly rooted in the old orthodoxy that was gradually breaking up. The mood was not that of an irreligious cynicism that is convinced that there is no longer means of contact between God and man, but rather a sense that all men are forgetting that we live *sub specie aeternitatis*. In a time of change there is perhaps inevitable confusion

as to whether it is progress or decay, but the more traditional branches of Jacobean society were inclined to view the
changes as decay caused by neglect of the older virtues.

Those who wrote tragedy produced ironic, reflective,
often cynical probings of the nature of man and society that
no doubt mirror in some way the tensions of the age. But the
connection between the societal changes and the tension expressed in the drama is complex. Few in the seventeenth century would have found the causes of tension in the economic,
political, or sociological changes that were producing a new
age. They simply did not have the terms or the theory or the
interest that would channel their thinking in that direction.
Instead all explanations were apt to be put in religious or
ethical terms. As the Civil War approached, religion was
not becoming less meaningful, as the Ellis-Fermor view implies; if anything it was becoming more important as the
people sought values more permanent than those they saw in
their rapidly changing society. When we turn to the theater
we find that the dramatists were still writing about the traditional themes—lust, ambition, and materialism—instead
of treating the new economic, political, and social problems
as a modern dramatist might. If we paid more attention to
the traditional way in which these playwrights handled these
themes in their non-tragic works, we might be less inclined
to talk about their disenchantment with older values in their
tragedies. It seems unlikely that these dramatists would be
quite conventional in their comedies, tragicomedies, and
other writings and then suddenly launch forth into original
philosophizing in their tragedies.[33]

In analyzing Jacobean tragedy we must face the paradox
that drama can be at once conservative and yet sensitive to
the new changes. The audience was conservative, and the
form itself features a moral structure in which vice is destroyed either by good or through its own excesses. But in
picking topics that will interest an audience, the dramatists
are apt to be *avant garde*. You can have an atheist's tragedy
when an audience has begun to conceive the alternative of
atheism or a tragedy about incest when it can be presented
as at least a remotely plausible possibility. Plays of this type
could both excite by presenting a graphic picture of a world

with new and frightening dimensions and reassure by showing the importance of the more traditional values. The particular position of each dramatist must of course be examined in the context of his own contribution since attitudes
can change even from play to play, but the assumption that
the dramatists' pessimism reflects their sense that traditional moral values were no longer viable is surely a modernist oversimplification.

In interpreting Jacobean pessimism one must enter into
the complicated dispute about the nature of Renaissance
stoicism, for it is clear that the Ellis-Fermor view is based
upon certain common assumptions regarding stoicism. Har-
din Craig, in a still influential article published in 1940,[34]
argues that Renaissance thinkers wavered between three
views of tragedy, the Aristotelian, the Senecan, and the
Christian. According to Craig, the Aristotelians held that
even though all that happens manifests a divine order, nothing is inevitable, and man can often through effort overcome
apparently insurmountable obstacles and live the life of reason; the Senecans held that man is "sure to be beaten" [35] and
can do nothing but endure by building up qualities that will
be sufficient to withstand anything; the Christians held that
man is responsible for his own fate and that catastrophe is
the result of sin. It is my belief that Craig underestimates
the extent to which thinkers in the eclectic Renaissance fused
these views into a philosophy of tragedy that is more consistent and more sophisticated than is commonly supposed.
One view has been that dramatists like Chapman, Webster,
and Middleton show that the world is so depraved that
almost everyone inevitably is corrupted by it. To make the
plays fatalistic in this way robs them of one of their most
distinctive qualities—their insistence upon the significance of
moral decision. On the other hand to make these plays into
simple illustrations of the theory that the wages of sin is
death is to underestimate the complexity of their vision of
evil and the extent of their stoicism. Most of the tragedies
of the period are filled with stoical ideas, but the philosophy
illustrated may be broadly stated as holding that man must
change what he can, endure what he cannot change, but, no
matter what happens, always remain virtuous. Although in

each of these tragedies the circumstances are different, and the exact blend of the mixture of stoicism and Christian responsibility varies considerably from author to author and play to play, the discussion goes on in a basically Christian humanist context. In their evaluations of the action the audience would be trying to discriminate between proper and improper responses to life's problems. There would be admiration for the virtuous, noble hero who accepts his tragic fate with courage and understanding; there would be disdain for the villain who postures stoically in facing a fate that he has brought on himself. There would be elements of sympathy, admiration, and disdain for the many cases that fall somewhere in between.

In an attempt to make more precise responses to the often bewilderingly complex protagonists in Jacobean tragedy, I have distinguished somewhat arbitrarily four different types of protagonists. They are: 1) the all-black villain; 2) the passionate sinner; 3) the noble victim; 4) the rationalizing fool. The protagonist, or antagonist, of the first type (the all-black villain) is a totally evil character who in the course of the play, either through his own excesses or through opposition from the forces of good, is brought to destruction. The protagonist of the second type (the passionate sinner) is a formerly great or potentially great person who submits himself to some passion and thus brings about his own destruction. The description "sinner" may appear too Christian to fit some of the secularized examples of the type, but the easy interchange of secular and religious terms and the tendency to think of all submission to passion as morally wrong makes the term generally accurate. The protagonist of the third type (the noble victim) is a virtuous victim who heroically endures some catastrophe not of his own making or who comes to an understanding of his own at least partial responsibility for his problem and accepts it with dignity and courage. The protagonist of the fourth type (the rationalizing fool) has adopted an unrealistic or immature conception of himself; his real nature is revealed to the audience in scenes that are invariably ironic and frequently satiric in a grotesque or even comic way.

One of the problems in interpreting Jacobean tragedy is

that, while the characters must be understood as representative types, they often are combinations of more than one type. Such combinations suggest a complexity that tempts us to apply psychological analysis, but we stay closer to seventeenth-century methods if we instead try to distinguish the types that are being combined. The four types I have mentioned are all grounded in the ethical thought of the time; in fact ultimately all are traceable back to the morality play with its stress on the significance of the kinds of moral response made to life's situations. Types one, two, and four represent responses that are inadequate in some way while type three represents an ideal. It should be clear that some of the types fit together easily while others do not. Mathematically there are six possible simple combinations of the four types: 1) all-black villain and passionate sinner; 2) all-black villain and noble victim; 3) all-black villain and rationalizing fool; 4) passionate sinner and noble victim; 5) passionate sinner and rationalizing fool; 6) noble victim and rationalizing fool. It should be clear that at least two of the combinations are impossible to achieve without a sudden switch in tone: normally you cannot have an all-black villain who is also a noble victim; nor can a character be at once an all-black villain, who evokes no sympathy, and a passionate sinner, with whom we sympathize. There might, however, be disagreements as to which category fits the case in question: presumably Richard III's deformity and Iago's elaborate self-justification will not win them sympathy, but a case like Shylock's is perhaps more questionable. In plays of this type, the director must decide whether to interpret a character as all-black or to suggest enough rounding so as to make his actions understandable and therefore at least partly sympathetic. We may conclude that if an author tries to combine an all-black villain with either a passionate sinner or a noble victim, he involves his play in serious problems of tone.

The all-black villain and the rationalizing fool are often combined so as to produce a kind of melodramatic stage villain who is at once frightening and grotesquely absurd. Richard III, the Jew of Malta (both of course pre-Jacobean), and Tourneur's D'Amville are the most obvious

examples. Richard III and the Jew of Malta would be perhaps closer to type one while D'Amville would be closer to
type four, but again the production could be slanted toward
the type desired. Discussions of combinations involving type
one are seldom applicable to Ford since there are very few
unmotivated villains in Ford. It is tempting to speculate that
his study of psychology led him to avoid that category, but it
may be simply a question of his not needing the type for the
themes he wanted to pursue.

The other combinations are more important to Ford studies. One of the most frequent combinations in Jacobean tragedy is that of the passionate sinner and the noble victim. In
some tragedies a great person is overcome through some passion or fault but comes to an understanding of himself and
reasserts his essentially noble nature before death. Picking
non-controversial examples is difficult since there is often
question as to whether self-understanding and true nobility
are achieved, but King Lear and Webster's Duchess of Malfi
are two examples that almost all would accept. Sometimes
the process can work in reverse, as in revenge plays where the
protagonist begins as a noble victim but steadily gets more
and more deeply involved in counterintrigues that bring
about his destruction. Vindice in *The Revenger's Tragedy* is
a good example. In all plays that combine types two and
three, a change in the character takes place during the course
of the play.

Another common combination is that of the passionate
sinner and the rationalizing fool. From one point of view we
can sympathize with such a character since we recognize him
as a fellow human being unable to control forces that are
present to some degree in all men. From another point of
view, however, he is only a grotesque shadow of his former
or potential self and reveals traits—hypocrisy, pride, self-
glorification, rationalization—that make him appear ludicrous or absurd. The tendency of a particular play might be
toward understanding or toward satiric exposure, with
again the slant of the production itself no doubt often determining which element was to be dominant.

While types two and three and types two and four can be
combined easily, types three and four cannot: rationalizing

fools and noble victims do not go together well since it is difficult to build up and tear down a character in the same play. When the passionate sinner and the rationalizing fool are combined, the tragic and the satiric can fuse; when the noble victim and the rationalizing fool are combined, the tragic and the satiric pull against each other. Respect for and exposure of the same person can be combined only by a sudden shift of tone within the play, and I am inclined to think that this seldom happens in Jacobean tragedy.

I do not propose to get involved here in the thorny controversies as to where each of the tragic protagonists in Elizabethan and Jacobean tragedy would fit. My scheme does not provide interpretations but only, I hope, a non-controversial framework that makes interpretation more manageable. I will permit myself only the generalization that major Shakespearean tragedy usually involves various combinations of types two and three while Jacobean tragedy more often combines type one or two with type four. Chapman's Clermont, Cato, and Chabot and Webster's Duchess are clearly in type three, but I would argue that the type is not so common as is usually supposed. The importance of type four in Marlowe, Chapman, Tourneur, Webster, and Middleton has, I think, too often been underestimated in evaluating characters like Faustus, Bussy, Byron, D'Amville, Vittoria, Flamineo, Brachiano, Beatrice-Joanna, and DeFlores.[36] Ford's protagonists have usually been thought of as combinations of the passionate sinner and the noble victim. It is clear that the main characters in *The Broken Heart* and *Perkin Warbeck* fit in that general category, but I am inclined to think that type four is more important in *'Tis Pity She's a Whore* and *Love's Sacrifice* than has been realized. Rationalizing fools are present in superfluity in Ford's early prose and poetry, in his tragicomedies, and in the subplots of his tragedies; the possibility that elements at least of this type are present in the main plots of *'Tis Pity* and *Love's Sacrifice* needs to be explored.

If we are to understand the characterization in a Jacobean play, we must recognize the representative types in their various combinations and, as readers, the variations in tone that a production can achieve through stressing one

type in a combination over another; perhaps more important, we must try to view the play as a unified whole in which
characterization is only one element in a larger symbolic
structure. A serious weakness in many interpretations of
Jacobean tragedies has been the tendency, perhaps inevitable because of the dominant influence of romantic theories
of art today, to think of the author as expressing himself
through his protagonists. Only through restoring theme to
its proper central position can we come to an understanding
of what these plays are about. A Jacobean dramatist deliberately patterns his material through a large number of
devices—type characterization, parallels between the main
plot and the subplot, significant juxtaposition of scenes, comparison and contrast of characters, image patterns that are
sometimes verbal but often visual in an almost emblematic
way, and allusions or more explicit references to traditional
concepts. In all of these ways the play is shaped into a
symbolic statement intended to illuminate the themes implicit in the story being told. If the play is a good one, the
story has implications beyond the relatively limited significance of what happens to these particular characters. The
individual analyses, far from being ends in themselves, are
used to illustrate what the dramatist thought of as universal
truths.

To become aware of the highly developed sense of form
in a writer like Ford, we must concentrate on a close analysis
of the text itself, always remembering that the "text," properly considered, is not just the language of the play as we
have it or the production of the play as we might see it
today, but the production of the play in a seventeenth-
century theater for a seventeenth-century audience. The
impossibility of restoring such a text should remind us to be
cautious; but we can assume that the dramatic company,
whether working closely with the playwright or not, would
be trying to develop a coherent interpretation of the play. In
the hands of a competent company, the actual production
would clarify meanings that may seem somewhat ambiguous
in the playwright's written text. On the other hand, we must
recognize that both the playwright and the company were
trying to present exciting theater and that there are many

possible pitfalls for all of them. Any drama assumes a degree of self-directing force which no playwright can entirely control since the plot that the dramatist chooses is a major factor in determining the play's form. The playwright may be forced to sacrifice character motivation to the exigencies of the plot; or he may simply fail to include enough information to show where his own sympathy lies or how he expects the audience to evaluate the action. In developing the characterizations to stress the full theatrical possibilities of the parts, dramatists and companies interested in successful theater may give them a depth and a suggestion of new dimensions of thought and behavior that go beyond what either the dramatist or his company may have thought possible. One speech or one scene may be given more emphasis for dramatic effect than it should have for moral or aesthetic consistency; improper attitudes may be expressed so eloquently that the audience becomes confused.[37]

It is my belief that the failure to understand the form of Ford's plays has led to many of the criticisms that he sacrifices consistency for dramatic expediency. Before assuming the judging role of critic, it is necessary to play the more modest role of interpreter. That role often will require modern readers to overcome an initial instinctive response in order to perceive the play in the form in which it was written. On the other hand, interpreting should force scholars to come to a play without rigid expectations based on knowledge of the author's other works or of ideas and dramatic techniques of the period. Unless each work is allowed to communicate its own form, we are in danger of forcing it into a preconceived mold. In what follows, I shall assume that Ford was a competent dramatist who arranged his materials as he did for good reasons.[38] My task is to examine all of the elements that influence and determine tone and form in the hope that we can discover, not Ford's probable intention, but the meaning that is actually present in each play.

IV

FORD'S TRAGICOMEDY

Since the chronology of Ford's plays is somewhat uncertain,[1] and since in any case they show little indication of any change or development in his ideas, I have decided to consider first the four tragicomedies, then the three tragedies, and finally the single history play. Ford's four tragicomedies, *The Lover's Melancholy* (1629), *The Fancies, Chaste and Noble* (1638), *The Lady's Trial* (1639), and *The Queen, or the Excellency of Her Sex* (1653),[2] are often dismissed as innocuous and conventional; but even casual examination reveals that they all deal with similar topics in a roughly similar way and that they are all influenced by ideas like those in Robert Burton's extremely popular *The Anatomy of Melancholy*. The recurrent pattern—the separation of lovers, the testing of their virtue, and their ultimate reconciliation—is conventional enough, but Ford's interest in ethical and psychological problems gives the plays a more than conventional cast. Scholars concerned with the sources of Ford's interest in such ideas have stressed his specific indebtedness to Burton. The debt is undeniable and has been documented thoroughly in Ewing's *Burtonian Melancholy in the Plays of John Ford* and in Sensabaugh's *The Tragic Muse of John Ford;*[3] but it must be remembered that Burton was writing a compendium of

68

the learning of his day. The specific debt to Burton may be far less than many have supposed simply because so many of his ideas were commonly accepted. It is not surprising that the theories of behavior found in Burton provide a natural supplement to the ethical ideas of Ford discussed in Chapter II, for in both the early Ford and Burton we find the same fusion of Christian and classical, the same ethical and rational faith that is characteristic of so much of Anglican thought during the late Jacobean and Caroline period. Before proceeding to the plays themselves a preliminary discussion of the cast of Burton's thought is essential, for his attitude toward love and ethics has frequently been misunderstood.

Burton's *magnum opus* was first published in 1621 and went through five editions by 1638. His diversity precludes any short, accurate description, for no matter what one says about the book, someone else will find a passage with a different emphasis. The expansive, eclectic method leads to the inclusion of much seemingly contradictory material, and source hunters must be particularly careful not to quote out of context. His section on love is no exception. In general it may be said that Burton's attitude toward love is a logical corollary to his discussion of passion and reason. He believed, along with most of the theorists of his time, that the passions were closely linked to the humours of the body, and that a disruption in the balance of the humours led to excesses which found release in the passions. Since a physical cause was involved, the dominance of passion was regarded as a disease. To avoid the danger of being ruled by passion, the reason must maintain control by turning the passions to proper ends and moderating their influence; or to put it in more Burtonian terms, the rational soul must control the sensitive soul.

Modern readers must constantly be aware of the ethical cast of Burton's thought. Although Burton and the medical and psychological writers of his time were searching for explanations, their methods were not truly scientific. Overemphasis upon their scientific methods can lead to a deterministic explanation of their psychology. Nothing could be further from the truth. Lawrence Babb, in his

useful introduction to Burton, comments: "Since the passions are in some degree due to physical causes, there are
physiological means of regulating them, for example, diet.
But the remedies on which every man must finally rely are
moral: unremitting vigilance on the part of the reason and
unremitting effort on the part of the reasonable will." [4] In
the opening of his section on the cure of melancholy Burton
stresses that cures are possible if the individual wants to be
helped: "It may be hard to cure, but not impossible, for him
that is most grievously affected, if he be but willing to be
helped" (*AM*, II, 5; 2, 1, 1, 1). Burton goes on to insist
that it is very important that prayer accompany treatment:
"we must first begin with prayer, and then use physick; not
one without the other, but both together . . . For all the
physick we can use, art, excellent industry, is to no purpose
without calling on God" (*AM*, II, 9–10; 2, 1, 2). Medical
psychology was still the handmaiden of Christian ethics.
Babb comments: "The knowledge of greatest worth and
dignity was that which served a religious or moral purpose.
Science was valued principally, therefore, for its religious
and ethical services. Its highest functions were the strength-
ening of men's belief and the rectification of their
conduct." [5] Burton may have been extremely interested in
the new science, but his methods were old-fashioned.

In his discussion of love Burton stresses that love is a
passion which is noble when controlled by reason but ignoble
when uncontrolled and refers with approval to the theory
traceable ultimately to Plato and made popular in the Renaissance by Ficino and others that there are two Venuses
and two loves. He quotes Augustine: *"two Cities make two
Loves, Jerusalem and Babylon, the Love of God the one,
the Love of the world the other; of these two cities are we
all Citizens, as by examination of ourselves we may soon
find, and of which"* (*AM*, III, 14; 3, 1, 1, 2). Adding that
"the one Love is the root of all mischief, the other of all
good" (*AM*, III, 14; 3, 1, 1, 2), Burton then quotes Lucian
on the same distinction: *"one love was born in the sea,
which is as various and raging in young men's breasts as the
sea itself, and causeth burning lust: the other is that golden
chain which was let down from heaven, and with a divine*

Fury ravisheth our souls, made to the image of God, and stirs us up to comprehend the innate and incorruptible beauty, to which we were once created" (*AM*, III, 14; 3, 1, 1, 2).

Burton distinguishes various kinds of worthy love, but his main concern is with love as a disease, commonly described as heroical love, or love-melancholy. "The part affected in men is the liver, and therefore called *Heroical*, because commonly Gallants, Noblemen, and the most generous spirits are possessed with it" (*AM*, III, 43; 3, 2, 1, 1). A constant target for Burton's condemnation is the noble gallant who professes that his love is noble when in actuality it is no more than lust. Heroical love

rageth with all sorts and conditions of men, yet is most evident among such as are young and lusty, in the flower of their years, nobly descended, high fed, such as live idly, and at ease; and for that cause (which our Divines call burning lust) this *ferinum insanus amor,* this mad and beastly passion, as I have said, is named by our Physicians *Heroical* Love, and a more honourable title put upon it, *amor nobilis,* as *Savanarola* styles it, because Noble men and women make a common practice of it, and are so ordinarily affected with it. (*AM*, III, 62; 3, 2, 1, 2)

A natural tendency of the time was for men to confuse, often deliberately, the honorable intentions of divine or Platonic love with their lustful desires for fleshly woman. Since beauty is the object of both kinds of love, men are able to mask their dishonorable intentions with exaggerated Platonic theorizing. As Burton says:

those two *Venus* twins, *Eros* and *Anteros,* are then most firm and fast. For many times otherwise men are deceived by their flattering *Gnathos,* dissembling Chamaeleons, outsides, hypocrites, that make a shew of great love, learning, pretend honesty, virtue, zeal, modesty, with affected looks and counterfeit gestures: feigned protestations often steal away the hearts and favours of men, and deceive them, *specie virtutis et umbra,* when as *revera* and indeed there is no worth or honesty at all in them, no truth, but mere hypocrisy, subtilty, knavery, and the like.[6] (*AM,* III, 25; 3, 1, 2, 3)

Burton himself is worried lest he will *"confound filthy burning lust with pure and divine Love"* (*AM*, III, 15; 3, 1, 1, 2).

Perhaps the most helpful way to begin a discussion of *The Lover's Melancholy* (1629) is to make a clear distinction between honest or natural love and heroical love. Since marriage involves bodies as well as minds, the physical attraction which exists before and in virtuous marriages must be acceptable and even honorable. Burton recognizes the existence of this kind of virtuous physical love when he writes:

> There is an honest love, I confess, which is natural, *laqueus occultus captivans corda hominum, ut a mulieribus non possint separari,* a secret snare to captivate the hearts of men, as *Christopher Fonseca* proves, a strong allurement, of a most attractive, occult, adamantine property, and powerful virtue, and no man living can avoid it. *Et qui vim non sensit amoris, aut lapis est, aut bellua.* He is not a man, but a block, a very stone, *aut Numen, aut Nebuchannezzar,* he hath a gourd for his head, a pepon for his heart, that hath not felt the power of it. (*AM*, III, 57; 3, 2, 1, 2)

Such love is not disease but is the natural prelude and accompaniment of marriage.

But how are we to distinguish natural love from violent heroical love? Burton does so by making an important moral distinction: love is heroical only when it threatens the established moral order of God and society. Describing heroical love, Burton says:

> But this love . . . is immoderate, inordinate, and not to be comprehended in any bounds. It will not contain itself within the union of marriage, or apply to one object, but is a wandering, extravagant, a domineering, a boundless, an irrefragable, a destructive passion; . . . it extends sometimes to corrivals, &c. begets rapes, incests, murders. . . . But it is confined within no terms of blood, years, sex, or whatsoever else. (*AM*, III, 59–60; 3, 2, 1, 2)

Natural lovers may suffer from melancholy until they are married but then will find a logical and harmonious solution to their malady (*AM*, III, 263–64; 3, 2, 5, 5). If the obstacles to marriage are insurmountable, the lover should try to forget his love since passion may overcome reason and lead to transgression of the moral law. But love can be termed natural as long as it remains moral.

No definite line exists between unnatural and natural love in life itself since the victim cannot be sure that he can stay within the bounds of morality; but in drama there is a clear line since melancholy lovers on their way to marriage belong to comedy or tragicomedy, while heroical lovers who threaten the moral order are most naturally treated in tragedy. When a villainous lover appears in comedy or tragicomedy, he either fails in his plans or else recognizes his faults and reforms. The lovers in *The Lover's Melancholy* with the exception of Thamasta are all conventionally moral in their approaches to their problems, and the only difficulty is that obstacles stand in the way of marriage to the desired partners. They are in varying degrees victims of melancholy, but they are not subjected to the moral struggle and temptation that befall those who are sick with heroical love. Instead they fall into a state of grieving inactivity which is a threat to order only in so far as the characters involved have responsibility in society.

At the beginning of *The Lover's Melancholy* we meet three lethargic but not rebellious victims of love-melancholy—Palador, Menaphon, and Amethus. Since each loves someone who is unmarried, the only problem is to produce the girls and gain their consent to marriage. The problems of Palador and Amethus are connected. Palador's love, Eroclea, has been forced to flee from Cyprus to avoid rape by Palador's father, who has since died. Eroclea's sister, Cleophila, is unavailable to Amethus since she must take care of the girls' father, Meleander, who has become melancholy because of Eroclea's absence and his own disinheritance for not having agreed to the rape. Quite obviously what is needed to bring a happy ending is to produce Eroclea, thereby curing both Palador and Meleander and releasing Cleophila for Amethus. Since Eroclea is present in male disguise from almost the beginning of the play, there is no difficulty in bringing her forward at the proper time. When her true sex is revealed, the other love conflict in the play is also resolved. Thamasta, who has loved the disguised Eroclea, realizes her folly and returns to her faithful melancholic lover, Menaphon, thereby curing him as well. The plot is a conventional romantic one, but it serves as a framework for Ford's analysis of the causes and cures of melancholy.

The result of the melancholy inactivity of Prince Palador is a fast deteriorating situation at the court. Sophronos attributes the country's problems to Palador:

> OUr Common-wealth is sick: tis more then time
> That wee should wake the Head thereof, who sleepes
> In the dull Lethargy of lost security.
> The Commons murmur, and the Nobles grieve,
> The Court is now turn'd Anticke, and growes wilde,
> Whiles all the neighb'ring Nations stand at gaze,
> And watch fit oportunity, to wreake
> Their just conceived fury, on such injuries,
> As the late Prince, our living Masters Father,
> Committed against Lawes of truth or honour. (D1ᵛ; II, i)

We shall see in our discussion of *Love's Sacrifice, The Broken Heart,* and *Perkin Warbeck* that Ford was extremely interested in what produces an ordered society, and we should not minimize the importance of the threat that Palador's melancholy constitutes for Cyprus. Without effective leadership disorder quickly arises and spreads. The virtuous Rhetias speaks of "the madnesse of the times" (B4ᵛ; I, ii), of "the Riots that embalme / Our wanton Gentry" (B4ᵛ; I, ii), and of "the vices / Which rot the Land" (B4ᵛ–C1; I, ii) and determines to renounce the pretensions of the court. The physician Corax speaks of "the sloth / Of sleepe and surfet" (D2ᵛ; II, i) that characterizes the court and laments the fact that he has "To waste my time thus Droane-like in the Court" (F4; III, i). Meleander's condemnation of the age's vanities is even more severe:

> fooles, desperate fooles,
> You are cheated, grossely cheated, range, range on,
> And rowle about the world to gather mosse,
> The mosse of honour, gay reports, gay clothes,
> Gay wives, huge empty buildings, whose proud roofes,
> Shall with their pinacles, even reach the starres.
> Ye worke and worke like Moles, blind in the paths,
> That are bor'd through the crannies of the earth,
> To charge your hungry soules with such full surfets,
> As being gorg'd once, make'ee leane with plenty.

And when ye have skimd the vomit of your riots,
Y'are fat in no felicity but folly,
Then your last sleepes seize on'ee. Then the troopes
Of wormes crawle round, &, feast, good cheare, rich fare,
Dainty delicious. (F1–F1ᵛ; II, ii)

His criticisms may be partly attributed to his melancholy, but Rhetias comments: "This is sence yet in this distraction" (F1ᵛ; II, ii).

The subplot illustrates the corruption by depicting the typical aspiring courtier's excessive concern for fine clothes and eloquent language rather than true virtue. Cuculus and Pelias are at once parodies of the courtier type and examples of the deterioration which has resulted from Palador's lack of concern for what is happening to his country. Throughout the play both are dressed in outlandish costumes that are meant to reflect their corrupt and immature values. In the scene in which Cuculus appears with his page Grilla, who is disguised as a woman, both are elaborately overdressed. In contrast, the virtuous Rhetias in the same scene is described as *"carelesly attyr'd"* (B4ᵛ; I, ii). If one is truly noble he is unconcerned about his appearance and remains natural in dress and manner. When Amethus advises Thamasta on how she should act, he tells her that she should be

> Not like a Lady of the trim, new crept
> Out of the shell of sluttish sweat and labour,
> Into the glittering pompe of ease and wantonnesse,
> Imbroideries, and all these antike fashions,
> That shape a woman monstrous; to transforme
> Your education, and a Noble birth
> Into contempt and laughter. Sister, sister
> She who derives her blood from Princes, ought
> To glorifie her greatnesse by humility. (C3; I, iii)

This simplicity of manner should also be reflected in simplicity of speech. Cuculus and Pelias are always ready with long and flowery speeches. When Grilla asks Cuculus if he is in love with all of the women that he courts, he replies: "Pish, I haue not a ragge of love about me. Tis only a foolish humour I am possest with, to be surnam'd the Conquerour. I will court any thing; be in love with nothing, nor no—thing" (F3; III, i). In contrast, when Amethus is about to court Cleophila, Rhetias tells him: "Few words to purpose soon'st prevaile: / Study no long Orations; be plaine and short" (F2; II, ii). Earlier when Amethus met Menaphon on his return to Cyprus, he told him "O, I want words / To let thee know my heart" (B2; I, i). We are clearly meant to see the close connection between the natural or simple and the virtuous and between the artificial or pretentious and the corrupt.

In the account of the music contest between Parthenophil (Eroclea in disguise) and the nightingale, Ford considers the relationship of the natural and the artificial in the artistic process itself. The section is of particular importance to a discussion of Ford's style since it is the only scene in his plays where a question of aesthetics is considered. No doubt the scene is intended in part to develop the characterization of Parthenophil, but the relevance of the art-nature conflict to the play's main themes makes it likely that Ford wants our close attention. It is significant that Parthenophil, who has developed her artistic talents to the fullest possible degree through many hours of practice, is able to win the contest with the nightingale, "Natures best skill'd Musicion" (B3ᵛ; I, i). In the stress on simplicity of expression in the rest of the play, Ford is not championing a naive primitivism in art or a passive innocence in life. Rather he implies that in both art and life the discipline of training and reason can lead to greater perfection. Parthenophil represents an ideal both as an artist and as a person. In her art she is able to express "Concord in discord, lines of diffring method / Meeting in one full Center of delight" (B3ᵛ; I, i). In her life Parthenophil maintains harmony despite the discord of her difficult experiences. The terms in which Menaphon praises her are worth noting:

> It was not strange, the musicke of his hand
> Did over-match *birds,* when his voyce and beauty,
> Youth, carriage, and discretion, must, from men
> Indu'd with reason, ravish admiration. (B4; I, i)

A cultivated grace of manner seems to be the inevitable expression of her inner maturity. But she is not coldly impassive; when the bird's heart breaks, Parthenophil is profoundly moved.

I suspect that the graceful simplicity of Ford's own style in *The Lover's Melancholy* is an attempt to reproduce in dramatic form Parthenophil's artful but still natural musical performance. When anyone in the play becomes excessively rhetorical, he is criticized. When depicting worthy people, Ford avoids elevated rhetoric and elaborate patterns of diction and imagery and concentrates instead on a direct and simple expression of their thoughts and feelings. Their speech could be described as natural, simple, rational, sensitive, and harmonious. A good example of these qualities is the speech of Menaphon when he describes the music contest. No words are wasted; no rhetorical or imagistic pattern is developed; what he says is straightforward and precise but still full of deep feeling:

> *The bird* ordain'd to be
> Musicks first Martyr, strove to imitate
> These severall sounds: which, when her warbling throat
> Fail'd in, for griefe, downe dropt she on his Lute,
> And brake her heart; it was the quaintest sadnesse,
> To see the Conquerour upon her Hearse,
> To weepe a funerall Elegy of teares,
> That trust me (my *Amethus*) I coo'd chide
> Mine owne unmanly weaknesse, that made me
> A fellow-mourner with him. (B3ʳ–B4; I, i)

It would seem that Ford was deliberately trying to find a poetic manner that would reflect the sensitivity and the serenity of his characters.

In Ford's treatment of all of the main characters in the play, we find the same sympathetic understanding of suffering that is present in this first scene. Melancholy is recognized as a dangerous illness, but cures are shown to be possible. As Corax explains it, melancholy is a disease which begins in the mind rather than in the body. It overcomes man's reason first and then is able to penetrate into the rest of the body. It is

> first begot i'th'braine,
> The Seate of Reason, and from thence deriv'd
> As suddenly into the Heart, the Seate
> Of our Affection. (F4ʳ; III, i)

If reason controls man's behavior, melancholy is no problem; but if passion becomes dominant, the effects can be serious. Corax tells Palador:

> Love is the Tyrant of the heart, it darkens
> Reason, confounds discretion, deafe to counsell:
> It runnes a headlong course to desperate madnesse. (H3; III, iii)

The play is throughout dependent on Burton, but the extremes of academic theory are satirized. Although Corax's theories are apparently accepted by all, his dogmatic reliance upon artificial cures is ridiculed by Rhetias, who feels that Corax too often treats the symptoms instead of getting at the causes of illness: "Thar't an excellent fellow. *Diabolo.* O this lousie close-stoole Empricks, that will undertake all Cures, yet know not the causes of any disease" (I2; IV, ii). Nevertheless Rhetias is a Burtonian too; despite their difference of opinion, he and Corax are able to work together in apparent harmony in curing the melancholy of Meleander.

Palador, even when he is most afflicted by melancholy, realizes the need to be rational and is never completely dominated by passion. He is melancholy only because he is absent from his loved one and believes that harmony will come from a virtuous union with her. After Palador has been reunited with Eroclea, he praises virtuous love in language which stresses the important distinction between love and lust:

> Blush sensuall follies,
> Which are not guarded with thoughts chastly pure.
> "There is no faith in lust, but baytes of Artes;
> "Tis vertuous love keepes cleare contracted hearts.
>   (K3–K3ᵛ; IV, iii)

Apparently we are intended to regard Palador's love for Eroclea as an exemplification of this ideal. Significantly he is worried about expressing his happiness in language which is too passionate:

> My extasie of joyes would speake in passion,
> But that I would not lose that part of man,
> Which is reserv'd to intertaine content. (K3; IV, iii)

Later when the virtuous Cleophila is reunited with her sister she too is worried that she might exceed proper bounds in showing too much joy:

> That I shew my selfe a Girle (Sister) and bewray
> Joy in too soft a passion 'fore all these,
> I hope you cannot blame me. (L2ᵛ; V, i)

The impression given in various other scenes is that man must strive by every means possible to free himself from excessive passion. When Menaphon is courting Thamasta too ardently, Sophronos sends him to Athens "to remove the violence of affection" (M2ᵛ; V, i).⁷ Palador is counseled by various people to bring his passion under control so that the state may be saved.

Perhaps the best indication of the moral position of the play is found in the treatment of Thamasta, the sister of Amethus and cousin of Palador. While the rest of the afflicted lovers in the play pine away in grief and do not even consider rebelling against conventional morality, Thamasta decides to solve her problem even though she must break the moral law. This rebellion makes Thamasta's love heroical, but since the play is a tragicomedy Ford avoids the tragic implications by having her love Parthenophil, who is really Eroclea in male disguise. When Thamasta discovers that she is attracted to Parthenophil, she does not struggle to suppress her passion but immediately gives in to it and laments the tyranny of love. Her analysis of her passion is conventional in describing herself as "base" and as a "traytor / To honour and to shame" (D1; I, iii), but her course of action is indicated when she says that "Love is a Tyrant / Resisted" (D1; I, iii), and begins plotting her appeal to Parthenophil. The attitude that love cannot be resisted or cured is the very view that Corax opposes so strenuously in this play. Three different times she defends herself by invoking fatalism:

> Tis a fate
> That over-rules our wisdomes. (D1; I, iii)

> True love may blush, when shame repents too late,
> But in all actions, Nature yeelds to Fate. (G2ᵛ; III, ii)

> *Parthenophill,* in vaine we strive to crosse
> The destiny that guides us. (G3ᵛ; III, ii)

Thamasta's insistence on the irresistible attraction that Parthenophil has for her is made absurd by the fact that she is expressing her fatalistic passion for a woman in disguise. The implication is that the basis of such heroical love is not the attraction of bodies but the vivid imagination of diseased minds. Significantly everyone opposes Thamasta's behavior except Kala, who also has a decidedly physical approach to love. Parthenophil tells Thamasta:

> If some few dayes have tempted your free heart,
> To cast away affection on a stranger:
> If that affection have so oversway'd
> Your Judgement, that it in a manner hath
> Declyn'd your soveraignty of birth and spirit:
> How can yee turne your eyes off from that glasse,
> Wherein you may new Trim, and settle right
> A memorable name? (G3; III, ii)

Amethus says: "You have sold your birth, for lust" (H4; IV, i). Thamasta herself repents in terms which reveal that she recognizes the sin of her earlier views:

> I have trespass'd, and I have been faulty:
> Let not too rude a Censure doome me guilty,
> Or judge my errour wilfull without pardon. (H4ʳ; IV, i)

Later she refers to the "grossenes of my trespasse" (K4ʳ; V, i) and to "The errors of my mistaken judgement" (L1ʳ; V, i). She finally sees that marriage and chaste love are positive virtues and must be sought diligently by the honorable.

At the end of the play all the characters have learned that reason must govern passion and that there are cures for melancholy. Corax, Rhetias, and the others have wisely recognized that marriage is the best cure if the participants have a mature attitude toward love and each other. Through the restoration of Eroclea to Palador, he is cured and order is reestablished in the state. Through Meleander's recovery Cleophila is freed for her marriage to Amethus. Through Thamasta's recognition of her earlier folly in allowing her passion to dominate her reason, she is ready to accept a marriage to her forgiving suitor, Menaphon.

Marriage is used by Ford as a symbol of order and happiness, and the audience is shown that the hopeful future is the direct result of having worked out cures for melancholy.

Ford scholars agree that *The Fancies, Chaste and Noble* (1638) is Ford's least successful extant play,[8] with the major objection being that Ford is less than fair with his audience when he conceals Troylo-Savelli's virtuous intention in bringing Castamela to his uncle Octavio's house as one of his "fancies." Not until late in the play do we learn that the other fancies are Octavio's nieces, not his harem girls, and that Octavio himself is a devoted uncle and not a prurient old man. Ford was usually above such crude theatrical tricks, and I can find no satisfactory explanation of his lapse in this play except the obvious one that he expected his audience to be amused. But Troylo's purpose in deceiving Livio, Castamela, and Romanello must be distinguished from Ford's purpose in deceiving his audience. Motivated by his love for Castamela, Troylo wants to test her virtue as well as that of her brother, Livio, and to get her suitor, Romanello, to give up his claim to her. The invitation to Castamela to join the fancies provides a perfect test. Both Livio and Castamela are forced to decide whether his advancement is worth the compromise of her virtue. Since Castamela will remain technically chaste even while in an atmosphere of licentiousness, each is given a chance to rationalize that all will be well. The strength of the play is in the subtle study of Livio's vacillation between ambition and love for his sister and of Castamela's polite but firm refusal to compromise herself. Livio too finally decides that virtue is more important than position, but he has to be shown, by another of Troylo's tricks, a changed and apparently corrupted Castamela before he recognizes the extent of his error. Even then his first instinct is to save the family's reputation by getting Castamela married to Romanello even though he had rejected him earlier as unsuitable. When that fails because Romanello also thinks that Castamela has been corrupted, Livio repudiates his position and challenges Troylo to a duel, thereby proving his virtue. In the world of tragicomedy Livio gets a second chance, and his new found dedication to virtue wins him

Octavio's trust as well as a chance to marry one of the fancies.

Romanello is a somewhat difficult character for a modern reader to understand, for the clue to his behavior is his victimization by love-melancholy.[9] Although his dedication to Castamela, even to the point of following her into the bower of fancies, might seem praiseworthy, there are clear signs that he is diseased. In his first scene with Castamela he vacillates between idolizing her and suspiciously condemning her ambition. This combination of jealousy and adoration is symptomatic of disease, and Castamela rightly concludes that "you would prove/A cruell Lord" (B2^v; I, iii) and gives him his freedom. When in disguise he follows Castamela into the court of Octavio, he seems concerned with proving his worst suspicions rather than saving Castamela. Nitido's response is to a victim of diseased love rather than to a defender of virtue: "love, oh love,/ What a pure madnesse art thou?" (E2; III, i). In his appearances to the fancies, he is the melancholy malcontent, jealously suspicious of the virtue of all women. Only when his sister Flavia convinces him of her own virtue does he begin to recover. Even then he is not worthy of Castamela, for Troylo and Octavio have concluded that his interest in her was all "Courtship" (K3^v; V, iii); in other words his interest had been less in Castamela than in expressing his own love-melancholy. By the end, however, he has learned much about love and women and thus is worthy to become a suitor for the hand of one of the fancies.

The situation of Flavia in the subplot is made to parallel that of Castamela. She too is a person from a lower class who has been placed in a difficult situation at the court of the noble because of someone else's avarice; in her case she has been sold by her husband, Fabricio, to a lord, Julio. She too is alienated from a brother, in her case Romanello, who thinks she has lost her virtue. She too is tempted by a courtier's advances, in her case by both Camillo and Vespucci. She too avoids outright refusals as long as possible but in the end proves her virtue and her right to nobility. Flavia's triumph comes when she takes Camillo and Vespucci to Romanello and reveals the whole situation. By handling her problem in this way Flavia stops the courtship, keeps two influential friends, and at the same time proves her virtue to her brother. By their wisdom and moral strength, Castamela and Flavia bring about the repentance of their betrayers (Livio and Fabricio, who goes into a convent), are reconciled with their brothers (Livio again and Romanello), and establish their credentials to be the wives of noblemen (Troylo and Julio). In the subplot the atmosphere of corruption is real, not contrived, but in both plots true nobility is shown to be a product of reason and virtue.

In the other subplot the barber, Secco, is revealed as a jealous and foolish lover who is suspicious of the virtue of his new wife, Morosa, the "guardianesse" of the fancies. Having Morosa's virtue suspect in the subplot contributes to the atmosphere of moral degeneracy in the main plot, since the role she plays there is of a corrupt guardianess. One can grant the cleverness of this double indictment of Morosa, but I cannot help feeling that this is controlling the response a little too completely and crudely. At any rate after much nonsense, extremely bawdy even for Ford, Secco finally realizes that he has been duped by Spadone and reasserts himself. The primary structural function of this subplot is to provide a parallel to the immature love of Romanello. Even though he is jealous and suspicious of her virtue, Secco idolizes Morosa and praises her in elevated Platonic terms. Only when Secco and Romanello avoid the extremes of idolatry and suspicion do they become capable of loving rationally. It is significant that when Octavio disguises himself as a melancholy, impotent old lecher in his advances to Castamela, he too utilizes Platonic arguments for love. He tells her that

> Love *deare Maid,*
> Is but desire of beauty, and 'tis proper
> For beauty to desire to be belov'd. (F4ᵛ; III, ii)

It should be noted both that Platonism is here associated with an attempt to corrupt a virtuous girl and that Castamela wins everyone's commendation by her resistance. It should be noted too that the marriages at the end of the play are promising only because reason and virtue have replaced idolatry and ambition.

What is probably Ford's last play, *The Lady's Trial* (1639), is more like the fashionable Cavalier plays of the court dramatists than are any of Ford's other plays. Although many of Ford's characteristic themes are considered, there is in the play an artificiality and refinement not found in the earlier plays but pervasive in the court drama of the time. In his subtle, often to a modern reader overly subtle, discrimination of what is proper behavior Ford has seemed to some to be struggling toward a new kind of psychological drama,[10] but it is perhaps better to see the play's techniques as a modification rather than a change of his earlier methods. Greater attention is paid to structure and theme than to psychological analysis.

Perhaps the key figure for the play's interpretation is Auria, for it is through him that Ford illustrates the fineness of moral discrimination that seems to be the play's main theme. Auria has shocked Genoa's traditional, aristocratic element, represented by his friend, Aurelio, by marrying Spinella, who is beautiful and virtuous but lacks money and a noble family. When Auria reports that he is going off to the wars in order to reestablish his depleted fortunes, Aurelio argues that leaving Spinella alone will inevitably lead to her temptation and corruption, since she lacks the breeding necessary for virtue. Auria is indignant but, in deference to his friendship for Aurelio, replies only by asserting his absolute trust in his wife. Aurelio also implies that the noble should depend on friends in time of need and that to seek war makes one appear to be a foolish adventurer. Auria replies that to stay in Genoa and seek help from others is to be "stoop'd to servitude" (B3^v; I, i). He wants to depend on no man but himself and to "merit / Preferment by employments" (B3^v; I, i). It soon becomes apparent that the men represent opposing views of nobility and virtue. Although both are aristocrats with firm commitments to traditional order and decorum, Auria believes that noble people must prove themselves through active virtue and that virtue is in no way dependent upon rank. Aurelio on the other hand is more narrowly aristocratic in his insistence on the outward forms of nobility and applies his code to every situation regardless of the circumstances. As the self-appointed guardian of traditional morality he forgets any concern for individuals in his zeal to preserve the rules of public decorum. But he does so with full confidence that he is doing the proper thing. His charge against Spinella is the natural outgrowth of his suspicion of all classes below the nobility. As he tells Castanna: "I finde [ ] / Co[a]rse fortunes easily seduc'd" (E3; II, iii). His recommendation that Auria seek revenge on his wife and Adurni reflects his assumption that Auria will be disgraced if he ignores an insult to his honor. His position may seem absurdly narrow to a modern audience, but it should be seen that Ford gives him the status of a representative figure. He is not simply a twisted human being who makes an interesting psychological study; rather he embodies the attitudes of an important segment of the society of Genoa. Significantly Auria finds it necessary to work out a solution that will satisfy Aurelio's aristocratic code of honor. What Auria questions is not the code itself but the rigid application of the code without regard to the persons involved. At the start of the play Auria sounds like Aurelio himself when he tells Spinella that she must do everything possible to preserve an unblemished reputation. He is just as insistent as Aurelio upon the obligations of friendship, and there are indications that he would follow Aurelio's suggestion to avenge himself if he were convinced that Adurni and Spinella were humiliating him. Auria is frustrated, even angered, by Aurelio's literal approach, but he never forgets the importance of maintaining moral and social order in Genoa.

Spinella and Adurni are more obviously stock figures. Spinella, like Cleophila and Eroclea in *The Lover's Melancholy,* Castamela in *The Fancies,* and the Queen in *The Queen,* is primarily a symbol of virtue and honor. Adurni is the courtly rake who uses the subtleties of Platonic love theory to try to persuade Spinella to submit to him. After an opening song intended to establish the atmosphere of dalliance, Adurni delivers a heavily Platonized speech pleading for her love:

> Plead not faire creature without sence of pity
> So incompassionatly gainst a service,
> In nothing faulty more then pure obedience,
> My honours and my fortunes are led captives
> In triumph by your all-commanding beauty,
> And if you ever felt the power of love,
> The rigor of an uncontrouled passion,
> The tyrannie of thoughts consider mine,
> In some proportion, by the strength of yours,
> Thus may you yield and conquer. (E2; II, iii)

The emphasis on the power of beauty, on the innocence of
serving beauty, on the need for pity, on the tyranny of love,
and on the victory found in submission are all typical of the
Platonists. Adurni invokes religious imagery as well when
he protests that

> that saint
> To whom I vow my selfe, must never want
> Fit offerings to her altar. (E2ʳ; II, iii)

Spinella promptly exposes the motive behind Adurni's noble
words and condemns him forcefully: "How poorely some,
tame to their wild desires, / Fawne on abuse of vertue"
(E2ʳ; II, iii). Adurni is so struck by her virtue that he
repents and changes his whole view of life. Formerly he had
assumed that all women were unchaste and had thus felt no
qualms about seducing them, but now he does what he can to
absolve Spinella. When Adurni confesses his advances to
Auria, Auria and Aurelio both seem to expect him to glorify
his love defiantly in the elevated terms of the courtier;
instead he asks forgiveness and proclaims

> The power of vertue, whose commanding soveraignty,
> Sets bounds to rebell bloods, and checke restraines,
> Custome of folly by example teaches
> A rule to reformation; by rewards,
> Crownes worthy actions, and invites to honour. (I1ʳ; IV, ii)

Auria, by this time convinced that the charges against Spinella are ungrounded, must decide whether he should follow
the letter of Aurelio's code and seek revenge for the wrong
done him or accept the repentance as sufficient. Adurni
states that he has "rob'd you / Of rigor (*Auria*) by my

strict self-penance" (I2; IV, ii), and Auria, although seeing that he is going against the letter of the old code ("The tricke is new" [I2; IV, ii]), accepts the explanation because he believes that Adurni is a man of integrity. People are more important to him than severe moral codes.

Many have questioned whether Auria needs to be as rigid as he is in the trial scene of Spinella herself. By modern standards no doubt he is rigid, but Auria by this time is not concerned with convincing himself but with convincing the others that no hint of scandal remains. By going through with a formal trial scene, he is able to prove for the record both that he has not glossed over a slight to his honor and that Spinella and her family can defend themselves nobly and convincingly. By proposing the marriage between Adurni and his sister-in-law, Castanna, Auria convinces everyone, even Aurelio, that the reconciliations are genuine. Although a modern audience might groan, a Caroline audience steeped in the subtle ethical discriminations of the Cavalier drama, was presumably expected to applaud this triumph of the highest qualities of nobility. Every subtle point is resolved. Although he might justly blame Spinella for fleeing he will not since she was in her kinsman's house, and "I honour / His hospitable friendship" (K3; V, ii).

The various subplots fill out and reinforce the themes of the main plot although their effectiveness in doing so might be questioned. The proud, blunt, but honest Malfato, Spinella's cousin, represents the true strength of the gentry, to whom Aurelio is always condescending. It is probably not surprising that his outspoken defense of his integrity as a gentleman (C3–C4; I, iii) sounds very much like Ford's own self-defense in his various prologues and dedications. Malfato is a victim of love-melancholy and at one point lapses into a heroic but somewhat absurdly romantic vow to champion Spinella's cause (G3ᵛ–G4; IV, i); but when Spinella rebukes him he promises never again to mention his "amorous folly" (G4; IV, i). Although he is outspoken and passionate, his basic integrity prevents more serious faults and wins him the respect of everyone.

The other subplots are intended mostly for comic relief, but they too contribute to the play's overall themes. Levidolche, the wife of Benatzi, had been corrupted by Adurni, and her subsequent immorality and broken marriage can be taken as a symbol of the disorder caused by following Adurni's code of conduct. When Benatzi returns to woo her in disguise, she recognizes him and determines to reform. Unfortunately she seems more concerned about getting Benatzi to seek revenge against Adurni and Malfato, who has also rebuffed her, than about rebuilding her marriage. The revenge is attempted, but its absurdity is emphasized by having the enraged Benatzi appear just after the reconciliation in the main plot is effected by avoiding hasty revenge. Benatzi's attempt is easily stopped, apparently with the help of a now genuinely reformed Levidolche, and there is hope for their marriage at the end. Significantly it is Auria, impressed by Benatzi's worth as a soldier, who helps plan Benatzi's disguised return to court his former wife.

The lisping Amoretta, like Spinella, of a lower social class, longs to marry someone courtly. Spinella of course had done so, but her motive was not ambition for position or money but love. Amoretta in contrast cares for nothing but the trappings of nobility. Futelli and Piero's involved machinations are primarily intended as comedy, but it should be noted that Futelli claims that "it may chance beside the mirth, / To worke a reformation on the mayden" (C3; I, ii). So it does, and when Amoretta has learned her lesson, it is Futelli who marries her. In her ridiculous wooers, Fulgoso and Guzmann, Ford again satirizes the language and techniques of foolish, would-be courtiers. They claim to be soldiers but, unlike Auria and Benatzi, they are cowards and would much rather posture heroically than fight. They also serve as further illustrations of what results when Adurni's code of love is allowed to become fashionable. It must be conceded that the ridiculous behavior of Levidolche, Benatzi, and Amoretta makes the marriages at the end seem like forced and conventional stage marriages, but it is the theme that is important. Marriage, represented in the four married couples at the end of the play, symbolizes the order that has been restored to Genoa through following reason and virtue.

In *The Queen, or the Excellency of Her Sex,* Ford illustrates the proper relationship between the sexes by depicting the modification of two unreasonable attitudes toward women. At one extreme is Alphonso, a dedicated misogynist, who has led an unsuccessful attempt to overthrow the Queen and who prefers death to marriage with her. When the Queen forces the marriage, Alphonso immediately asserts his sovereignty, assumes control of the state, and insists upon living apart from his wife. At the other extreme is Velasco, a successful general who idolizes a rather ordinary young widow, Salassa. The absurdity of the two attitudes is emphasized by the fact that the Queen is the epitome of virtue while Salassa's morality is somewhat dubious. The action of the play involves the education of the two misguided men in the proper attitude toward women and marriage.

Alphonso's hatred of women is motivated by his belief that all women are fickle and will be unchaste at the first opportunity. When Almada says that Alphonso's irresponsible attitude is the result of melancholy, he states the view that the audience is apparently intended to accept: "What can you hope from one so wholly drown'd / In melancholy and sowre discontent" (B3; I, ll. 446–48). Alphonso's follower Muretto sees that the cure must be gradual. First Alphonso must become interested in the Queen as a person instead of as just another example of a fickle sex. By telling Alphonso that the Queen is having an affair with Petruchio, Muretto arouses the needed interest and gets Alphonso to admit that the Queen would be an ideal wife if only she were chaste. Then by proving that she is in fact chaste, Muretto removes Alphonso's only objection and persuades him to accept the Queen. An element of Fletcherian suspense is added by the audience's ignorance of what Muretto is up to and gives Ford a chance to present a realistic temptation scene obviously based on *Othello*. Nevertheless there are hints of Muretto's virtue, and an audience experienced in the ways of tragicomedy would probably not be unduly concerned.

Ford utilizes the Queen herself to establish the proper attitude toward marriage. At the beginning of the play she sees the possibilities in Alphonso if he can be brought to a mature view of man's relationship to woman. In his belief that man must have unquestioned sovereignty over woman, Alphonso has the support of Christian tradition,[11] but he is misguided in thinking that sovereignty includes the right to treat women disrespectfully. Throughout the play the Queen recognizes that Alphonso is right in asserting man's natural dominance over woman, but she also is emphatic about her right to be respected.[12] When she marries him her statement of his responsibility is apparently intended to win audience approval:

> I yeeld to you (my lord) my Crown, my Heart,
> My People, my Obedience; In exchange
> What I demand is Love. (B4; I, ll. 646–49)

Nevertheless the woman must obey even if love is not forthcoming. After Alphonso has banned her from his bed, the Queen remains true to him:

> Away, ye are all Traytors to profane
> His sacred merits with your bitter terms.
> Why, am I not his Wife? A wife must bear
> Withal what likes her Lord t'upbraid her with,
> And yet 'tis no injustice. (C3; II, ll. 1248–55)

After Alphonso has been cured and has vowed his devotion to the Queen, she once again declares her submissive role. She apparently is concerned that Alphonso's praise of her is exceeding the desired moderation, for she tells him:

> Be not so low, my lord, in your own thoughts:
> You are, as you were, Soveraign of my heart;
> And I must kneel to you. (F3; V, ll. 3654–58)

Muretto had expressed the same point of view earlier when he told Alphonso: "women (my lord) are all creatures, not Gods nor Angels" (E1; IV, ll. 2466–67). Alphonso accepts the Queen's restatement when he defines his new role:

> now I am King
> Of two rich Kingdoms, as the world affords:
> The Kingdom of thy beauty, and this land. (F3; V, ll. 3670–74)

Man is to retain the sovereignty but woman is to be highly respected both as a creature of God and as a subordinate helper to man in this world.

This interpretation of the main plot gains support from the way in which Ford treats Velasco in the subplot. He is a Platonist whose worship of woman has deprived him of his rightful sovereignty and of his noble attributes as a man. He tells Salassa:

> You, Lady, are the deity I adore,
> Have kneell'd too in my heart, have vow'd my soul to,
> In such a debt of service, that my life
> Is tenant to your pleasure. (C3ʳ–C4; II, ll. 1383–88)

When Salassa taunts him by accusing him of mocking her by such effusive speech, Velasco replies: "Mock you? Most fair *Salassa*, if e're truth / Dwelt in a tongue, my words and thoughts are twins" (C4; II, ll. 1391–94). To prove his love Velasco offers to do any service that will win her favor. Salassa, finally convinced of his sincerity and tempted by this chance to assert her power over a man, asks him to give up all fighting for two years as an expression of his love for her. Velasco is forced by his vow to agree and thus through submission to love becomes a pathetic and cowardly figure who abdicates everything that has made him great. Paradoxically, Velasco can prove himself worthy of Salassa's love only by abandoning his excessive adoration. When he will do anything she wants she treats him as a fool, but when he repudiates his passionate former self he achieves maturity as a man and wins both her respect and her love. His analysis of his weakness in allowing Salassa to have sovereignty over him is a reassertion of his reason:

> Too late I finde,
> How passions at their best are but sly traytors
> To ruin honour. That which we call love,
> Was by the wisest power above forethought
> To check our pride. Thus when men are blown up
> At the highest of conceit, then they fall down
> Even by the peevish follies of their frailties. (E2ʳ; IV, ll. 2726–39)

When Salassa, thinking that she still controls Velasco, rashly promises that she will provide a champion for the Queen's honor, Velasco refuses because he sees that she is using him to get the money offered to the Queen's champion. He finally stands up for Salassa when she is about to be put to death for not producing a champion, but he will still have nothing to do with her. It is only after Salassa has repented of her avarice and ambition for sovereignty that Velasco consents to be married to her. Velasco's statement accepting Salassa is another expression of the proper attitude toward marriage:

> I must confess I love you, and I hope
> Our faults shall be redeem'd in being henceforth
> True votaries to vertue, and the faith
> Our mutual vows shal to each other ow. (F4; V, ll. 3856–60)

The reasonable approach to marriage is to avoid the excesses of Alphonso's cynical misogyny on the one hand and of Velasco's Platonized idolatry on the other and to strive to achieve a mean which recognizes that man should be dominant but that woman is worthy of respect.

The common theme in the four tragicomedies is love, but Ford treats so many kinds of love in so many different ways that generalization is dangerous. Some of the lovers are cynical rakes who reform, some are foolish courtiers, some are victims of melancholy who remain virtuous, some are melancholics with more dangerous tendencies, some are idealized virtuous lovers. The debt to the Burtonian section on love-melancholy is great, but the plays resist any attempt to make them simply applications of Burtonian theory to imagined situations. Even in *The Lover's Melancholy,* where the major theme is melancholy, the cures are effected more by common sense than by academic techniques. What is common to all of the plays is the stress on the need for both moral decision and sympathetic understanding of the victims of passion. Ford is insistent that man can by wise choices build a virtuous, meaningful, and happy life, but he also sees that external and internal pressures make such choices difficult. Today we are apt to translate the consideration of external pressures into sociological discussion of environment, and of internal pressures into psychological discussion of man's complex drives. In both cases the result is apt to be emphasis on man's helplessness. If we are to understand Ford's plays, we must see that the psychological analysis goes on in a traditional context. In Christian terms the world has been corrupted by the Fall, with the result that both man's society and his own being are pervaded by sin. Although that makes man's situation difficult, he cannot excuse his sin by pleading that his society is corrupt or that he is the victim of the original sin present in all men; in Christian theology each person is responsible for his failures no matter what the extenuating circumstances may be. Christians responding to the faults of others, however, must avoid moralistic judgment in the awareness that life is difficult and that all men are sinners; instead the Christian should hate the sin and understand and love the sinner.

Even though Ford's analysis is carried on in primarily secular terms, the terms are analogous. The imperfection of society's institutions and the difficulty of channeling passions to constructive ends make man's plight hard indeed. But he cannot excuse himself by blaming his society or the way he was made. In all that he does he must attempt to remain rational. Ford never suggests that since following reason is so difficult, man's submission to passion can be excused. There can and should be sympathy for victims of passion, but there should never be glorification of the passion itself or of the person who is overcome. In the tragicomedies, Ford's characters are seldom faced with easy moral decisions. Instead, Ford shows that all people are subject to pressures to submit to passion. Ford seems to see that even the most villainous behavior can be understood if we seek out the causes. There are some foolish, some immature, even some potentially disastrous views expressed in these plays, but there are no unmotivated evils and no simple solutions. But there are solutions. In each of the plays the resolution comes about partly because of practical solutions but also because education and experience have brought about greater maturity and understanding. At the end the main characters are always wiser than they were at the beginning, and we are allowed to see that their marriages will succeed because tendencies toward disorder have been overcome through reason and virtue.

In this chapter I have dealt almost exclusively with what has been too often ignored—that Ford's tragicomedies are more than superficial romantic plays. I should close by saying that they also have the theatrical vitality that we expect from a professional dramatist of Ford's stature. We should remember that the intellectual context that must be reconstructed for a modern reader would be immediately obvious to a sophisticated Caroline audience. To them the plays would have appeal partly because of Ford's insights into the nature of melancholy and love but also, and for many primarily, because of the delights of a well told tale. The separation and reunion of lovers, the excitement of catastrophes avoided, the poetic expression of noble and not so noble sentiments, and the color of a well staged spectacle would undoubtedly be the dominant impression of the play that many would have. In our search for the deeper meaning we must not overlook the more obvious vitality of language and scene.

V

'Tis Pity She's a Whore

After hearing a brief summary of the plot, a Caroline play-goer might expect *'Tis Pity She's a Whore* to be a sensa-tional melodrama with Giovanni portrayed as an all-black villain who outrageously violates all standards of decency. As an atheist, an incestuous lover, a revenger, and a mur-derer, Giovanni has many of the characteristics of a stage villain; but Ford chooses to develop him in a quite different way. Instead of stressing the villainy, Ford portrays Gio-vanni as a talented, virtuous, and noble man who is over-come by a tumultuous passion that brings about his destruc-tion. Most modern readers, steeped in the literature of romantic love, are so impressed by the noble side of Gio-vanni that they respond to the play as the tragic story of two courageous lovers trapped by a transcendent passion that an inflexible society cannot hope to comprehend. Ac-cording to this view, Giovanni and Annabella are victims of a situation that is largely beyond their control. When the play is read historically, this interpretation of the lovers must be seen as inadequate. If one tries to interpret the play as celebrating a Giovanni who remains throughout his trou-bles more noble, more courageous, and more sensitive than those in the corrupt society around him, he is forced to qualify that judgment until it has little meaning. From a traditional point of view an incestuous love would by its very nature deteriorate and end in destruction. When we see Giovanni steadily becoming more blasphemous, jealous, irrational, and vengeful, we must recognize that the traditional formula for tragedy is operating. Scholars, however, after admitting or implying that some reservations about the love may be necessary, still maintain that Giovanni's glorification of passionate love and his heroic stance in accepting his destruction make him a worthy figure, even in degradation.[1] No doubt there is some truth in this view in that Giovanni retains his courage, his pride, and his eloquence; but my analysis of Ford's presentation of Giovanni's arguments for love and fatalism suggests to me that there is more satiric undercutting of Giovanni's position than has been realized.

According to my classification of types of character developed in Chapter III, Giovanni is a combination of the passionate sinner and the rationalizing fool. In so far as he is ruined by his inability to control his unruly passions, we can pity him, since all men after the Fall are susceptible to beauty, quick to justify their actions, and insufficiently rational in overcoming their weaknesses. In so far as he justifies himself through twisted logic and pseudo-heroic posturing, he transforms himself into a grotesque and almost ludicrous figure who elicits our shock and at times amusement at his arguments. The exact nature of the fusion of the two types would depend in part on the way Giovanni is presented; also some in the audience would no doubt be more inclined to pity him and others to scorn him. But Giovanni never becomes a noble victim. The structure and tone of the play make clear that the pressures on him are the usual temptations of a world corrupted by the Fall and that Giovanni's moral collapse is an example of how passion can corrupt and degrade even the worthiest individual. Annabella falls too, but, in contrast to Giovanni, repents and becomes at the end of the play an example of the noble victim; unfortunately she has learned too late what proper values are and must die as a consequence of the tragic events initiated by the earlier sin.

While this traditional moral framework operates in *'Tis Pity,* it would be wrong to put all of the stress there. Giovanni is a sinning and foolish everyman who must be evaluated by traditional Christian humanist assumptions, but he is also a vehicle for sophisticated, satiric comment on issues of the day. In his arguments in defense of love and fatalism, Giovanni twists various contemporary theories of love, ethics, and psychology. A Caroline audience aware of the topicality of his arguments could be expected to see that satirizing Giovanni also means satirizing the perverted arguments that he uses. In achieving such a response to Giovanni, Ford is aided by the air of melodramatic unreality that pervades the play. Giovanni is no ordinary sinner. In making him an incestuous lover, a blasphemous atheist, and a sensational murderer, Ford makes his problems so extreme that an audience would inevitably feel less emotionally involved. Ford's intention seems to have been to write an exciting entertainment that would add melodramatic and satiric elements to his basically morality-play structure. The result is a witty, ironic, often cynical appraisal of man's capacity for evil and for absurdity, all made delightfully, at times scandalously, sensational by the very outrageousness of the deeds. If we are to appreciate *'Tis Pity,* we must take it on its own terms and avoid the temptation to fit it into any preconceived notion of what a play on this subject should be.

The brilliant opening scene in which Giovanni boldly but illogically defends atheism and incest to the shocked but understanding Friar Bonaventura does much to shape our reaction to Giovanni's love. Scholars who view the friar as a muddled, narrow-minded moralist should notice that Ford carefully associates him with the virtues of Giovanni's former life. It is the friar who as Giovanni's tutor over a long period shaped him into "that miracle of Wit,/ Who once within these three Moneths wert esteem'd/ A wonder of thine age, throughout *Bononia*" (B1ʳ; I, i). It is the friar to whom Giovanni naturally turns in his trouble, and the references to him as "Gentle Father" (B1; I, i) and "deare Confessor" (B1ʳ; I, i) seem to indicate that he does so with great respect. Giovanni, far from regarding his advice as narrowly dogmatic, twice refers to his counsel as life-giving; he also notes the "pitty and compassion" (B1ʳ; I, i) in the friar's eyes. But the friar, despite his sympathy for Giovanni's plight, is completely opposed to Giovanni's clever but perverted arguments. He insists that the course Giovanni is following can only lead to death and destruction: "hast thou left the Schooles/ Of Knowledge, to converse with Lust and Death?" (B1ʳ; I, i). His life-giving counsel is that Giovanni's only hope is to "Begge Heaven to cleanse the leprosie of Lust/ That rots thy Soule" (B2; I, i). In his simple refutation of Giovanni's involved arguments the friar states that Giovanni is forgetting or ignoring that in the Christian scheme the order of nature and the order of grace are fused. Certainly man should reason (and we should remember that it was the friar who taught Giovanni his philosophy), but man's reason, according to the friar, is misguided unless it is directed by God. If you depend upon reason alone, you are apt to fall into perversions of right reason:

> wits that presum'd
> On wit too much, by striving how to prove
> There was no God; with foolish grounds of Art,
> Discover'd first the neerest way to Hell. (B1; I, i)

The friar, by implication here and explicitly later (E1; II, v), goes so far as to admit that incest could be defended according to the natural law,[2] but he is emphatic in stressing that that proves only that the opposition to incest is based on the divine law.

Ford's contemporaries, aware of the Platonic fashions of the time, would recognize Giovanni and the friar as studies of Platonists of different types. They would understand the logic of the friar's suspicion that it is Giovanni's perverted love that has twisted his reasoning on religion as well. Instead of worshiping God, he has substituted an earthly "Idoll" (B2; I, i), his sister. Giovanni has learned his lessons on Platonic love imperfectly; instead of proceeding from the admiration of earthly beauty to the worship of God, Giovanni inverts this natural order and even suggests that the gods would bow down to Annabella if they had the chance:

> Must I not praise
> That beauty, which if fram'd a new, the gods
> Would make a god of, if they had it there;
> And kneele to it, as I doe kneele to them? (B1; I, i)

Although the friar does not go into a long explanation, his attitude is clear. Proper love is always beneficial, but Giovanni's passion can never find fruition in marriage and will lead him inevitably into mortal sin.

The friar remains sympathetic to Giovanni's plight because he recognizes that Giovanni is suffering from what Burton calls love-melancholy and that Giovanni's illogical rationalizations are indications of a mind twisted by passion. The indications of passion are unmistakable. When Annabella first sees Giovanni cross the stage her description of him stresses his unhealthy appearance:

> This is some woefull thinge
> Wrapt up in griefe, some shaddow of a man.
> Alas hee beats his brest, and wipes his eyes
> Drown'd all in teares: me thinkes I heare him sigh. (B4; I, ii)

Giovanni's later description of his love reveals the symptoms of heroical love:

> I have too long supprest the hidden flames
> That almost have consum'd me: I have spent
> Many a silent night in sighes and groanes. (C1ʳ; I, iii)

The friar has been criticized for his practical approach to solving Giovanni's problem,[3] but his dual remedy of prayer and practical cure is exactly what is recommended by Burton to cure love-melancholy. The friar tells Giovanni to pray but that if prayer is unsuccessful "I'le thinke on remedy" (B2; I, i). Burton says: "we must first begin with prayer, and then use physick; not one without the other, but both together" (*AM*, II, 9; 2, 1, 2). The friar's advice throughout the play is invariably that of a wise Burtonian spiritual counselor who realizes that Giovanni's love is a passion that is corrupting him morally and physically and that demands immediate cure if disaster is to be avoided. One possible criticism of the friar in this first scene is that his advice to Giovanni to satisfy his passion with another woman is immoral. But the friar does not defend such a course as right: "Leave her, and take thy choyce, 'tis much lesse sinne,/ Though in such games as those, they lose that winne" (B2; I, i). His point is the practical one that it is far better to put down his concupiscence with any woman of the streets than to involve his whole being in a serious affair that is justifiable only through open revolt against God's moral law. The difference is the same as that in the Catholic distinction between venial and mortal sin,[4] and the charge that the friar is being legalistic overlooks an important Renaissance theological distinction. Another charge is that the friar advocates a kind of divine magic in prescribing Giovanni's regimen of prayer. But what the friar suggests is a program of disciplined meditation that follows a general pattern widely accepted in the Renaissance.[5]

Even though Giovanni's love might be described as a kind of disease, a Caroline audience would have been suspicious of his fatalistic defenses of his actions since a common view of the time was that prayer and planning can effect cures even in the most difficult cases. As Burton says: "It may be hard to cure, but not impossible, for him that is most grievously affected, if he be but willing to be helped" (*AM*, II, 5; 2, 1, 1, 1). But Giovanni glorifies his condition instead of trying to overcome it. His fatalistic speech at the end of the first scene is not a legitimate defense but an abdication of his moral responsibility:

> All this I'le doe, to free mee from the rod
> Of vengeance, else I'le sweare, my Fate's my God. (B2; I, i)

He has told the friar that he realizes the need for moral striving, but he appears to have given up hope; he is going to pray only to satisfy God that he has tried but is incapable of conquering his desire. This rationalizing fatalism is to be Giovanni's excuse throughout the play. Some have argued that the fatalistic arguments of Giovanni and of various other characters in the tragedies are an indication of Ford's sympathy for the stoical argument that adversity is the common lot of man and that man can do nothing but accept and endure whatever befalls him. Ford in *The Golden Mean* states in direct opposition that man should endure if he is guiltless but repent and reform if he is guilty.[6] Burton, as we have seen, also opposes Giovanni's view. More important, in the play itself, Giovanni's fatalism is presented in a way that stresses his lack of logic and his submission to passion.

A good example is his soliloquy just before he reveals his love to Annabella. When the speech is studied carefully the contradictions become apparent. He has attempted to repent, but his description suggests that reason and sincere sorrow for sin were perhaps less apparent during the period of prayer and fasting than his passionate assurance that his case was hopeless and that fate controlled his destiny. He still wants to make love his God:

> O that it were not in Religion sinne,
> To make our love a God, and worship it. (B4–B4ʳ; I, iii) [7]

Giovanni is aware of his sin and seems to realize that the inevitable result will be his destruction; but instead of continuing to struggle he capitulates. Recognizing that he must choose between God and Annabella, he argues illogically that since God has not cured him Christianity has no validity; hence he is free to love Annabella and blame fate for what he seems to realize will be a tragic end: "tis not I know,/ My lust; but tis my fate that leads me on" (B4ʳ; I, iii). Atheism and the belief that man cannot control his actions go together in Giovanni, and we see that his atheism and his fatalism are the result, not of a dispassionate search after truth, but of passionate lust which has overcome his reason. Giovanni is a sick, confused, and irrational sinner rather than a rational rebel.

In these first scenes Ford seems to be striving to get the full shock effect of Giovanni's outspoken but troubled immorality. In the courtship scene with Annabella, we see a new Giovanni—a courtly lover who has cast aside all his uncertainty and has determined to act courageously even if it leads to the destruction he expects. Now the troubled melancholic appears as the exultant lover, and the Platonic theories, stated in the first interview with the friar, are translated into the glowing full-blown language of romantic courtship. Giovanni is not to be an ordinary melancholic

lover. In this scene we see that Ford is going to combine his
Burtonian analysis with a treatment of the same Platonic
themes found in the Cavalier drama. Although there is a
connection between melancholy and Platonism in that the
victim of love-melancholy is apt to launch into effusive
praise of his loved one, Ford in this scene seems more
interested in the contemporary fashion of Platonic love than
in illustrating Burtonian theories. Professor Sensabaugh in
his book on Ford is right in showing that Giovanni's case
must be seen in light of the current furor over Platonic love,
but, as I have shown in Chapter III, he is wrong in his
conclusion that arguments like Giovanni's would be approved by the love cult. At one time or another during the
play, Giovanni does base his arguments on all of the theo-
rems that Sensabaugh describes as the coterie's system of
love: *"Fate rules all lovers. . . . Beauty and goodness are
one and the same. . . . Beautiful women are saints to be
worshiped. . . . True love is of equal hearts and divine.
. . . Love is all-important and all-powerful. . . . True love
is more important than marriage. . . . True love is the sole
guide to virtue. . . . True love allows any liberty of action
and thought."* [8] But the audience would be apt to criticize
such positions just as they probably did the arguments of the
perverted Platonists discussed in Chapter III. As the friar
and presumably the audience realize, Giovanni is simply not
a good Platonist. In his theories of love he has forgotten the
most important point—that love must be rational and moral.

The atmosphere of the proposal scene is shrewdly designed to reveal the absurd quality of Giovanni's courtship.
Using a series of formulistic images and phrases, Giovanni
eulogistically praises Annabella's beauty. At the start he
seems to be only half serious; but, although he instinctively
falls back upon an ironic tone when speaking in this exaggerated way, he is unable to direct this sense of the ridiculous to
the arguments themselves. Baffled by his uneasy self-
consciousness, Annabella is unsure as to whether he is jok-
ing. If we are to judge by her reaction to Soranzo's similar
courtship later, she is not used to taking such extravagance
seriously, and it is probably even more surprising to her to
have these praises come from her virtuous brother, Gio-

vanni. This is not the way a brother should talk to his sister. But is soon becomes apparent that Giovanni is serious, and Annabella's own passionate love for Giovanni prompts her to respond in the same way. The result is an extended celebration of their mutual love that culminates in the pseudo-religious ritual of their exchange of vows at the end of the scene. In their worship of each other and of their love both have forgotten the basis of moral order. Earlier in the scene Giovanni went so far as to lie in claiming that the friar has approved their love:

> I have askt Counsell of the holy Church,
> Who tells mee I may love you, and 'tis just,
> That since I may, I should; and will, yes will. (C1ᵛ; I, iii)

At the end of the scene the ultimately physical basis of their love is stressed by their passionate kiss and their not-too-subtle declaration that they are off to an incestuous bed.

One device Ford uses to accentuate the perversion of their love is to have the amoral Putana comment on what is happening. When Giovanni in the proposal scene asks Putana to leave, the idea of an affair between them is unthinkable even to her depraved mind: "If this were any other Company for her, I should thinke my absence an office of some credit" (B4ᵛ; I, iii). In their next appearance at the beginning of Act II, Giovanni and Annabella are the honeymooners fresh from bed, jesting bawdily about their love and feeling no guilt. To accentuate the perversion that the lovers are forgetting Ford brings in Putana to comment crudely on the inconsequence of kinship when love is involved: "and I say still, if a young Wench feele the fitt upon her, let her take any body, Father or Brother, all is one" (C4; II, i).

In his next scene with the friar, Giovanni seems to be flaunting his immorality. It can be argued that his irrational logic is the product of his disordered mind, but he is too flippant in his manner and too deliberately outrageous in his arguments to justify the claim that he expects his arguments to be taken seriously. Rather his passion has made him so reckless that philosophy itself seems like so much useless casuistry that may be true but is inconsequential when compared with the overpowering transcendence of his love. The arguments he does use are filled with twisted Platonic jargon:

> It is a principall (which you have taught
> When I was yet your Scholler) that the F[r]ame
> And Composition of the *Minde* doth follow
> The Frame and Composition of [the] *Body:*
> So where the *Bodies* furniture is *Beauty,*
> The *Mindes* must needs be *Vertue:* which allowed,
> *Vertue* it selfe is *Reason but refin'd,*
> And *Love* the Quintesence of that, this proves
> My Sisters *Beauty* being rarely *Faire,*
> Is rarely *Vertuous;* chiefely in her love,
> And chiefely in that *Love, her love to me.*
> If *hers to me,* then so is *mine to her;*
> Since in like Causes are effects alike. (D4ᵛ–E1 ; II, v)

Giovanni's reasoning in this speech is a good example of the perversion of sound doctrine that Ford parodied in *Honor Triumphant.* The third position of *Honor Triumphant* is that *"Faire Ladie was never false,"* and it opens with the same argument that Giovanni cites: *"The temperature of the mind follows the temperature of the bodie.* Which certaine axiome (sayes that sage Prince of Philosophers *Aristotle*) is ever more infallible" (*HT*, D1ᵛ). As I have pointed out in Chapter I, Ford shows ironically that this position is absurd. Giovanni's sophistical argument, like the logic of *Honor Triumphant,* is patently false, and we must agree with the friar when he describes Giovanni's reasoning as "O ignorance in knowledge" (E1 ; II, v).

Nevertheless we should beware of putting their love in an oversimplified context. At this point in the play Giovanni and Annabella themselves still regard their love as something pure and lovely and believe that they can make it lasting and ennobling. Any audience would have to grant that Annabella's virtues make her worthy of idealization, if not of worship, and that Giovanni is attracted not only by physical longing but also by admiration of these real virtues. If there were no moral barrier one could imagine a happy and lasting marriage, and Giovanni and Annabella are indeed unfortunate to love where the natural fruition of marriage is impossible. But without that fruition corruption is inevitable, as they would have realized if they could have been more rational. One of the major interests of the play is in showing the progressive degeneration of Annabella and Giovanni as they become more and more inextricably trapped by events initiated by their passionate love. We have already seen that Giovanni's love for Annabella has led him to atheism, blasphemy, incest, fatalism, deceit, and a complete abrogation of his former power of reason. As the drama proceeds these faults are intensified and others—jealousy, adultery, and finally murder—are added. Giovanni, the paragon of reason, is turned into a foolish madman by his love. Annabella recovers her moral sense before the play's end, but she too is for a time consumed by passion. When she first appears, she is on the balcony observing with apparent detachment and superiority the chaos of the scene following the duel between Grimaldi and Vasques. But when Giovanni crosses the stage she breaks into lyric praise of his noble qualities, and we are made to see that her silence has been a reflection, not of her detachment from the immoral world about her, but of her preoccupation with her love for her brother. When she goes down to meet Giovanni, her literal descent may be taken as a visual image of the moral descent that is to follow.

The play's subplots are more important than has usually been recognized, for they parallel the action in the main plot and help create the play's moral atmosphere. Annabella's three suitors are obviously much inferior to her in everything except status; but her father is concerned primarily with wealth and position, and her other main adviser, her corrupt "*Tutresse*" (B3; I, ii), Putana, is preoccupied with the physical and the material. Under these circumstances it is not surprising that Annabella turns to Giovanni, the one admirable person in her circle. Since her three suitors, Grimaldi, Bergetto, and Soranzo, have respectively influence, money, and worldly honor, they are treated seriously even though it means that a virtuous girl must be subjected to indignities. The cowardly soldier Grimaldi's hope is that his connection with the Pope and the local Cardinal will make him desirable, but in his duel with Vasques in the second scene of the play he is exposed as both a coward and a weakling. From that point on he gives up all pretense of nobility and depends entirely on underhanded methods and influential friends. Persuaded that he must kill Soranzo if he is to win Annabella, he decides to attack even though he knows such a course is dishonorable. When the plan backfires and Bergetto is killed, he uses his connections with the Cardinal to avoid punishment.

Bergetto is the type of the rich but frivolous fool, and his only hope for Annabella is his uncle Donado's money. Having him rich serves to expose the motives of people who deal with him. His uncle Donado sees him primarily as a means of making a marriage that will increase his own wealth. Putana says to Annabella, Donado "meanes to make this his Cozen a golden calfe, thinkes that you wil be a right *Isralite,* and fall downe to him presently" (B4; I, ii). Hippolyta's disguised husband, Richardetto, tries to marry his niece to Bergetto so as to get some of his money. All view Bergetto as a means to their own selfish ends; as his servant, Poggio, comments: no one has ever considered elder brothers fools "as long as they had either land or mony left them to inherit" (B3ᵛ; I, ii). His pathetic murder just before he is about to achieve some measure of happiness through marrying Philotis serves as a further indictment of a society in which the innocent too often suffer for the misdeeds of the evil. Florio is never serious about letting Annabella marry him but feels that he cannot risk offending the wealthy Donado. Consequently he suggests that Annabella has free choice as to whom she shall marry even though he has made it clear earlier that Soranzo has already been chosen.

The third suitor, Soranzo, is both more successful and more dangerous because he is able to present a more impressive exterior than either Grimaldi or Bergetto. Soranzo is a clever dissimulator, as the duel between Grimaldi and Vasques indicates. Grimaldi had apparently been spreading some scandalous yet plausible rumors about him, and the shrewd Soranzo sees that sending Vasques to start a fight will vindicate himself by showing his concern for his honor and disgrace Grimaldi by showing his ineffectiveness as a soldier. He succeeds in both ends, and the audience is permitted to see Soranzo's devious methods as well as one reason why the honor-conscious Florio has been convinced that Soranzo would be the best husband for his daughter. In this scene Florio's reasons for preferring him are not made clear but later he makes them explicit:

> My Lord *Soranzo,* though I must confesse,
> The proffers that are made me, have beene great
> In marriage of my daughter; yet the hope
> Of your still rising honours, have prevaild
> Above all other Joynctures; here shee is. (E4; III, ii)

Florio's lack of concern about moral qualities should be obvious, and Annabella's expected response is clear when he tells her "And heare you daughter, see you use him nobly" (E4; III, ii). The issue of who is to decide on the marriage partner does not become a major one since Annabella herself decides that a marriage to Soranzo would be wise. Nevertheless it should be clear that Florio's handling of his daughter's marriage does not make her situation any easier.

But Soranzo's chief importance in the structure of the play is as a parallel to Giovanni as a lover, for we find that he too utilizes all the standard devices of the Platonic lover. When we first see him alone he is reading the Italian poet, Sannazar, "This smooth licentious Poet" (C4^v; II, ii), and we see that he too is an overenthusiastic admirer of female beauty. In his rewriting of Sannazar's couplet about the pain, unrest, and disdain associated with love, Soranzo hymns the joys of satisfied love, and indicates that the present object of his fancy is Annabella. She is described in the same exaggerated Platonic love terminology that Giovanni had utilized in courting Annabella. Both Soranzo and Giovanni combine sensuality with elevated language. Although it should be clear that Soranzo's fine speeches are in part merely a means to an ignoble end, there can be no doubt of his appreciation of feminine beauty. Worldly honor and love are Soranzo's idols.

The quality of his love is revealed in the following scene in which the forsaken Hippolyta confronts him with her

misery. She describes herself as a chaste girl who was seduced by the smooth charms of a lover who used all of the
stock Platonic arguments:

> Thou knowst (false wanton) when my modest fame
> Stood free from staine, or scandall, all the charmes
> Of Hell or sorcery could not prevaile
> Against the honour of my chaster bosome.
> Thyne eyes did pleade in teares, thy tongue in oathes
> Such and so many, that a heart of steele
> Would have beene wrought to pitty, as was mine. (D1; II, ii)

But now she recognizes that the real motivation was not
love but "distracted lust" (D1; II, ii) and "sensuall rage of
blood" (D1; II, ii), and that his promises to marry her
after her husband's death were meaningless. Even in this
situation in which his duplicity has been completely un-
masked Soranzo tries to maintain the appearance of virtue
by appealing to the letter of the Christian moral code:

> The vowes I made, (if you remember well)
> Were wicked and unlawfull, 'twere more sinne
> To keepe them, then to breake them; as for mee
> I cannot maske my penitence. (D1ʳ–D2; II, ii)

Hippolyta is not deceived and even Vasques is shocked by
his legalism, but Soranzo's habit of trying to appear honorable has become so interwoven into his being that he has
perhaps managed to convince even himself that his course is
the proper one.

In the later scene in which Soranzo courts Annabella, he
uses the same stock literary Platonic phrases that he apparently had used earlier with Hippolyta and that Giovanni
used in his courtship of Annabella. The difference in result is
significant. When the girl feels the same passion that the
man does, she accepts the Platonic trappings as sincere; but
when she views the arguments in a rational way, they become ridiculous and the speaker is exposed as a fool. Feeling
no love, Annabella exposes Soranzo, and we should remember that in the earlier scene Annabella was ready to treat
Giovanni's ravings as a joke until she became convinced that
he reciprocated her own passion. It should be clear that the
element of the ridiculous is never far removed from Fordian

courtship scenes; they are saved from descending to comedy in cases where we recognize a worthy person victimized by passion, but Ford allows the comic full scope whenever the situation is not inherently tragic.

Although the corruption in the society around them makes the attraction of Giovanni and Annabella to each other more understandable, it must be emphasized that they are not absolved from blame simply because their situation was difficult. The initial contrast of their nobility with the degradation around them does not lead to a defense of their immoral relationship as something purer and more ideal. Rather it reveals their weakness in betraying their earlier values and descending to the level of the society around them. Ford skillfully depicts the deterioration that results from their abandonment of reason and virtue. As the play progresses, we see that a steady decline in the spiritual quality of their relationship accompanies their continuing revolt against the moral order.

The deterioration of Giovanni's love is perhaps best indicated by his compulsive jealousy. Instead of trusting the person with whom he has established this supposedly idealized spiritual relationship Giovanni repeatedly suspects that she will desert him for another lover. In the first scene after the consummation of their love he first brings up the subject of her marriage, and it is clear that he is unalterably opposed. At this point his concern seems quite natural but it soon develops into an obsession. Before Annabella's conference with Soranzo he warns her: "Sister be not all woeman, thinke on me" (E4; III, ii). This cynical comment on woman's fidelity does not sound at all like his earlier praise, but we should remember that Burton has a long section in *The Anatomy of Melancholy* which stresses that jealousy frequently accompanies heroical love (*AM*, III, 295–357; 3, 3). It is likely that Ford included Giovanni's jealousy as an indication of the steady decline of his moral character. Even after Annabella becomes pregnant and desperate measures are necessary. Giovanni is violently opposed to any marriage not only because he does not want to degrade their relationship by sharing her with another man, but also because he does not trust Annabella's love for him. The physical relationship has become such an important part of their love that he fears that another man might easily replace him in her favor. Thus when Annabella repents in the last act, Giovanni's first response is to suspect her motive:

> What chang'd so soone? hath your new sprightly Lord
> Found out a tricke in night-games more then wee
> Could know in our simplicity? (14; V, v)

Giovanni's jealousy and his preoccupation with the physical are connected, and both indicate that he is a victim of heroical love.

Friar Bonaventura has received unjustified criticism for his part in persuading Annabella to marry Soranzo.[9] Throughout the play the friar does everything in his power to stop the incestuous relationship, and his support of the marriage should be seen as another practical attempt to stop the affair. Certainly the friar does not counsel a marriage simply to preserve appearances; his continued demands for repentance prove that he sees Annabella's marriage as a means of ending rather than hiding the affair. Nor is the friar to be blamed for supporting a marriage that is almost certain to end in disaster because of Annabella's pregnancy. For he knows nothing or at least appears to know nothing of the pregnancy. If, as the friar assumes, Annabella is truly repentant and is ready to end her affair with Giovanni, there is no reason why the marriage to Soranzo will not work. Admittedly there is no evidence of love for Soranzo in Annabella, but a common Renaissance view was that love came as a result of marriage. From the audience's point of view Soranzo will hardly make an ideal husband, but it should be noted that neither the friar nor Annabella has much choice as to the groom. Earlier Florio had talked about letting Annabella choose her own husband, but at this point Florio has decided that the marriage will go through, and Annabella would have to rebel openly to prevent it. There is no indication of the friar's attitude toward Soranzo, but presumably he would support any plausible marriage that would stop the affair.

Another charge made against the friar is that his lecture on hell is an "exercise in terror"[10] that Ford does not ap-

prove. But the passage is apparently lifted directly from the
passage on hell in *Christ's Bloody Sweat*, since the corre-
spondence of details is very close.[11] If Ford's authorship of
Christ's Bloody Sweat is accepted, the debt suggests Ford's
approval of the friar's stand since it is unlikely, though
admittedly possible, that an author would lift a passage
from his earlier work that he no longer approved. More
important is that the speech is a standard exposition of the
Christian view of hell and is designed to encourage Annabella's repentance. Only after Annabella has convinced him
that she is truly penitent does the friar come forward with
his practical suggestions as to what can be done:

> 'tis thus agreed,
> First, for your Honours safety that you marry
> The Lord *Soranzo,* next, to save your soule,
> Leave off this life, and henceforth live to him. (F4; III, vi)

The progression is chronological and does not imply that
the friar is less concerned about her soul than about getting
her married. His repeated insistence on her repentance re-
futes such a view. As for the reference to "your Honours
safety," the friar probably does not mean "for the safety of
your reputation" but rather "for the safety of your true
honor—that is, your moral integrity and virtue." As the
friar has maintained throughout the play, the safest and
surest way for Annabella to forget Giovanni and insure her
virtue and honor is to marry someone else and and then stay
true to him. We must distinguish between the friar's sense
of honor and the concern for worldly honor that motivates
Annabella when she later tells Soranzo " 'twas not for love
/ I chose you, but for honour" (H1; IV, iii).

The question of whether Annabella's repentance in this
scene is sincere is troublesome but is not crucial to the play's
interpretation. The best answer seems to be that she is so
deeply disturbed that she lets circumstances control her responses, but it may be that she feigns repentance so that the
friar will consent to the marriage. An actual stage production could easily clarify the nature of her attitude. Certainly
she is unfair to Soranzo to marry him without revealing that
she is pregnant. Also it is clear that even if she does feel

some penitence in this scene she quickly resumes the affair with her brother. Giovanni himself describes loving her after the marriage (I2; V, iii). Also Putana apparently does not think she is sincerely penitent for she tells Vasques that Giovanni "will not be long from her" (H4; IV, iii).

Nor does Annabella seem very repentant in the scene in which Soranzo discovers her pregnancy. There her rebellious behavior parallels Giovanni's in insolence and moral confusion. Soranzo justifiably demands some explanations, but Annabella argues only that she is faultless since fate is beyond her control: "Beastly man, why 'tis thy fate: / I sued not to thee" (H1; IV, iii). Even though her defiance may be calculated to get Soranzo to kill her, it should be apparent that she believes what she says. If you cannot justify an action, do it anyway and blame fate: that would seem to be Giovanni and Annabella's moral code. Her fault is the same as his; she has elevated her lover to a position of dominance and worships him:

> This *Noble Creature* was in every part
> So angell-like, so glorious, that a woeman,
> Who had not beene but human as was I,
> Would have kneel'd to him, and have beg'd for love.
> You, why you are not worthy once to name
> His name without true worship, or indeede,
> Unlesse you kneel'd, to heare another name him. (H1 ; IV, iii)

They both treat other human beings as means of achieving their lustful ends. Thus she can tell Soranzo to feel happy that he has had a part in such an affair:

> Let it suffice, that you shall have the glory,
> To *Father* what so *Brave a Father got*. (H1ᵛ; IV, iii)

She can meet his threats of death with blasphemous exclamations:

> *Che morte [piu] dolce che morire per amore?* [12] (H1ᵛ; IV, iii)

In Christian terms death for love of the celestial Venus would be sweet, but Annabella would be dying for love of the earthly Venus. Her inversion is blasphemous, as is her next phrase:

Morendo in gratia [dee] morire senza dolore.[13] (H1ᵛ; IV, iii)

Her grace is not the grace of God but the grace of Giovanni. The atmosphere of approaching tragedy is clearly mirrored earlier in the scene describing Annabella's wedding feast, for none of the characters closely involved approaches the celebration in the right spirit. The scene opens with the friar commenting on the ritual significance of the feast as a celebration of the joy and plenitude of marriage; he suggests that the saints of the church are there in spirit and urges that the feast may be an emblem of their future happiness. Unfortunately this proper wedding spirit is perverted at every turn. Soranzo is still preoccupied with his recent escape from murder and self-righteously proclaims that God has protected him and rewarded him with Annabella. Donado is reluctant to drink because of his grief for his dead nephew, Bergetto. The brother-lover, Giovanni, rudely refuses to drink the ceremonial toast. Even the wedding masque, ostensibly performed by lovely virgins honoring the marriage, is in reality Hippolyta's device for exposing and murdering her former lover. Instead of toasting their happiness, she reminds everyone of Soranzo's affair with her; then after realizing that she herself has been poisoned with the wine intended for Soranzo, she curses the marriage in terms that are particularly ominous since the audience knows of Annabella's incestuous pregnancy:

> Take here my curse amongst you; may thy bed
> Of marriage be a racke unto thy heart,
> . . . maist thou live
> To father Bastards, may her wombe bring forth
> Monsters, and dye together in your sinnes
> Hated, scorn'd and unpittied. (G4; IV, i)

Although the appearance of order is reestablished at the end of the scene, we must agree with the friar who closes the scene with a choral comment on the bad omen of a bloody marriage feast and a warning to Giovanni to "take heed" (G4; IV, i). Unfortunately Giovanni does not take heed, and the second banquet, a birthday feast, supposedly a celebration of life, also becomes a feast of death. After Hippolyta's death Richardetto comments: "Here's the end/ Of lust and pride" (G4; IV, i). After the second banquet, he makes a similar comment; he has disguised himself "To see the effect of *Pride and Lust* at once/ Brought both to shamefull ends" (K4; V, vi). Richardetto, perceiving what Soranzo and Giovanni do not, that tragedy results from revenge, determines to change his life and give up his revenge: "there is one/ Above begins to worke" (G4; IV, ii). The implication that he would still act if God does not makes it questionable whether Ford regards the reformed Richardetto as a norm; but certainly his decision to quit seeking revenge and his evaluations of the deaths of the four principal characters are sound. Lust was the initial cause of the tragedies, and pride, expressed in a compelling desire to assert greatness of spirit, is a strong motivating force behind the revenges of Hippolyta, Soranzo, and Giovanni.

The moral attitude suggested by the handling of the revenges in the play is important for establishing the moral context of the ending. As Fredson Bowers has shown in his study of revenge tragedy, Ford, like most of the dramatists of the 1620's, disapproves of revenge and treats it as "a cruel, mistaken, or useless motive." [14] All of the revenges in the play end in tragedy. Two misfire completely: Grimaldi and Richardetto's plot to kill Soranzo results in the death of Bergetto, ironically the means by which Richardetto had hoped to get some wealth; Hippolyta's plot to kill Soranzo results in her own death. Also the innocent suffer: in addition to the innocent Bergetto, Florio dies of grief at his children's actions. Nor in the cases in which the revenge is carried out successfully is there justice, unless one judges by the same code of values that prompted the revenges in the first place. The motivation of each of the revenges is the reassertion of one's nobility in the face of an action which has questioned it. But the concern with only the appearances of grandeur and honor is shown to be empty and misguided. The revenger takes justice into his own hands and invariably produces tragedy for all concerned. A thinking person of Ford's own time would be more concerned with living a truly honorable life under God's moral law.

Annabella in Act V finally does see the folly of her sinful

ways. In a long soliloquy which the friar overhears she
reveals what her mistake has been:

> My Conscience now stands up against my lust
> With dispositions charectred in guilt,
> And tells mee I am lost: *Now I confesse,*
> *Beauty that cloathes the out-side of the face,*
> *Is cursed if it be not cloath'd with grace.* (H4ᵛ; V, i)

Annabella in this complete recantation admits that her former love was lust and that beauty without the grace of God
is *"cursed."* She also makes clear that she no longer believes
in the fatalistic argument that man cannot be blamed for his
fate since all is predetermined:

> *But they who sleepe in Lethargies of Lust*
> *Hugge their confusion, making Heaven unjust,*
> And so did I. (I1; V, i)

The sincerity of this repentance after the falseness or at
least shallowness of her repentance in Act III is certain
because she is alone, and the friar discovers her penitence
only by overhearing. From this point on all that Annabella
does is nobly conceived; because of her repentance she will,
as the friar suggests, "dye more blessed" (I1ᵛ; V, i). Incidentally the friar's genuine surprise and happiness at the
change in her are further rebukes to those who claim that the
friar himself has been somewhat Machiavellian in his methods. Also the repentant Annabella's wholehearted praise of
the former advice of "that *Blessed Fryar*" (I1; V, i) implies that he never deviated from sound morality.

In contrast to Annabella's repentance, Giovanni rises to
even greater defiance. Although he maintains the pretense
of lofty Platonism, it has become clear that the motivation
of his love is primarily physical pleasure and that Annabella
has become an idolatrous heaven on earth for him:

> Let *Poaring booke-men* dreame of other worlds,
> My world, and all of happinesse is here,
> And I'de not change it for the best to come,
> *A life of pleasure is* Elyzeum. (I2; V, iii)

To incest is added adultery, but Giovanni finds "no change/
Of pleasure in this formall law of sports" (I2). His atti-

tude to the friar and religion has now become flippant and condescending:

> Father, you enter on the *Jubile*
> Of my retyr'd delights; Now I can tell you,
> The hell you oft have prompted, is nought else
> But slavish and fond superstitious feare;
> And I could prove it too—. (I2; V, iii)

When the friar gives Giovanni the letter from Annabella telling of the discovery of their affair and apparently also imploring him to repent,[15] Giovanni refuses to take the letter seriously and goes so far as to call it a forgery. When in spite of the warning Giovanni accepts an invitation to dinner with Soranzo, the friar realizes that Giovanni's state of mind is desperate and beyond control.

In the final act Soranzo and Giovanni, parallel earlier in their techniques of courtship and their valuation of love, are shown to have similar ideas about revenge and honor as well. The moral code of both is based on worldly rather than spiritual values: both feel that the self is more important than any moral law. Since both of them are more concerned with outward appearances than with inner truth, they react to any trivial assault upon their honor, not with reason and common sense, but with the self-aggrandizing act of revenge.

Soranzo, a more practical and less reflective person than Giovanni, is so hardened in his villainy that he never faces the contradiction between his noble appearance and his corrupt actions and manages to convince himself, with the help of Vasques, that even his most treacherous actions are honorable. Thus the proposed murder of Giovanni and Annabella is seen as a ritual punishment that not only purges corruption but also proves Soranzo's nobility. When Vasques recites the long list of Annabella's misdeeds, Soranzo replies by stressing his resolution and nobility:

> I am resolv'd; urge not another word,
> My thoughts are great, and all as resolute
> As thunder. (I1; V, ii)

When later Vasques again tells him to be resolute and not to pity Annabella, Soranzo says firmly that "Revenge is all the

Ambition I aspire" (I1ᵛ; V, ii). Later he tells the banditti: "what you do is noble, and an act of brave revenge" (I3; V, iv), and Vasques tells him "nothing is unready to this *Great worke,* but a great mind in you" (I3ᵛ; V, iv). In planning the banquet Soranzo and Vasques have been attentive to every detail, and we can probably assume that they would have succeeded if Giovanni had not acted first. Soranzo would dramatically reveal the incest and the pregnancy and would pose as a champion of moral order; probably his power-conscious friend, the hypocritical Cardinal, would agree, and if the Cardinal agreed, the rest would follow.

When Giovanni's actions in the last act are compared with Soranzo's it can be seen that he is struggling to accept the moral code of his corrupt society so that he can justify his depraved actions as glorious and courageous. He wants to prove his greatness by a final gesture of heroic nobility, but beneath the eloquent rhetoric is a depraved and troubled sinner now approaching madness. When Annabella tells him of her repentance he jealously suspects that Soranzo has replaced him in her favor and launches into a grand assertion of his ability to overcome fate if only Annabella had been true:

> why I hold Fate
> Clasp't in my fist, and could Command the Course
> Of times eternall motion; hadst thou beene
> One thought more steddy then an ebbing Sea. (I4; V, v)

In his irrationality, Giovanni does not notice that this contradicts his previous position that man is helpless in the power of a malevolent universe.

Not surprisingly the passionate Giovanni himself seems unsure of his rebellion. He shifts from rebellion to conventional speeches about life, death, and immortality and even urges Annabella to pray so that she will go to heaven. Underneath his defiance is a deep consciousness of sin. Giovanni is not a study of a man in intellectual revolt against God but of a sinner who desperately tries to justify what even he himself subconsciously knows is wrong. His naive hope that the strength of their love "will wipe away that rigour" (K1; V, v) of the just condemnation of the laws of morality is both a recognition that a moral law does exist and a repetition of his old fault of elevating their love above that moral law. Ford would probably expect the audience of "after times" to see the mitigating circumstances in their situation, but he has revealed far too much of the weakness in their passion to permit anyone to accept Giovanni's romanticized view of their love.

Our final attitude toward Giovanni should probably be close to that of Annabella in their last interview. She now sees their affair as deadly sin, is unimpressed by his heroic rhetoric, and insists on breaking off their relationship. Nevertheless she is sympathetic to him: she sees him as tormented by "Distraction and a troubled Countenance" (I4^v; V, v), and she without reservation forgives him, somewhat ironically in light of what happens, "With my heart" (K1; V, v). But significantly there is no romanticizing of their love and no thought in her mind of a counterrevenge against Soranzo. She wants to find a way of avoiding the catastrophe that she knows is being planned for them, but she is insistent that the most important factor is their relationship to God. She dies while imploring mercy for both Giovanni and herself.

Irony is heavily operative throughout the murder scene. Giovanni speaks of saving Annabella's fame, but it is difficult to see how killing her can save her reputation, particularly since in the next scene in the banquet hall Giovanni flaunts their immorality. Giovanni also speaks of the honor of his revenge: *"Revenge is mine; Honour doth love Command"* (K1^v; V, v). The revenge can only be on Annabella herself for her defection from him and to a lesser extent on Soranzo for his treatment of Annabella. Such revenge is hardly honorable, and yet Giovanni refers to honor as commanding love. Perhaps he refers to their vows when they first made their pledge of love; each vowed: "Love mee, or kill mee . . ." (C2; I, iii). Even though the vow itself was sinful and Annabella no longer approves, there is a perverted kind of honor in Giovanni's carrying out the letter of the terms they had agreed on. Giovanni himself seems to see the weakness of his abstractions, for he then tells Annabella that he will explain later:

> When thou art dead
> I'le give my reasons for't; for to dispute
> With thy (even in thy death) most lovely beauty,
> Would make mee stagger to performe *this act*
> Which I most glory in. (K1ᵛ; V, v)

Giovanni's final melodramatic entry into the hall with
Annabella's heart on his sword is the ultimate depravity of a
man approaching madness.[16] In his deluded concern with
dying a glorious death, Giovanni sacrifices all decency. First
he breaks the heart of his father and shames the memory of
Annabella by revealing his incestuous love; then he is much
more impressed by the appropriateness of his father's death
than he is with his own guilt in causing it; finally he glories
in his "brave revenge" on Soranzo even though what Soranzo has actually done hardly justifies such gloating language. In his final welcome of death Giovanni is concerned
only with seeing Annabella again; the romantic grandeur of
his death is more important to him than the state of his own
soul. If we allow ourselves to be impressed by passionate but
vacuous rhetoric we can perhaps see even these final actions
as noble, but to do so we must ignore Giovanni's twisted
logic, self-conscious role-playing, and lack of concern for
others. We should pity the lovers since their situation was
difficult and since passions are hard to control, but I can find
no historical justification for romanticizing their love as
something noble and transcendent.

The moral chaos of the last scenes is symbolized by the
friar's departure after his final warning to Giovanni. The
friar has stood for religion's promise of repentance and
regeneration. When he departs after being rejected by Giovanni, all hope of a new life for Giovanni is gone and the
tragic ending is inevitable.[17] Evil has assumed control of the
society of Parma, and the result must be a bloody conclusion. A criticism made of the friar is that his flight indicates
his lack of sincere concern about Giovanni's problem. Such
an argument fails to account for the friar's repeated warnings of impending tragedy and his obviously sincere pleasure
when Annabella repents. He leaves Giovanni only when he
sees that there is no chance of getting him to reconsider. His
physical departure serves a double function: it prepares us

for the tragedy of the final act and it suggests that the entire society of Parma has been corrupted beyond hope of restoration.

After the friar, the symbol of true religion, leaves the city, corruption and hypocrisy go unchallenged, and the powerful Cardinal is made a kind of symbol of the society's venality. His perverted sense of justice was revealed in the earlier scene in which he protected Grimaldi after the murder of Bergetto. The justice that he dispenses at the end is similarly corrupt. He orders Putana put to death even though she was only indirectly connected with the incest, whereas the villainous Vasques is only banished since he is able to appear virtuous through eloquent but hypocritical speeches about the duty of servants to masters and the glories of revenge. If any doubt remains about the Cardinal's moral values it is dispelled when he confiscates the gold and jewels from the bodies for the church. His final speech about Annabella should probably be viewed ironically as well. The Cardinal thinks in worldly terms, and his glib, clever summary is consistent with his character: *"Of one so young, so rich in Natures store,/ Who could not say, 'Tis pitty shee's a Whoore?"* (K4; V, vi). Although the Cardinal's summary of Annabella's position has a superficial truth that all would grant, it is a view which fails to account for the deeper truth of Annabella's guilt and sincere repentance. Ford's use of the final phrase for his title may be taken as an indication of the extent of the irony that pervades Ford's view of the entire play, particularly this last scene. In his dedicatory letter Ford himself calls attention to the difference between the lightness of the title and the gravity of the play: "The Gravity of the *Subject* may easily excuse the leightnesse of the *Title:* otherwise, I had beene a severe Judge against mine owne guilt" (A2ᵛ). The effect of the ironic ending is to suggest the danger of falling back on moral platitudes without examining the realities they represent. Reason and faith should be allies, but if the faith is hypocritical the situation is made worse rather than better. A society in which the friar can find no place is in a deplorable state, and Ford suggests no easy solution. No doubt this cynicism, witty but at bottom traditionally moral, would appeal to an audience aware of the hypocrisies in their own society. The extent of Ford's detachment from moralizing tragedy is indicated by this ironic handling of the conclusion. If we are to understand the nature of Ford's achievement we must distinguish the melodramatic, satiric, and tragic elements. The play is at once an exciting entertainment, a witty but serious analysis of important ideas of the time, and a study of two human beings caught in a situation that they cannot handle.

VI

Love's Sacrifice

In *Love's Sacrifice* Ford returns to the theme of illicit love
but treats it in a more restricted way. In *'Tis Pity* Ford goes
beyond love to consider such diverse topics as incest,
atheism, blasphemy, ambition, materialism, and hypocrisy.
The scope is so broad that the play might be said to be about
the justice of the moral laws of God and of society. In
Love's Sacrifice Ford deals almost exclusively with love and
seldom suggests larger dimensions. Although there is disorder in Pavia the cause is not ambition or materialism or
hypocrisy but only the improper views of love held by its
leaders. The implication is that if these views could be cor-
rected order would be possible. At the end of the play
tragedy occurs, but a stable order is reestablished. One
consequence of the more limited subject is a lighter tone; it
is doubtful that a Caroline audience would get very emotionally involved with the play's collection of extravagant suitors and all too frail ladies. The satiric impluse dominates,
and the audience would probably have come away from the
play as much amused by the foolishness of love as appalled
by the tragedy of it. Fernando, Bianca, and the Duke are
combinations of the passionate sinner and the rationalizing
fool, and the stress in *Love's Sacrifice* is as much on exposing
their folly as on developing sympathy for them. Because the

characters represent less, their tragedies imply less, and the audience could relax and enjoy the satire and the melodrama without being forced to consider the more profound questions posed by *'Tis Pity.*

Despite its comparative simplicity, *Love's Sacrifice* has aroused even more perplexity than *'Tis Pity,* for scholars have found little justification for its supposedly immoral main plot and indecent subplot. Stuart Sherman found it less successful than *'Tis Pity* and *The Broken Heart* and more reprehensible morally: "Now the conclusion of this play must seem to every person of normal sense singularly wrong, weak, and futile. In the beginning of it everyone knows what is decent; in the middle Fernando and Bianca grow skeptical as to what is decent; in the end no one knows what is decent—not even the author." [1] More recent scholars have questioned the extent of Ford's sympathy for Bianca and Fernando but have been just as bewildered as to the play's intention. Most conclude that Ford, in his desire to create exciting theater, sacrificed logic for dramatic effect and produced an inconsistent, inartistic failure.[2]

Much of the difficulty has arisen because of failure to understand the play's relationship to the Platonic love cult discussed in Chapter III.[3] The views of the cult are quite different from those of Fernando and the other Platonists in *Love's Sacrifice,* and what happens to the court in *Love's Sacrifice* is the direct opposite of what the queen intended for the English court. The utilization of Platonic doctrines to glorify passionate love would have been viewed by Henrietta Maria's group with aghast disapproval or more likely with amused superiority. In all of his plays, but particularly in *Love's Sacrifice,* Ford illustrates the effects of using such twisted arguments. Far from glorifying passion, Ford ridicules it by showing its absurd, but unfortunately also tragic, effect on individual lives.

Almost every person that we see in the first scenes of the play has an improper view of love and is acting foolishly as a result. The Duke and Fernando are serious advocates of a heavily Platonized theory of love that glorifies physical love and beauty, while Mauruccio is a parody of this serious courtly type. Ferentes and Fiormonda see the fallacies but they also see that Platonic arguments can serve as a useful mask for libertinism. Even the reasonable Roseilli is a victim of love, but he differs from the others in that he finally sees the folly of passionate idolatry of women and asserts his natural sovereignty over Fiormonda at the end of the play. The others are less capable of ordering their passions and meet tragic ends as a result.

The somewhat pompous Petruchio's evaluation of the Duke's marriage to Bianca is misguided in implying that someone of Bianca's background could not make a good duchess, but it turns out to be accurate as a description of the Duke's motives. Instead of choosing Bianca for her real virtues, he picked her because "her inchanting face" appealed to "His roving eye" (B2ᵛ). Other details also emphasize the physical basis of the Duke's love:

> Fortune (Queene to such blind matches)
> Presents her to the Dukes eye, on the way
> As he pursues the Deere. (B2ᵛ–B3; I, i)

Renaissance moralists frequently warned against the fruits of Fortune, while the image of the deer hunt can be taken as an icon of the search for a bestial love.[4] When the Duke enters, his first words verify Petruchio's analysis of the lustful motive of his love:

> Come my *Biancha,* revell in mine armes,
> Whiles I, wrapt in my admiration, view
> Lillies and Roses growing in thy cheekes. (B3; I, i)

The combination of delight in the physical and eulogistic romantic praise reveals the Duke as a typical heroical lover. Despite the ultimately physical basis of his love, the Duke uses all of the stock Platonic defenses of love and beauty. When Fernando suggests that Bianca is virtuous "If credit may be given to a face" (B3ᵛ; I, i), the Duke agrees and argues eloquently that royalty should be encouraged to marry for beauty (B3ᵛ–B4; I, i). The Duke also invokes the Platonic belief in the virtuous union of true souls when he suggests that Bianca should treat Fernando just as she does him:

> in all respects to him
> Be as to me: onely the name of husband,
> And reverent observance of our bed
> Shall differ us in persons, else in soule
> We are all one. (B3–B3'; I, i)

Perhaps the major interest of the play is the study of the moral deterioration of the characters in the play who claim to follow this code of rational love but who allow their passions to corrupt their ideals. As the play reveals, neither the eloquent Duke nor the attractive Fernando nor the beautiful Bianca is able to keep love on a rational level. Ford's intention seems to be to provide both a psychological study of the influence of love on human behavior and a satirical exposure of the absurdities of the arguments used to justify love.

In the first section of the play the satirical dominates as each lover in turn is made to look foolish by his submission to passion. The cases of Fernando and Bianca have a tragic dimension, however, in that we are led to believe that their virtues at the beginning of the play are real. If there had been no barrier separating them they undoubtedly would have found natural expression for their love in marriage. Since the Duke has few qualities that would win a young girl's love, the audience probably would be even more sympathetic to Bianca's plight. She is quite naturally attracted to the virtue and beauty of Fernando just as he is to her. But what must be recognized is that their relationship never becomes the rational love that the Duke had suggested but is instead a destructive passion that steadily corrupts them and helps bring about final tragedy. The Duke is presented as an inadequate husband and ruler from the very start, while Fernando is portrayed as a virtuous courtier who at first struggles to suppress his passion. His return from travel abroad brings hope of a restoration of order to the court of Pavia, which has become degenerate through the influence on the pliable Duke of corrupt men like Ferentes. The general moral chaos is made specific when Petruchio tells his nephew, Fernando, that Ferentes has corrupted Petruchio's own daughter, Colona, and implores Fernando's help. By having Petruchio make this specific plea, Ford establishes a moral responsibility for Fernando, who has learned of the moral corruption of the court and now is told something that he can do about it. Twice the issue of Fernando's duty comes up, and twice Fernando is more concerned about his own obsessive love than about the unfortunate Colona. After Petruchio's original plea Fernando promises help but quickly shifts the conversation to Bianca:

> Unckle, I'le doe my best; meane time pray tell me
> Whose mediation wrought the Marriage
> Betwixt the Duke and Dutchesse? (B2ᵛ; I, i)

The second mention of Fernando's duty to Colona puts his failure to act in an even more clearly unfavorable context. Just after Ferentes' depraved conversations with Colona and Julia, Fernando enters and says:

> My Lord *Ferentes,* I should change some words
> Of consequence with you; but since I am,
> For this time, busied in more serious thoughts,
> I'le picke some fitter opportunity. (C2; I, ii)

In his soliloquy which follows, Fernando reveals that these "more serious thoughts" are his passionate desires for Bianca. Ford must have included the passage to indicate that Fernando's love for Bianca causes him to evade his responsibilities. The trust that Petruchio has placed in him proves to be unwarranted, and the moral tone of the society deteriorates even further with Fernando's return.

Ford's treatment of the more obviously corrupt Fiormonda and Ferentes serves as a commentary on the Platonic doctrines espoused by the Duke and Fernando. Both Fiormonda and Ferentes are interested in the techniques of courtship, and both see eloquence as a camouflage for lust. In portraying their viciousness, Ford can allow his satiric impulse full expression, for there is less need to make their villainy psychologically credible. One of the comic highlights of the play is the elaborate parody of courtship in the scenes in which Fernando refuses the circuitous advances of Fiormonda. By taking the Platonic euphemisms as the reality Fernando is able to avoid recognizing what D'Avolos and later Fiormonda actually intend. There is always a disparity between appearance and reality when idealization

is used as a mask for passion. By refusing to acknowledge
the convention that he, D'Avolos, and Fiormonda all know
is being used, Fernando can avoid committing himself.

Ferentes' technique is more successful than Fiormonda's,
as is revealed in his juxtaposed interviews with Colona and
Julia. Once again the satiric intention is the controlling factor. Since Colona has not yet been seduced, she is treated
with great respect; she is "sweet *Colona*, faire *Colona*,
young and sprightfull Lady" (C1; I, ii). Since Julia has
already submitted, Ferentes' manner with her is directly
opposite; he calls her "wench" and tells her to meet him
again in her "Ladies backe lobby" (C2; I, ii). There is no
relation between the language used by Ferentes in courtship
and his true feelings. When by himself he says, "Chastity! I
am / An Eunuch, if I thinke there be any such thing; or/If
there be, 'tis amongst us men, for I never found it / In a
woman, throughly tempted, yet" (C2; I, ii). This is the
reality that Ferentes finds underneath the beautiful appearance of women. D'Avolos had expressed a similar view
earlier (B4^v; I, i). The relevance of these cynical appraisals
to the belief of Fernando and the Duke that beauty is an
indication of virtue is immediately obvious, and the audience
is naturally interested in seeing which view will prove accurate.

In Act II Ford develops his main theme, the folly of love,
by deliberately juxtaposing scenes in which the foolish Mauruccio and Fernando express their love for noble ladies. In
his depiction of Mauruccio, Ford parodies the courtly lover
who spends his time looking in the mirror, worrying about
his appearance, reciting love poetry, and developing elaborate conceits to express his love. It is no coincidence that his
idolatrous attitude toward Fiormonda is strikingly similar
to the attitude of the Duke and Fernando toward Bianca.
All three believe that women are saints to be worshiped and
that a series of noble speeches is the best way to win their
favor, but in each the ultimate motivation is physical rather
than spiritual. Their Platonizing is at once a blasphemous
perversion of religious doctrine, a subtle rationalization of
lustful intentions, and an indication of what Burton calls
heroical love. Mauruccio's ineffectiveness makes him only

ridiculous, and the Duke is apparently unaware of the moral problem, but Fernando is intelligent enough to see that his love is both a sin and a kind of disease. His self-awareness makes him more sympathetic because we see the struggle that he is going through, but the close parallel with the other two Platonic lovers makes it clear that he is descending to their level by submitting to his passions. In Act II we see that his excessive love has reduced him to the pathetic state of Mauruccio, for the same courtly manners, fine speeches, and preoccupation with the physical are present in both men.

Mauruccio's plan to enclose his picture in a looking-glass for Fiormonda provides a satiric parallel to the later scene involving Fernando and the picture of Bianca. Both Fernando and Mauruccio are impressed by the appearance of beauty and consequently are much influenced by pictures. Mauruccio believes that a picture accompanied by an elaborate conceit is the best means of ingratiating himself to Fiormonda, and Fernando with his similar courtly ideas behaves ridiculously when he sees the picture of Bianca. D'Avolos describes Fernando's reaction as *"plaine passion"* (D4; II, ii) and as "Love in the extreamest" (D4; II, ii), and Fernando himself says, after D'Avolos has gone: "I feare I spoke or did I know not what, / All sense of providence was in mine eye" (E1; II, ii).

Ford's deliberate comparison of the two lovers is hard to ignore, for Mauruccio makes courtly love to Fiormonda just after Fernando leaves the stage, and Fernando makes his first courtly addresses to Bianca after Mauruccio's first ridiculous appearance. The same elaborate conceits found in Mauruccio's speeches are in Fernando's:

> Please but to heare
> The story of a Cast-away in love;
> And ô let not the passage of a jest
> Make slight a sadder subject, who hath plac'd
> All happinesse in your diviner eyes. (D3; II, i)

Significantly Bianca recognizes Fernando's speeches for what they are, a mask for a plea for physical love.[5] She

interrupts him with admonitions to stop and finally breaks
into an outspoken condemnation:

> No more; I spare
> To tell you what you are; and must confesse,
> Doe almost hate my judgement, that it once
> Thought goodnesse dwelt in you: remember now
> It is the third time since your treacherous tongue
> Hath pleaded treason to my eare and fame;
> Yet for the friendship 'twixt my Lord and you,
> I have not voyc'd your follies; if you dare
> To speake a fourth time, you shall rue your lust:
> 'Tis all no better; learne, and love your selfe. (D3ʳ; II, i)

Perhaps Bianca's decision not to reveal Fernando's love
may be seen as a sign of her own love for Fernando, but she
does know what right and wrong are. So does Fernando, as
his words spoken after her departure indicate:

> Gon! oh my sorrowes! how am I undone?
> Not speake againe? no, no, in her chast brest
> *Vertue* and *resolution* have discharg'd
> All female weaknesse. (D3ʳ; II, i)

He recognizes that his appeal has been to female weakness
and that it is her virtue, resolution, and chastity which have
overcome him; he also realizes that passion dominates him
and that he must try to regain control of himself:

> I must resolve to checke this rage of blood,
> And will; she is all ycie to my fires,
> Yet even that yce inflames in me desires. (D3ʳ; II, i)

When by himself, Fernando admits that he is a victim of
heroical love. He realizes that the passions of his body are
trying to overcome his reason and protests weakly that he
will attempt to fight.

But when he is next with Bianca, Fernando again woos in
the exaggerated phrases of Platonic courtship. Again
Bianca reduces his argument to its lustful presuppositions:

> looke on our face.
> What see you there that may perswade a hope
> Of lawlesse love? Know, most *unworthy man,*

> So much we hate the basenesse of thy lust,
> As were none living of thy sexe but thee,
> We had much rather prostitute our blood
> To some invenom'd Serpent, then admit
> Thy bestiall dalliance. (E4ᵛ; II, iii)

Perhaps the audience would think that her continued condemnation is weakened by her failure to carry out her threat
to reveal Fernando to the Duke, but there is no uncertainty
in her moral evaluation. By giving the virtue of Bianca such
emphasis early in the play Ford provides a norm against
which to measure her later actions. She is a symbol of chastity in the first part of the play, and her subsequent change
could be taken as a partial verification of the cynical appraisal of women by Ferentes and D'Avolos. But from another more mature point of view, her fall is an illustration
of original sin in all men and an implied criticism of the
excessive glorification of woman by extremists among the
Platonists of the day. Women are worthy of respect, but
they are human and are not to be worshiped as embodi-
ments of virtue.

Bianca's approaching fall is depicted allegorically in the
chess game just before Fernando's second scene with her.
D'Avolos invites the audience to interpret the game allegorically when he says just before the game starts that " 'tis a
Rooke to a *Queene,* she heaves a *pawne* to a *Knights place;*
by'r lady, if all be truly noted, to a *Dukes place"* (E3ᵛ; II,
iii). The audience, prepared by this speech, would almost
certainly notice the allegorization when Fernando takes
Bianca's queen, and she says:

> My Clergy helpe me;
> My Queen! and nothing for it but a pawne?
> Why then the game's lost too. (E4; II, iii)

Translating we read that Bianca, lacking the help of her
moral standards (the clergy or the bishops), will lose her
virtue (the queen) with nothing to show for it but Fernando
(a pawn). With her virtue gone, the game, or the value of
her life, is gone as well. After the first bedchamber scene
with Fernando, her taste in games changes; now she wants

"to try a set at Maw" (G2ʳ; III, ii). Fiormonda replies disdainfully:

> 'Tis a peevish play,
> Your *Knave* will heave the *Queene* out, or your *King;*
> Besides, 'tis all on fortune. (G2ʳ; III, ii)

Again the allegorical references in the second line are clear; the mention of the part chance plays in the game should perhaps be taken as an indication of Bianca's submission to the chance fortunes of life. Her trust is no longer in the eternal certitudes of God's moral law.

When Bianca comes to Fernando in the controversial bedchamber scene she still regards submission to him as morally wrong:

> With shame and passion now I must confesse,
> Since first mine eyes beheld you, in my heart
> You have beene onely King; if there can be
> A violence in love, then I have felt
> That tyranny; be record to my soule,
> The Justice which I for this folly feare. (F1ʳ–F2; II, iv)

Here Bianca expresses openly the guilt that Fernando has granted only in private, but clearly both see their love as a shameful passion. Fernando has overcome his moral scruples, but Bianca, still conscience-stricken by the thought of sin, wants a way to have Fernando's love and be moral at the same time. Fernando naturally refuses her offer to submit to him, since she adds that she will kill herself afterwards, and it becomes clear that what Bianca really wants is a non-physical relationship that will conveniently permit her to satisfy everyone. She can enjoy the love of Fernando, she can defend that love as something noble and pure since it is not physical, and she can remain true to her vow to be faithful to her husband.

Although both Bianca and Fernando had been ashamed of the passionate basis of their love, both now defend it by arguments that imply complete acceptance of the Platonic glorification of love expounded by Fernando during his courtship. But this obsessive, passionate love is far removed from the innocent, rational Platonic love cult of Henrietta Maria's circle and must be seen rather as a perverted de-

fense of a diseased and passionate love. Earlier Fernando
had had no idea of an innocent Platonic relationship, for he
is obviously surprised when Bianca opposes the actual consummation after going so far:

> Oh me—Come, come, how many women pray
> Were ever heard or read of, granted love,
> And did as you protest you will? (F2ʳ; II, iv)

In the terms of the play, Bianca and Fernando are not
rational rebels but passionate sinners.

The problem of determining when playing with temptation becomes sinful is inevitably an issue, and it is a question
upon which Christian ethical doctrine is clear. Sin is not a
matter of action only; if a person sins in intention it is just
as unmistakably a sin as the actual commission of a sinful
act.[6] Bianca cannot escape moral criticism by refusing to
consummate her love since the love itself is a violation of
the spirit of her wedding vows to the Duke. Only romanticization and glorification of passionate love can excuse their
affair, but neither is a characteristic seventeenth-century attitude. We should perhaps feel pity for two formerly virtuous and noble persons who are being destroyed, but we
should also note that their passionate self-justifications are
based on foolish rationalizations rather than calm reasoning.

The scene which immediately follows the interview of
Bianca and Fernando is that in which Nibrassa and Petruchio discover the pregnancies of their daughters. When we
remember that Fernando, because of his preoccupation with
Bianca, had neglected to warn Ferentes to stay away from
Petruchio's daughter, the significance of this juxtaposition
of scenes becomes evident. In this scene we see what happens
when people fail to realize that the Platonized speeches of
courtly lovers are frequently only a mask for libertinism.
Nibrassa's rebuke to Julia for believing the vows of Ferentes is applicable to all of the lovers of the play and should
be seen as a key speech for the play's interpretation. He tells
her: "Why thou foole, thou wickedly credulous foole, Canst
thou imagine Luxury is observant of Religion? No, no, it is
with a frequent Lecher as usuall to forsweare as to sweare,

their piety is in making idolatry a worship, their harts and their tongues are as different as thou (thou whore) and a Virgin" (F3–F3ʳ; III, i).

When we next see Bianca she is almost overcome with passion for Fernando. She seriously considers stealing a public kiss from him, and it is not a chaste kiss: "Speake, shall I steale a kisse? beleeve me, my Lord, I long" (G2; III, ii).⁷ Fernando too is becoming increasingly foolish. When Roseilli warns him that D'Avolos and Fiormonda are plotting against him and that he ought to be sure that they can find nothing to use against him, Fernando pays no heed and asserts his own independence in a speech which is strongly reminiscent of the argument of Giovanni near the end of *'Tis Pity* (*TP*, I4; V, v). Fernando says:

> Pish; should he or hell
> Affront me in the passage of my fate,
> I'de crush them into Atomies. (G3ʳ; III, ii)

Now Fernando sees himself as controlling his fate. In *'Tis Pity* Giovanni's pretentious claim that he could control his fate was the final raving of a man who had lost his reason. Roseilli warns Fernando to be "nearest to your selfe" (G3ʳ; III, ii); Fernando has allowed passion to cloud his reason and has lost all awareness of the implications of his position.

At this point the revenge theme becomes dominant. Revenge has already been in the air with D'Avolos and Fiormonda's plottings against Fernando, Bianca, and Roseilli, but now two more revenges are considered. The Iago-like D'Avolos plays on the Othello-like jealousy of the Duke and stirs him to a revenge on Bianca and Fernando. Throughout the play the Duke is portrayed as a weak and vacillating victim of his corrupt counselors, and his revenge on Bianca is always viewed as evil and unjustified. D'Avolos and Fiormonda plant the idea of jealousy, nurture it carefully, and bring it to fruition in the final act by emphasizing that the Duke's honor requires that he seek revenge. The Duke is reluctant, but he is too weak to provide effective resistance.

The other revenge is that of the three deceived women upon Ferentes. In this case the murder, enacted in a ritualistic masque reminiscent of *Antonio's Revenge* and *The Re-*

venger's Tragedy, approaches the tone of a sacrifice to effect a purging of a corrupt society. The Abbot, who may have been included by Ford to provide a moral comment analogous to that of the friar in *'Tis Pity* and Tecnicus in *The Broken Heart,* summarizes: "Here's fatall sad presages, but 'tis just, / He dyes by murther, that hath liv'd in lust" (H2; III, iv). This view recognizes the justice of the death of the sinner without condoning the means utilized. As we shall see, in Act V the Abbot once again provides a moral comment.

Act IV is filled with the sense of impending catastrophe. Fiormonda makes a final offer to Fernando and is rebuffed. The Duke makes a last plea to Bianca by relating an extremely graphic dream which warns her against adultery. Finally Roseilli tells Fernando that their love is known. All three episodes should serve as warnings to the lovers, but none has any effect even though both lovers have speeches which imply a conventional evaluation of their position. Bianca tells the Duke:

> for did such a guilt
> Hang on mine honour, 'twere no blame in you
> If you did stab me to the heart. (I3; IV, ii)

Fernando is more defiant but he uses conventional phrases to describe guilt and does not attempt an intellectual justification of their love:

> yet I vow
> Shee is as loyall in her plighted faith,
> As is the Sunne in heaven: but put case
> She were not; and the Duke did know she were not,
> This Sword lift up, and guided by this Arme,
> Shall guard her from an armed troupe of Fiends,
> And all the earth beside. (I3ᵛ–I4; IV, ii)

Fernando tries to have it both ways. Bianca is innocent, but if she were guilty, and the very mention of possible guilt seems to indicate a sense of real guilt in Fernando, he would defend her. The noble posture, the heroic gesture, and the faulty logic all reflect the growing irrationality of Fernando. His final lines in the scene are an assertion of his individual power in controlling his own fate by rising above it:

> Let slaves in mind be servile to their feares,
> Our heart is high in-starr'd in brighter Spheres. (I4; IV, ii)

Ford allows no chance for misinterpretation, for the reasonable Roseilli soliloquizes:

> I see him lost already,
> If all prevaile not, we shall know too late,
> No toyle can shun the violence of Fate. (I4; IV, ii)

In their passionate discussion in Bianca's bedchamber Fernando and Bianca fail to consider either the error of their passion or the danger of continuing their affair. The entire scene is designed to emphasize the excessive physical attraction of the lovers for each other. Bianca is *"discovered . . . in her night attire, leaning on a Cushion at a Table, holding Fernando by the hand"* (I4; V, i). Her first words reveal that her love for Fernando now impels her to question the moral law itself:

> Why shouldst thou not be mine? why should the laws
> The Iron lawes of Ceremony, barre
> Mutuall embraces? what's a vow? a vow?
> Can there be sinne in unity? (I4; V, i)

In the earlier bedchamber scene there had been no doubt in Bianca's mind about the justice of God's moral law. The only question then was whether she should submit to her weakness and face punishment for breaking that law. Now she wonders if union with Fernando would be a sin:

> Could I
> As well dispense with Conscience, as renounce
> The out-side of my titles, the poore stile
> Of *Dutchesse;* I had rather change my life
> With any waiting-woman in the land,
> To purchase one nights rest with thee *Fern[a]ndo,*
> Then be *Caraffa's* Spouse a thousand yeares. (I4–I4ᵛ; V, i)

She is still troubled by the moral problem but seems to be getting closer to physical submission to Fernando. An unfortunate lacuna in the text makes it difficult to analyze Fernando's reply, but clearly his vow to bury himself alive in Bianca's coffin if she dies before he does is not the approach of a rational man. Ford accentuates the physical basis of their love by having them kiss to seal Fernando's vow and continue kissing until they are interrupted by the Duke *"Whiles they are kissing"* (I4ᵛ; V, i). Since Bianca now seriously questions the moral law and since the intensity of their physical passion appears to be even greater than in the preceding bedchamber scene, it seems clear that Ford is dramatizing the moral deterioration of two people under the influence of heroical love.

The interpretation of the final act depends in part upon the values that have been established for the leading characters in the first four acts. Since we have been shown the contrast between the Bianca who has submitted to dalliance with Fernando and the Bianca who seemed to be a paragon of virtue in the first two acts, we should be extremely suspicious of any glorification of her virtue. Since Fernando has been treated as a study in the excesses of heroical lovers and the Duke as a passionate and weak-minded old man, we should expect the same kind of behavior in the final act. No reading can be certain because Ford includes no character representing the norm to comment on the action until the Abbot appears late in the act. But when we judge the characters by the values that have been established in the first four acts, the final act becomes consistent with the rest of the play, and what has been thought of as a somewhat ludicrous melodramatic ending can be seen as a serious analysis of the effects of excessive passion. Bianca, Fernando, and the Duke all strive for honorable deaths, but all meet their fates in the same passionate and illogical way in which they have lived.

Bianca's tempestuous words with the Duke after the discovery are a strange combination of honest recognition of guilt, of denial of guilt, of rationalization of the causes of her sin, of excuse for Fernando but not for herself, and of rhetorical posturing in an attempt to provoke murder. The scene is psychologically incisive: Bianca is not a logical person and her ravings have the passionate unreasonableness that has characterized her behavior since her love for Fernando was first revealed. When the Duke asks her what she now hopes for, Bianca requests death and admits that the Duke's dream warning her against sin does apply to her:

> Death; I wish no lesse:
> You told me you had dreamt; and, gentle Duke,
> Unlesse you be mistooke, you are now awak'd. (K1; V, i)

Her denunciation of the Duke and praise of Fernando seem to be more than just an attempt to provoke the Duke's anger since these evaluations are consistent with her attitudes earlier in the play. She defends her preference for Fernando by arguing that she has been motivated by the same appetites which motivated the Duke in marrying her. Why did the Duke marry her?

> But why? 'twas but because you thought I had
> A sparke of beauty more then you had seene.
> To answer this, my reason is the like,
> The selfe same appetite which led you on
> To marry me, led me to love your friend. (K1ᵛ; V, i)

Since we have had an uncomplimentary picture of the Duke's lustful motives in marrying Bianca, such a comparison hardly elevates Bianca. Rather it reveals her as another Platonic who worships beauty of person over all moral values.

Until Bianca shifts to the question of responsibility her argument has been an honest attempt to tell the Duke what she thinks of him. She begins to falsify only when she tries to assume all of the guilt in her plea for pardon for Fernando. Significantly her assertion of what Fernando did is very close to what Fernando should have done:

> I must confesse I mist no meanes, no time,
> To winne him to my bosome; but so much,
> So holily, with such Religion,
> He kept the lawes of friendship, that my sute
> Was held but, in comparison, a jest;
> Nor did I ofter urge the violence
> Of my affection, but as oft he urg'd
> The sacred vowes of faith 'twixt friend and friend. (K2; V, i)

The passage puts the actual behavior of Fernando in a decidedly bad light. But what of the nobility of such a self-sacrifice by Bianca? Ford is not concerned with having Bianca articulate rational reasons for her action since the stress throughout the play is that the victim of heroical love will act irrationally. One motive is her feeling that life for her would be useless with Fernando dead through the Duke's revenge. She tells the Duke: "For life to me, without him, were a death" (K2ᵛ; V, i). Other possible motives are that death is preferable to life burdened with suspicion of infidelity, that she could not be happy with the Duke even if she could win his forgiveness, and that the people would regard her death as a martyr's death even though they would severely criticize her for her dalliance if she were alive. Her dying words, "Live to repent too late" (K3; V, i), reveal her assurance that the Duke will discover her "innocence" and honor her memory. But the honor that comes to her after her death is based upon the Duke and Fernando's slanted accounts of her virtue.

A natural question is why Fernando falsifies his account of their love. When he tells Nibrassa and Petruchio that passion played no part in their relationship, he is still hopeful of saving Bianca's life; but in the next scene with the Duke, when he knows that Bianca is dead, Fernando still defends her virtue:

> Unfortunate *Caraffa;* thou hast butcher'd
> An Innocent, a wife as free from lust
> As any termes of Art can Deifie. (K4; V, ii)

This praise fits the chaste Bianca of the first part of the play, but it bears little resemblance to the Bianca of the bedchamber scenes or to the Bianca who has just revealed her motivations to the Duke. As a self-confessed victim of lustful, physical love, Bianca can make no claim to being "free from lust." Why then does Fernando describe her in such elevated terms? Perhaps it is sufficient to think of him simply as a loyal lover instinctively defending his mistress. But at least two other reasons are apparent. He has elevated her to the level of a goddess and is incapable of providing an impartial evaluation of her moral worth. Since Bianca was reluctant to consummate their affair, Fernando, already passionately in love with her, easily convinces himself that she is completely virtuous. Fernando no doubt does believe in Bianca's virtue, but that proves his irrationality rather than Bianca's virtue. Another reason is that since his guilt or innocence is linked to that of Bianca, it is to his advantage to claim that she is innocent. Since no one else knows what their relationship was, Fernando shifts the emphasis from their lustful passion to their supposedly reasonable restraint in not consummating their affair. His legalistic analysis sounds like Bianca's legalism in the first bedchamber scene. Neither of them will admit that dalliance, kissing and fondling, lustful desires, and improperly placed love are an indication of the weakness and sin that accompany heroical love. Fernando and Bianca have not consummated their love, but they have done and said much more than innocent lovers would.

Fernando, supported by the naive but virtuous old men, Petruchio and Nibrassa, convinces the Duke of Bianca's innocence and drives him to repentance and self-condemnation. Although his praise of Bianca's virtue is slightly absurd in that he ignores all the evidence of her unfaithfulness in spirit, the Duke is right to recognize D'Avolos' villainy in tempting him and his own fault in carrying out the murder. His words near the end of the scene are words of wisdom: "No counsaile from our cruell wils can win us, / 'But ils once done we beare our guilt within us" (K4ᵛ; V, ii).

In the scene at the tomb, however, the Duke is far from being a portrait of a repentant man now at last restored to sanity. In fact, the behavior of both the Duke and Fernando is so preposterous that the scene is saved from becoming comic only by the pathetic quality of their irrationality. The Duke's memory of Bianca is already sentimentalized beyond recognition:

> So chast, so deare a wife was never man,
> But I, enjoy'd: yet in the bloome and pride
> Of all her yeares, untimely tooke her life. (L1ᵛ; V, iii)

The description bears little resemblance to the Bianca who has insulted the Duke's appearance and stated her preference for Fernando or to the Bianca who told Fernando in the second bedchamber scene that she would trade her position as duchess and a thousand years as the Duke's wife for one night of love with Fernando. The Duke can maintain his faith in Bianca only by ignoring everything that Bianca told him before he killed her.

Then Fernando suddenly appears in the winding-sheet at the tomb and delivers a passion-crazed attack on the Duke:

> Forbeare; what are thou that dost rudely presse
> Into the confines of forsaken-graves?
> Has death no privilege? Com'st thou, *Caraffa,*
> To practise yet a rape upon the dead? Inhumane Tyrant;
> Whats'ever thou intend'st, know this place
> Is poynted out for my inheritance:
> Here lyes the monument of all my hopes. (L2; V, iii)

The intrusive reality of a competitor who claims that he has sole right to Bianca is more than even the Duke can rationalize into a favorable picture. His reply to Fernando is significant. He does not question Fernando's claim to Bianca but only deplores the loss of his own honorable name because Fernando's presence destroys the fiction of Bianca's chastity:

> *Fernando,* man of darknesse,
> Never till now (before these dreadfull sights)
> Did I abhorre thy friendship; thou hast rob'd
> My resolution of a glorious name. (L2; V, iii)

The greatest curse that the Duke can think of is that Fernando "hast rob'd / My resolution of a glorious name." The Duke had succeeded in assuming the role of the duped and mistaken murderer of an innocent wife, but the appearance of Fernando with his claims upon Bianca's love restores the sordid quality of illicit love.

Fernando's speech warning the Duke to stay away from the tomb is the final irrationality of a heroical lover. The overstatement, the possessive attitude toward Bianca's body, the insulting attacks upon Caraffa, and the perverted insistence upon staying with the corpse are all proof of Fernando's inability to face his problems in a reasonable way. We should perhaps feel pity for a man who has lost control of his reason, but there can be no admiration for either his words or his actions. Before the Duke can seize him, Fernando drinks poison and delivers a death speech which is a final assertion of the grandeur of heroic love:

> O royall poyson? trusty friend? split, split
> Both heart and gall asunder; excellent bane!
> *Roseilli* love my memory; well search'd out
> Swift nimble venome, torture every veyne.
> I, come *Biancha,*—cruell torment feast,
> Feast on, doe; Duke farewell. Thus I—hot flames
> Conclude my Love—and seale it in my bosome, oh—*dies*.
>
> (L2ᵛ; V, iii)

At this point the Abbot exclaims: "Most desperate end!" (L2ᵛ). When spoken in reference to suicide the word "desperate" has a theological denotation of ultimate sinfulness and perhaps should be taken as an indication of Fernando's sin in choosing suicide as a way out of trouble.[8] But Ford does not emphasize a religious context, and the Abbot's role is much too small to justify viewing him as the moral norm of the play. What is significant is that the evaluation of the Abbot is the same as the evaluation of the play itself. Fernando is at once a passionate sinner, a rationalizing fool, and a disturbed melancholic. Ford does not find it necessary to limit the portrait by concentrating on a single element to the exclusion of the others.

This evaluation of Fernando's final speeches and death receives support from *The Golden Mean,* which stresses the need for repentance and a moderate conception of individual honor. Speaking of men who are excessively proud, Ford says: "but when a very little alteration of their pomp waineth their pompe to a decay, then like Bladders, they burst with venting their owne breath; chiefely for that they were alway cursed with that mischievous flatteries of themselves that they were too great to fall. *Securitie* in the possession of Honor and prosperitie is a head-long running to ruine; he who hath in himself worth and worthinesse will so moderate the course of his resolutions and actions as that his resolutions shall be directed to doe well, as his actions may prove that he meant well; and then whatsoever the end fall out to be, repentance cannot buy afterwit too deare, nor after-wit have cause to repent too late" (*GM*, C3–C3ᵛ). This description of the foolishly proud man is an accurate description of Fernando just before his death.

With Fernando dead, the Duke immediately reverts to his earlier sentimentalizing: "And art thou gone? *Fernando*, art thou gone?/ Thou wert a friend unmatch'd, rest in thy fame" (L2ᵛ; V, iii). This stand is a complete reversal of the Duke's anger a few lines earlier. Apparently he senses that with Fernando dead, the "glorious name" that he covets is again a possibility. The Duke continues:

> Sister, when I have finisht my last dayes,
> Lodge me, my wife, and this unequall'd friend,
> All in one monument. (L2ᵛ; V, iii)

The Duke's request is in direct conflict with his friend's earlier insistence that the Duke not invade the privacy of Bianca's tomb. The Duke stabs himself and after a final sentimental speech dies. Significantly there is no statement of praise but only shocked disapproval from the Abbot.

The play closes with an image of the need for the repentance of lust and the reassertion of reason. Roseilli, dominated by love at the beginning of the play, has now seen his error and asserts the natural superiority of the man over the woman in marriage and of reason over passion. Fiormonda, now somewhat implausibly repentant, accepts Roseilli's rule and laments her own earlier lust. Reason is restored to control of the state, the corrupt D'Avolos is condemned to death, and the future is one of hope. The Abbot's advice to Fiormonda is to "Purge frailty with repentance" (L3ᵛ; V, iii); this would have been the proper course of action for all of the lovers in the play. Instead of facing the irrationality at the core of their lives, Bianca, Fernando, and the Duke all try to glorify their actions so that their grandeur in adversity rather than their folly will be remembered by posterity. The Abbot concludes the play: "No age hath heard, nor Chronicle can say, / That ever here befell a sadder day" (L3ᵛ; V, iii). The day was sad because passion overcame reason. The tomb that Roseilli will build for the lovers will honor their memory but should also serve as a warning to future men. To suppose that Ford and his audience were taken in by the sentimental excesses of the speeches in the final act is to underestimate Ford's craftsmanship and his audience's sophistication. While I have here indicated a fairly serious tone in the last act, I must admit the possibility that it might have been played as at least closer to farce by emphasizing the wild irrationality in speeches like Fernando's at the tomb. We must, I think, recognize that the ending of *Love's Sacrifice* is open to more diverse interpretations than any other ending in Ford. I would even grant that a serious glorification of the lovers is not so inconsistent with the written text as we have it that it would be unplayable. By very carefully cutting out the more glaring revelations of confused weakness in the characters and by playing down the symbolic significance of the ending, you might make such a reading stand. But it would be completely inconsistent with what had preceded and would destroy the carefully developed structure of the play. Such a sudden switch from treating Bianca, Fernando, and the Duke as combinations of passionate sinners and rationalizing fools to treating them as noble victims would be surprising in a playwright of Ford's competence. Even though we cannot be sure of the blend of tragedy and satire in the final act, I suspect that a Caroline production would have followed the general pattern that I have suggested. That makes the play coherent as well as more consistent with Ford's other plays and his thought as a whole.

VII

The Broken Heart

The satiric element that plays such an important part in *'Tis Pity She's a Whore* and *Love's Sacrifice* is almost entirely absent from *The Broken Heart*. Ford here is concerned less with how irrational behavior leads to tragedy than with how people react to a tragedy that has already occurred. In concentrating less on the exposure of weakness and more on the understanding of suffering, Ford produces a tragedy that is at once his most ambitious and his most complex. Despite its occasional sensationalism, the tone of the play is remarkably subdued. In trying to account for the play's "coldness and restraint," its "grave and chill dignity," and its emphasis on "continence, courage and chivalry," scholars have called attention to Ford's use of spectacle, music, dance, and ritual.[1] But no one has sufficiently stressed that these devices are like the symbolic techniques of the masques and the emblem books. When we remember that Ford had collaborated with Dekker on *The Sun's Darling,* the fact of the influence becomes more plausible. When we recall that emblem books and masques made use of an iconographical tradition that invariably linked the visual and the moral, the significance of Ford's debt becomes apparent. Ford, in *The Broken Heart,* seems to have been consciously trying to make fuller use of what we can call emblematic methods as a

means of defining the nature and significance of the suffering
that is the play's main theme. Although Ford treats all of his plays as symbolic struc-
tures, he is in *The Broken Heart* moving away from the
more realistic presentation of the professional dramatists
toward the more symbolic techniques of the masque. He
always uses type characterization; in *The Broken Heart* it is
important enough as a controlling factor in the play's form
so that in the list of characters the names are even translated to make their qualities clearer. Perhaps more than in
any other play by Ford, the characters represent abstractions which they embody throughout the action. If we are to
understand the play's form, we must recognize the importance of the descriptions of Orgilus as *"Angry,"* Penthea as
"Complaint," Bassanes as *"Vexation,"* Ithocles as *"Honour
of lovelinesse,"* Calantha as *"Flower of beauty,"* Crotolon
as *"Noyse"* (A4), etc. In addition the speech of most of the
characters is more elevated and formal in *The Broken
Heart* than in any other Ford play. This serves in part to
reinforce the stylized tone of the play; it also allows Ford to
examine the differences between outward appearance and
inner reality. In many of the scenes there is very little action
in the sense of advancing the plot; but there is always an
enriching of our understanding of the quality and significance of the emotions being depicted. To achieve this depth,
Ford uses music to help set the mood; in one famous in-
stance he uses a formal dance to help express Calantha's
reaction to tragedy; in the final scene he uses a masque-like
formal ritual complete with music and an elaborate setting.
In this movement toward the masque we can perhaps recognize the influence of Beaumont and Fletcher, the most emblematic of the major dramatists, and of the Cavalier play,
but Ford still manages to retain his own characteristic handling of themes. Despite the changes in technique, the play is
more similar to Ford's other tragedies than it is to any other
play of the period.

The tragic fact that lies behind all the suffering in the
play is that Ithocles has forced the marriage of his sister
Penthea to Bassanes even though she was already betrothed
to Orgilus.[2] As a result of this misalliance several lives are

in danger of being ruined. Penthea cannot love Bassanes because she still loves Orgilus and regards him as her real husband; Bassanes is jealous because he knows Penthea does not love him; Orgilus is melancholic because his happiness has been destroyed; Ithocles is troubled by the results of his villainy. Later in the play the princess Calantha too must cope with tragedy, in her case with the deaths of three people who are close to her. The play is in large part a study of the characters' struggles to maintain honor under these conditions that make rational and moral behavior difficult.

If we are to avoid oversimplification, we must see that Ford stresses both the near impossibility of starting a new life after such a crushing experience and the absolute necessity for making the effort. To emphasize the characters' weakness in being unable to solve their problems rationally is to underestimate the extent of the original tragedy. Orgilus, Penthea, and Calantha cannot be expected to forget relationships that have given their lives their deepest meaning; Ithocles and Bassanes cannot win acceptance simply by apologizing and reforming. But to regard the characters as helplessly and heroically struggling against fates that are largely beyond their control is to accept their own descriptions of their motivations instead of listening to more objective voices. Judged by the standards of Tecnicus and Armostes, Orgilus and Ithocles are too preoccupied with individual glory and honor: Orgilus hears what Tecnicus tells him about true honor but still acts dishonorably; Ithocles, despite warnings from Armostes, is more concerned with personal power, wealth, and pleasure than with reconciliation, love, and friendship. Bassanes swings from absurd jealousy to a posturing, sentimental stoicism. Calantha and Penthea are more fully sympathetic since they remain devoted to Spartan principles of virtue and honor and carry out no active evil; but even if we see their tragedies as too profound to be met rationally and approve their courage in accepting their fate, we must grant that their tragedies occur in part at least because the Spartan ideals encourage an unyielding acceptance of one's fate. From one point of view they help bring on their own final tragedies by the very rigidity of their insistence on dying as tragic victims rather than trying to begin new lives. That view gets support from Tecnicus' demand for a rational approach to tragedy and would seem to coincide with Ford's own attitude on how to overcome misery expressed in *The Golden Mean*. To insist on this view, however, is to moralize the play in a way that oversimplifies its meaning. In his presentation of the heroic endurance of Calantha and Penthea as well as in his study of the courage of Ithocles and Orgilus in the final act, Ford reveals both achievement and limitations and thereby demands a complexity of response from his audience. In the last analysis there can be no evaluation that fits the four leading characters into tidy moral compartments but only understanding of their human struggles with misery. Nevertheless we must beware of reading the play like a modern novel. Ford's characterization may seem more modern in *The Broken Heart,* but he has not tried for three-dimensional psychological realism: each character is still an amalgam of representative qualities and must be analyzed in terms of seventeenth-century rather than modern psychology. Ford has placed them in such complex situations that inevitably they seem to be more fully rounded portraits than are present in other Ford plays, but the complexity is ultimately more thematic than psychological.

In the first scene of the play Orgilus behaves as a reasonable man should. He and Penthea have been badly treated by Ithocles, but he tells his father that he will leave Sparta to go to Athens rather than endanger Penthea, Bassanes, and himself by staying. Since travel was thought to be a good cure for love-melancholy and since Athens was associated with wisdom,[3] his apparent decision to go must be seen as a wise way to begin rebuilding his life. Conversely his actual decision to remain in Sparta can only lead to more trouble, particularly since he himself seems to realize that he should go.[4] The one remaining hope for Orgilus is his friendship with the philosopher Tecnicus, but Orgilus deceives him as well when he tells him that his motives for staying in Sparta in disguise are virtuous. Tecnicus sees signs of danger and warns Orgilus that man cannot hide from the gods' "quicke-piercing eyes, which dive at all times / Downe to thy thoughts "(C1; I, iii),[5] but Orgilus proclaims his good intentions. Not until he is alone for the first time does Orgilus reveal his true motivations. Then we see the extent of his preoccupation with his now impossible love for Penthea:

> Love! thou art full of mystery: the Deities
> Themselves are not secure, in searching out
> The secrets of those flames, which hidden wast
> A breast, made tributary to the Lawes
> Of beauty; Physicke yet hath never found
> A remedy, to cure a Lovers wound. (Cᴵᵛ; I, iii)

The claims that love is a mystery that even the gods cannot understand and that a person in its grasp has no chance of finding a remedy for his plight indicate that Orgilus is developing the symptoms of heroical love. Significantly he talks of love in terms of disease and cure even when he is glorifying it. Since Orgilus is the victim of a tragic situation there must be sympathy for him as a person who under great stress is unable to maintain his rationality, but there can be little respect for the passionate arguments that he uses. What formerly was a chaste and virtuous love is being twisted into a destructive passion.

His attitude toward the love of his sister Euphranea for Ithocles' friend, Prophilus, must be regarded as a further indication of his passion. His insistence that he has the right to decide whom Euphranea is to marry is a repetition of Ithocles' fault in determining Penthea's marriage partner for her. Orgilus' motivation is also the same: Ithocles wanted revenge on Orgilus' family for wrongs done him during their feud, and Orgilus opposes Euphranea's marriage because Prophilus is a friend of Ithocles. Glenn Blayney has shown that the position of both Ithocles and Orgilus is wrong when measured against Nearchus and Amyclas' view that free choice is essential.[6] Since Orgilus has seen the tragic results of Ithocles' interference, his attitude is even less defensible. His violent soliloquy at the end of the scene insisting on his right to stop the marriage and rejoicing in the chance fate has given him in his role as messenger between the two lovers leaves no doubt as to the passion which impels him.[7]

In his pathetic appearance to Penthea in Act II, Orgilus, while in disguise as a scholar, praises her in long and heavily Platonized speeches that are so exaggerated that she suspects the speaker of madness. When he reveals himself to her and claims his right to her affections because of their betrothal, her response is a mixture of anger that he would presume to approach her and pity because she loves him and understands what he has gone through. But even though she had been legally betrothed to Orgilus and cannot regard Bassanes as her husband, she sees that she must forget Orgilus and try to make a success of her marriage. From her point of view Orgilus' love for her has degenerated into a passion that is both unhealthy and immoral. She regards his elevated rhetoric as a symptom of his irrationality rather than as proof of the nobility of his love:

> Unworthy man,
> If ever henceforth thou appeare in language,
> Message, or letter to betray my frailty,
> I'le call thy former protestations lust,
> And curse my Starres for forfeit of my judgement. (EIᵛ; II, iii)

And she insists on the need to subdue weakness that threatens to overthrow higher duties: "Honour, / How much we fight with weaknesse to preserve thee" (EIᵛ; II, iii). Despite these evidences of strict principles, she still loves Orgilus, however, and the extent of her pity for him makes their situation seem even more tragic:

> 'A sigh'd my name sure as he parted from me,
> I feare I was too rough: Alas poore Gentleman,
> 'A look'd not like the ruines of his youth,
> But like the ruines of those ruines. (EIᵛ; II, iii)

Orgilus, by forcing his attentions upon her, is partly responsible for driving her into the morbidity that eventually leads to her death; but their love remains tragic even if its manifestations in Orgilus are anything but noble. If their mutual vows had been allowed to proceed to marriage, they probably would have been as happy as Prophilus and Euphranea.

The powerful image of the tragedy of their love forces us to remember the injustice that Ithocles perpetrated. Orgilus' bitter denunciation of Ithocles in the first scene is apparently justified:

> For *Ithocles* her brother, proud of youth,
> And prouder in his power, nurisht closely
> The memory of former discontents.
> To glory in revenge, by cunning partly,
> Partly by threats, 'a wooes at once, and forces
> His virtuous sister to admit a marriage
> With *Bas[s]anes,* a Noble-man, in honour
> And riches, I confesse beyond my fortunes. (B1ᵛ; I, i)

This sweeping condemnation of Ithocles as proud, tyrannical, revengeful, cunning, avaricious, and ambitious is our introduction to him. Although Ithocles does become more concerned about others as the play develops, viewing him as a reformed and noble hero oversimplifies the complexity of his character. He is no doubt sincerely sorry that he has mistreated Penthea, but he is never able to overcome his ambition for power and material pleasures. His selfishness prevents him from ever becoming genuinely interested in anyone except as a means of furthering his own advancement.

The public image of Ithocles is quite different. When we first see him, he is the conquering general returning from glorious victories that have won him the admiration of the beautiful princess Calantha and the entire court. Not only is he a great soldier, but he is also an eloquent speaker who modestly minimizes his own part as only his patriotic duty while praising his soldiers as being primarily responsible. After hearing Orgilus' outspoken attack in the first scene and then the eulogistic praise of the court, we naturally wonder which account of Ithocles is correct. Somewhat paradoxically, both are. As Ford presents him, there is no question that Ithocles is a great leader who is entitled to the respect he has won. Ford never undercuts this scene's conventional image of Calantha's love for him as that of the fair princess for the noble hero. Nor does he question the quality of the again conventional image of the friendship of the worthy Prophilus. Both admire Ithocles for his greatness of soul and his virtuous accomplishments, and there is no reason to doubt that he possesses both. As a result of this approval of undeniably virtuous characters as well as by the court as a whole, Ithocles is usually interpreted as a heroic figure who can justifiably claim our full support. That view is an oversimplification. In his early prose and poetry, Ford returned again and again to the theme of the great man who under the pressure of flattery, pride, and ambition is unable to retain his sense of moral values. Ithocles is no small-minded Machiavellian; rather he seems to be Ford's dramatic version of his earlier account of greatness with insufficient goodness. Ithocles is conceived in the mold of Essex, Byron, and Barnevelt—great men with heroic ideals that we can admire but with personal weaknesses that we must lament. If we are to understand Ithocles, we must give full weight to both elements in his nature and avoid making him either a study in villainous ambition or a portrait of a valiant hero ruined by a mistake he cannot rectify.

The difference between public virtues and private vices is perhaps hinted at in the scene in which the public Ithocles is praised so extensively. Two of the soldiers that Ithocles praises for their virtue and sincere regard for honor detain two of Calantha's women, brag of their military exploits, and make crude propositions of love. The scene serves as an ironic comment on the Spartan martial honor that all have praised. Greatness like that of Ithocles is to be admired, but there is no necessary connection between public and private virtues or between the full-blown rhetoric of noble appearances and the underlying reality of true motivations.

We get a better look at Ithocles' motivations when in his next appearance on the stage he reveals in soliloquy that he is "Broken with griefes" (D2; II, ii). First in a series of emblem-like images, Ithocles presents an accurate analysis of the ambition that is perhaps the central facet of his character:

> Ambition? 'tis of vipers breed, it knawes
> A passage through the wombe that gave it motion.
> Ambition? like a seeled Dove, mounts upward,
> Higher and higher still to pearch on clouds,
> But tumbles headlong downe with heavier ruine.
> So squibs and crackers flye into the ayre,
> Then onely breaking with a noyse, they vanish

In stench and smoke: Morality appli'd
To timely practice, keeps the soule in tune,
At whose sweet musicke all our actions dance;

then he comments on the inadequacy of traditional morality
in dealing with a sickness that is as extreme as his own:

But this is forme of books, and schoole-tradition,
It physicks not the sicknesse of a minde
Broken with griefes: strong Feavers are not eas'd
With counsell, but with best receipts, and meanes:
Meanes, speedy meanes, and certaine; that's the cure. (D2; II, ii)

The statement about the evils of ambition and the necessity
of morality expresses the dominant moral position of Ford's
time, and Ithocles' dismissal of "books, and schoole-
tradition" is tantamount to a dismissal of reason and wisdom. The obvious question is what is wrong with Ithocles;
the answer is complex. Later he attributes his illness to his
grief for the wrong to Penthea and to his love for Calantha,
and they undoubtedly are factors; but since Ithocles has just
been discussing his ambition, it seems likely that he refers to
his ambitious fever as well.[8] It would be wrong to attribute
his malaise to one or the other. When he returns from the
wars he finds that Penthea's situation has become intolerable (as the audience has seen in the scene immediately
preceding this soliloquy), and that he is strongly attracted
to the king's daughter and perhaps even more to the life
that marriage to her would bring for him. Consequently he
decides that traditional moral solutions are inadequate in
dealing with his ambition and that he will achieve his objects
through "Meanes, speedy meanes, and certaine."
      There is no reason to believe that Ithocles' later pleas to
Penthea for forgiveness are insincere, but it would be naive
to think that that is all he wants. Her forgiveness will not
only mollify the guilt that he feels for marrying her to
Bassanes but will also give him an ally for his courtship of
Calantha; and we should note that Ithocles manages to
direct the development of their conversation so that at the
end Penthea promises to help him as much as she can. Later
it becomes clear that Ithocles is worried about Orgilus too,

and it may be that he hopes that peace with Penthea will lead to better relations with the dangerous Orgilus as well. Ithocles is full of plans for his own advancement and seems to be interested in the people around him primarily as means to his own largely selfish ends.

Further proof of Ithocles' questionable motives in his dealings with Penthea and Calantha is the suspicion of both Armostes and Orgilus about Ithocles' intentions. Armostes stands in relation to Ithocles as Tecnicus does to Orgilus: both are unheeded moral counselors. In the first scene of Act IV, Armostes apparently has been accusing Ithocles of insincerity in his love for Calantha, for Ithocles replies:

> Forebeare your Inquisition; curiosity
> Is of too subtill, and too searching nature:
> In feares of love too quicke; too slow of credit:
> I am not what you doubt me. (G2ᵛ; IV, i)

Armostes again questions his sincerity but expresses the hope that Ithocles' intentions are now worthy. Ithocles continues his defense: "I did the Noble *Orgilus* much injury, / But griev'd *Penthea* more: I now repent it" (G2ᵛ; IV, i). He goes on to regret that his repentance may be too late and to hope that Orgilus' friendship is sincere. Armostes replies in a speech which stresses the difference between appearance and reality:

> Yet Nephew, 'tis the tongue informes our eares;
> Our eyes can never pierce into the thoughts,
> For they are lodg'd too inward. (G2ᵛ; IV, i)

Armostes is referring to the question of whether Orgilus is sincere in his newly stated loyalty to Ithocles, but his statement is a general one that applies to his doubts about Ithocles' motivations as well.

Ithocles in a long speech in the same scene reveals more about what these motivations are; Calantha, by throwing her ring to him and favoring him over Nearchus, has just given him clear evidence that she loves him, but Ithocles reacts, not as a virtuous lover overcome by this sign of favor, but as an ambitious man who now sees some hope of getting what he wants:

> Looke 'ee Uncle:
> Some such there are whose liberall contents
> Swarme without care in every sort of plenty;
> Who, after full repasts, can lay them downe
> To s[l]eepe; and they sleepe, Uncle: in which silence
> Their very dreames present 'em choyce of pleasures:
> Pleasures (observe me Uncle) of rare object:
> Here heaps of gold, there Increments of honors;
> Now change of garments, then the votes of people;
> Anon varieties of beauties, courting
> In flatteries of the night, exchange of dalliance,
> Yet these are still but dreames: give me felicity
> Of which my senses waking are partakers;
> A reall, visible, materiall happinesse. (G3; IV, i)

This candid revelation should be sufficient proof that Armostes' fears are justified and that Ithocles is primarily interested in getting the material possessions and pleasures that he now lacks. In interpreting this speech we should remember that Ford in *The Golden Mean* says that "the desire of money or large Lordships, argues but the filthinesse of an unsatisfied covetousnesse" (*GM*, F1ᵛ–F2). Ambition was not thought to be wrong if motivated by proper ends, but no one could miss the improper motivation in Ithocles' blatantly materialistic philosophy of life.

Later Ithocles says that

> To be any thing
> *Calantha* smiles on, is to be a blessing
> More sacred than a petty-Prince of *Argos*
> Can wish to equall, or in worth or Title. (G3ᵛ; IV, i)

But the advantage of Calantha's favor is that it brings the material prosperity that Ithocles describes so graphically. Significantly Armostes' strongest warning against ambition follows directly after this speech:

> Containe your selfe, my Lord, *Ixion* ayming
> To embrace *Juno,* bosom'd but a cloud,
> And begat *Centaures:* 'tis an usefull morall,
> Ambition hatch'd in clouds of meere opinion,
> Proves but in birth a prodigie.[9] (G3ᵛ; IV, i)

His final words to Ithocles are in the same vein: "Hee deserves small trust / Who is not to privy Counsellor to himselfe" (G3; IV, i). Armostes is portrayed as a shrewd and accurate observer, and his doubts should not be taken lightly.

Even stronger accusations are made by Orgilus before he kills Ithocles. To Orgilus the *"Engine"* (Ia; IV, iv) that he uses to entrap him is a "throne of Coronation" (I2ᵛ; IV, iv) that provides an ironically appropriate setting for the fall of an ambitious man. Ithocles is described by Orgilus as a "foole of greatnesse" and Penthea as "a beauty wither'd by the flames / Of an insulting *Phaeton* her brother" (I2ᵛ; IV, iv). When we remember that Phaeton in his ambition had foolishly tried to drive the chariot of the sun but had succeeded only in scorching the earth and endangering the sisters who were riding with him, the significance of his identification with Ithocles becomes apparent. Orgilus goes on to accuse Ithocles of ambition for the throne and power, of a primarily physical interest in Calantha, and of no concern at all for Penthea or Orgilus himself:

> You dream't of kingdomes, did 'ee? how to bosome
> The delicacies of a youngling Princesse,
> How with this nod to grace that subtill Courtier,
> How with that frowne to make this Noble tremble,
> And so forth; whiles *Penthea's* grones, and tortures,
> Her agonies, her miseries, afflictions,
> Ne're toucht upon your thought; as for my injuries,
> Alas they were beneath your royall pitty,
> But yet they liv'd, thou proud man, to confound thee. (I2ᵛ; IV, iv)

One might argue that Orgilus in his passion is unjust except that Ithocles' final speech is a tacit admission that the charges are true:

> *Penthea,* by thy side thy brother bleeds:
> The earnest of his wrongs to thy forc'd faith,
> Thoughts of ambition, or delitious banquet,
> With beauty, youth, and love, together perish
> In my last breath. (I3; IV, iv)

When he thinks of Penthea he thinks of his guilt, not of their reconciliation. When he thinks of becoming king, the attitude is the same as in the speech to Armostes in Act IV;

ambition and sensual and material pleasures are mentioned, but Calantha is not. The tone is the same as in Orgilus' charge that Ithocles has studied "how to bosome / The delicacies of a youngling Princesse." Calantha seems to be an object of desire in so far as she is anything more than a means of becoming king. Orgilus is right in his cynical analysis of Ithocles even though he is wrong to seek his death.

Earlier we had another glimpse of Ithocles' methods in the scene in which Calantha receives the king's permission to marry Ithocles. After she has won approval, she says to Ithocles in an aside: "Th'art mine,—Have [I] now kept my word" (I1; IV, iii). The inference that Ithocles has obtained Calantha's promise to approach the king about their marriage is not to Ithocles' credit and suggests once more that he is using Calantha as a means of becoming king. All of this evidence—Calantha's compliance with his request to talk to her father, Orgilus' outspoken condemnation, Armostes' continued suspicion, and most important Ithocles' own confession that he is driven by ambition for power and material pleasures—indicates that there is little change in Ithocles' private character in the course of the play. He should not be interpreted as a study of the tragic inefficacy of repentance. But we must also remember the qualities that make it impossible to regard him as an all-black villain. He has served the state well; he has won the friendship of Prophilus and the love of Calantha; and he wins Orgilus' respect for his courage in facing death. In Orgilus' explanation to the court of his reasons for revenge, there is recognition of both the personal faults and the heroic greatness of Ithocles:

> the reasons
> Are just and knowne: quit him of these, and then
> Never liv'd Gentleman of greater merit,..
> Hope, or abiliment to steere a kingdome. (K1; V, ii)

We cannot and should not forget the private faults that Orgilus himself had catalogued earlier, but we must try to understand his virtues as well. Perhaps Ithocles is incapable of disinterested patriotism or friendship or love, and perhaps the Spartans' admiration of him reflects in part their own preoccupation with greatness; but his heroic accomplishments are not hollow, and his outstanding personal qualities are worthy of admiration.

Bassanes, the third person who helps drive Penthea to madness, is easily understood as the conventional stage old man, incapable of winning his wife's love and jealously hiding her from all potential lovers, but he should also be seen as an almost clinical analysis of the heroical lover who falls victim to jealousy.[10] When Penthea appears immediately after his long tirade on the faithlessness of woman, Bassanes breaks into hyperbolic praise: "Shee comes, she comes, so shoots the morning forth, / Spangled with pearles of transparent dew" (C4ᵛ; II, i). The scene is comic, and one of the comic elements is the juxtaposition of Platonic lyricism with worried concern about Penthea's fidelity. Bassanes' jealousy reaches such an extreme when he suspects Penthea of incest with Ithocles that he himself finally realizes his absurdity and determines to change.

The madness and subsequent death of Penthea is the focal point of the tragedy, for it is Penthea who has best embodied the rational approach needed for overcoming misery. In her reaction to the problems caused by earlier tragedy she has been easily the most mature in trying to find constructive solutions. She urges Orgilus to forget her and try to reconstruct his life with another woman; she remains scrupulously loyal to Bassanes and does all she can to make the marriage work; and she forgives Ithocles and even becomes his advocate with Calantha. But Orgilus' continued pressure, Bassanes' wild jealousy, and her own suffering from Ithocles' earlier villainy finally force her collapse. Her mad scene serves to develop Penthea as a powerful symbol of the evil that all three—her brother, her husband, and her former lover—have done. In her madness she reverts to her elemental distaste for both Ithocles and Bassanes: "Oh my wrack'd honour ruin'd by those Tyrants, / A cruell brother, and a desperate dotage!" (H2ᵛ; IV, ii). She refers to the marriage that might have been, the children that were never born, and the happiness that her forced marriage prevented; and she blames Ithocles and Bassanes for what has happened. Bassanes admits everything and tries to appear as the repentant husband who becomes a tragic figure himself when he realizes his fault. But he remains such a posturing sentimentalist that his change is more ludicrous than affecting. Ithocles at first tries to minimize the seriousness of Penthea's condition but later finds it necessary to emphasize her madness. Penthea's sisterly sympathy for Ithocles breaks through on occasion, but the directness of her charge, "That's He, and still 'tis He" (H2ʳ; IV, ii), forces Ithocles to call attention to her irrationality: "Poore soule, how idely / Her fancies guide her tongue" (H2ʳ; IV, ii). Even Orgilus, who tries to avoid recognizing his own responsibility for Penthea's madness, is criticized by Penthea:

> Remember
> When we last gather'd Roses in the garden
> I found my wits, but truly you lost yours. (H2ʳ; IV, ii)

Unfortunately instead of taking her present condition as a warning of the results of following passion, Orgilus decides that it is a just reason for seeking revenge:

> She has tutor'd me:
> Some powerfull inspiration checks my lazinesse. (H2ʳ; IV, ii)

Penthea has struggled as valiantly as possible to remain rational in the face of her problems, but the combination of a tyrannous brother, a jealous husband, and a doting former lover is too much for her to bear, and her reason is destroyed. Her death is pathetic rather than noble, but Ford makes clear that the responsibility for her breakdown is not hers. Burton follows what was probably a widely accepted view when he states that a person who commits suicide while mad or melancholy will be saved if he was a good Christian before going mad.[11] Although the Christian context of course is absent, this description would seem to fit Penthea exactly. We should admire Penthea's courage, pity her tragic plight, and excuse her irrationality.

Before discussing the final act, the importance of Tecnicus' role as a moral commentator should be stressed. His speech to Orgilus on the true conception of honor establishes the attitude by which we should judge not only Orgilus but also Ithocles:

> But know then *Orgilus* what honour is:
> Honour consists not in a bare opinion
> By doing any act that feeds content;

Brave in appearance, 'cause we thinke it brave:
Such honour comes by accident, not nature
Proceeding from the vices of our passion
Which makes our reason drunke. But reall Honour
Is the reward of vertue, and acquir'd
By Justice or by valour, which for Bases
Hath Justice to uphold it. He then failes
In honour, who for lucre o[r] Revenge
Commits thefts, murthers, Treasons and Adulteries,
With such like, by intrenching on just Lawes,
Whose sov'raignty is best preserv'd by Justice.
Thus as you see how honour must be grounded
On knowledge, not opinion: For opinion
Relyes on probability and Accident,
But knowledge on Necessity and Truth:
I leave thee to the fit consideration
Of what becomes the grace of reall Honour,
Wishing successe to all thy vertuous meanings. (E2ʳ-E3; III, i)

If any speech in Ford's plays could be said to represent the core of his ethical views, this is that speech. Here we find explicitly stated his insistence on distinguishing between the code of honor based on grand but hollow assertions of individual nobility and the true honor that is based on virtue.[12] When measured against this norm, the attitudes of too many of the Spartans are inadequate. Orgilus tries to defend a rash revenge and desperate suicide; Ithocles pursues an honor based on riches and fine appearances; the Spartans as a group are perhaps too easily impressed by the appearance of nobility and too little concerned about virtue and truth.

The theme of the play receives emphatic statement in the scene in which Tecnicus warns both Ithocles and Orgilus of impending doom. The situation is closely parallel to the scene in *'Tis Pity* in which the friar's departure after a final warning to Giovanni was a symbol of the impossibility of averting the final catastrophe. The same symbolism of departure is utilized in this scene when Tecnicus, after explaining the moral chaos which exists in Sparta, speaks of his journey to Delphos, an obvious symbol of wisdom:

The hurts are yet but mortall,
Which shortly will prove deadly: To the King,

Armostes, see in safety thou deliver
This seal'd up counsaile; bid him with a constancy
Peruse the secrets of the gods:—ô *Sparta,*
O *Lacedemon!* double nam'd, but one
In fate; when Kingdomes reele (marke well my Saw)
Their heads must needs be giddy: tell the King
That henceforth he no more must enquire after
My aged head: *Apollo* wils it so;
I am for *Delphos.* (G4–G4ᵛ; IV, i)

Tecnicus, having heard the voice of the oracle, a transparent symbol for the judgment of God, knows that there is no longer any hope for change. His view is not fatalistic in the sense that man has no chance to determine his own actions. Tecnicus' advice throughout the play has been a rebuke to such a doctrine; rather he suggests that when man gives up trying to control his passions, tragedy is inevitable. Unfortunately Orgilus has become so set in his self-centered concept of honor that change is no longer possible. Orgilus is warned explicitly: "Let craft with curtesie a while conferre, / Revenge proves its owne Executioner" (G4ᵛ; IV, i). He refuses to take the warning seriously: "Darke sentences are for *Apollo's* Priests: / I am not *Oedipus*" (G4ᵛ; IV, i). Later he adds: "It shall not puzzle me; / 'Tis dotage of a withered braine" (G4ᵛ; IV, i). The replies reveal that he is enveloped by an all-consuming passion which makes reasonable thought and action impossible. Instead of listening to this oracle, Orgilus regards the mad Penthea as an oracle: "If this be madnesse, madnesse is an Oracle" (H2ᵛ; IV, ii). With the warning and departure of Tecnicus, we are prepared for a conclusion in which the actions of the characters will reflect the moral chaos that Tecnicus has described.

Since Orgilus is at once a victim of forces beyond his control, an initiator of an unwise course of action, and a believer in a questionable code of honor, it requires some care to sort out the complexities of response to him in the final act. Even if Tecnicus is right about what Orgilus should do, there are various reasons for sympathizing with what he does do. First Orgilus is a figure whose plight is truly tragic. Penthea's death further aggravates his already disturbed state of mind and makes understandable his decision to seek the death of the man who he thinks is primarily responsible. More important to a sympathetic reaction to Orgilus are the inevitably mixed emotions one must have about the revenge code to which he appeals for justification. Since attitudes toward revenge will always be ambivalent in any situation where there is some cause for revenge,[13] we would be unwise to minimize the sympathy and even admiration that would be felt for Orgilus. Morally if not legally a case can be made that his revenge on Ithocles is a noble execution rather than a foul murder. From Orgilus' point of view, Ithocles has caused Penthea's death just as surely as if he had actually killed her, but he will escape punishment unless Orgilus himself takes on the role of both judge and executioner. If Ithocles had sincerely reformed, murdering him would seem less defensible, but his continued pride and ambition make his fall appropriate. When you add Orgilus' belief that his honor has been insulted, it is easy to see how he can convince himself that he is an unimpassioned and honorable seeker of justice. As Orgilus has said earlier: "In point of honour / Discretion knowes no bounds" (G4; IV, i). By viewing himself as morally justified Orgilus can even defend himself against the charge that giving Ithocles no chance to fight back was treacherous. As Orgilus puts it: "I durst not / Ingage the goodnesse of a cause on fortune" (K2; V, ii). In both his actions and his speeches Orgilus is so heroic that we must be impressed. He is charitable to Ithocles, just in accepting his own punishment, and courageous in facing death. These are in Ford's world not inconsiderable virtues. When he executes himself in the presence of the court, he satisfies both the law of the state and the revenge code by which he must die for having killed Ithocles. Thus Orgilus can be seen as effecting a purgation of the evil that has been corrupting the state and as providing the basis for a new and more stable society.

But there are other factors that must be considered. In the murder scene Orgilus is less calm and rational than he later claims to have been; he kills Ithocles as much or more in wrath for ruining his life than because justice requires his death. And the *"Engine"* (I2; IV, iv) that he utilizes does indicate an element of baseness and cowardice, as Ithocles had pointed out. In his high praise of Ithocles in the death scene and later to the Spartan court, Orgilus minimizes the bitterness and anger that led him to the murder. We can only suppose that he is perhaps unconsciously falsifying his motivations so that his actions will seem to be a dignified revenge followed by an honorable suicide. When Orgilus is about to die, he recalls Tecnicus' prophecy:

> Oh *Tecnicus,* inspir'd with *Phoebus* fire,
> I call to mind thy Augury, 'twas perfect;
> Revenge proves its owne Executioner. (K2; V, ii)

Never mind that Orgilus had scornfully dismissed this prophecy when it was given, and never mind that Tecnicus' words were entirely devoid of the noble grandeur that Orgilus gives them: Orgilus is about to die, and Spartan nobility is more important to him than a realistic appraisal of his situation.

An even more important factor is the moral context for revenge that is established through the thematic patterns of the play. From the very start revenge is associated with death and disorder: the feud begun by Crotolon and Thrasus and continued in turn by Ithocles and finally Orgilus has brought tragedy both to the individual and to the state. In contrast marriage is made a symbol of order and peace: a good marriage stabilizes both the warring melancholic impulses within the individual and in this play the warring factions in the country as well. The marriages of Orgilus and Penthea, of Prophilus and Euphranea, and of Ithocles and Calantha would all be hopeful bases for moral and political stability. Ithocles stops the first and substitutes a disastrously disordered marriage; Orgilus attempts to ruin the second (and finally allows it for reasons that are not made clear but may be connected to his desire to keep his opposition secret); Orgilus destroys the third by killing Ithocles and announces his triumph of disorder at Euphranea's wedding feast. Only through the calm, rational actions of the matchmakers is there hope for the individuals involved and for the state. Amyclas supports all three weddings; Penthea and Nearchus both subdue their personal feelings and support Ithocles' marriage to Calantha. In doing so they become images of the new code of forgiveness, peace, and love that must replace the revenge code of hate and chaos. In the scene in which Orgilus executes himself the efficacy of the Spartan legal system is stressed and Orgilus' personal justice is deplored. In contrast to the law, virtue, reason, and knowledge exemplified in this scene, Orgilus' action must be seen as unlawful, vicious, passionate, and unwise. If we pay attention to the thematic patterns of the play, the natural sympathy felt for Orgilus as a wronged revenger will be seen in the wider context of the need for love and justice. Even though there must be sympathy for his plight and admiration for his courage, there can be only regret and pity that such a noble figure would add to the already immense tragic burden.

When we turn to consider Calantha's dignified endurance in the last act, we realize the extent of the tragedy of Ithocles' death. The recognition of a certain appropriateness in his fall should not blind us to the real courage of his final moments and to the horrible meaning of his death both to the state, which has lost a great leader, and to Calantha, who has lost a husband. Like Penthea before her, Calantha becomes a symbol of the useless suffering that results from dependence on a revenge code. Like Penthea she is largely a passive victim of circumstances that are beyond her control. In the final act she bravely but somewhat naively tries to carry out her responsibilities as the Spartan queen. When she is told of the deaths of three of her loved ones, she shows no outward emotion and goes on with the festive wedding dance. Armostes, Bassanes, and Orgilus, the bearers of the tragic news, express amazement at her exemplary Spartan self-control, and all see Calantha as a strong figure who is able to overcome her natural feelings through strength of character. Later Armostes once again expresses surprise: " 'Tis strange, these Tragedies should never touch on / Her female pitty" (K1ᵛ; V, ii). Bassanes refers admiringly to her "masculine spirit" (K1ᵛ; V, ii). But in the final scene Calantha reveals that her strength was a deception:

> ô my Lords,
> I but deceiv'd your eyes with Anticke gesture,
> When one newes straight came hudling on another,

Of death, and death, and death, still I danc'd forward,
But it strooke home, and here, and in an instant,
Be such meere women, who with shreeks and out-cries
Can vow a present end to all their sorrowes,
Yet live to vow new pleasures, and out-live them:
They are the silent griefes which cut the hart-strings;
Let me dye smiling. (K3ᵛ; V, iii)

Calantha swings from one extreme to the other. After first expressing no feeling for the dead she now glorifies profound feeling and even justifies a death out of grief as superior to mourning for a time and then resuming a normal life. In this speech that has been so much admired since it was praised by Charles Lamb,[14] Calantha raises a basic question that suggests again the complexity of Ford's moral vision of the characters in *The Broken Heart*. One instinctive and, I think, proper response is to regard the speech as a poignant expression of the positive side of the Spartan celebration of individual integrity over all other values. If love is a value, it is an absolute value, and to die for it is proof of its depth. There is honor in Calantha's death for love, just as there was honor in Orgilus and Penthea's unwillingness to cheapen their relationship by accepting something less satisfactory. The error is not in seeing this point as basic to the play's meaning; the error comes rather in making it the entire meaning. The last act is too full of moral ironies to permit us to accept any single vision of the play as normative. Perhaps the central irony is the recognition that a selfless and devoted love can become so important to a person that loss of the loved one destroys all reason for living. In theory it is easy to hold the stoic (and Christian) view that man should not become too attached to anything in this world, but in practice it is much more difficult to apportion one's loyalties without falling into either the selfish superficiality of independence from others or the tragedy of dependence on that which is mortal. Viewed from an orthodox moral perspective, Calantha's death is a direct result of her attempt to live according to a rigid Spartan code instead of expressing her natural human reactions. We can assume that the audience would have been aware of the traditional view that the mean should be followed in mourning for loved ones. Burton recalls a long tradition when he cites the authorities for moderation: "'twas *Germanicus's* advice of old, that we should not dwell too long upon our passions, to be desperately sad, immoderate grievers, to let them tyrannize, there's *indolentiae ars,* a *medium* to be kept: we do not (saith *Austin*) forbid men to grieve, but to grieve overmuch" (*AM,* II, 207; 2, 3, 5). Some in the audience might even see a causal connection between her refusal to express sorrow and her death, for a common belief was that the heart had to open a little to let out sorrow or else death might result.[15] But most would probably feel that she is hardly to be blamed for not responding wisely since there are so many mitigating circumstances. One reason she does not express her grief is her sense of responsibility to the state since she is now the Spartan queen. As Calantha herself indicates at the start of the final scene, a woman cannot be expected to rule both herself and her country:

> A woman has enough to governe wisely
> Her owne demeanours, passions, and divisions.
> A Nation warlike and inur'd to practice
> Of policy and labour, cannot brooke
> A feminate authority. (K2^v; V, iii)

Calantha realizes that she has been trying to act a role that is beyond her capabilities. From this point of view her death is in part the tragedy of a person who tries to follow a moral code that makes unnatural demands upon self-control, particularly for a woman.

Nevertheless an audience would admire the courage with which Calantha faces her situation. Despite her fears about her ability to govern she is both fair and wise in her decisions regarding the future of the kingdom. She remains loyal to Ithocles with a love that is both deep and sincere, and her self-evaluation, in contrast to the elaborate rhetoric of Orgilus and Ithocles, is both honest and simple. She recognizes her weakness and the causes of her death and makes no attempt to falsify her nature. The dirge which she has commanded to be sung as she approaches death is a conventional call for recognition that earthly honor and beauty quickly pass away. In the final scene there is a message of hope for the future as well as tragic proof of what submission to passion brings. Calantha is related to both themes—to the tragedy as a pathetic symbol of the suffering caused by passion and to the hope through her wise distribution of power before her death and her recognition of what values are lasting.

If one is inclined to moralize the ending by stressing what the characters should have done, he should pay closer attention to the way Ford handles the moralistic Bassanes. In his determination to seek help from Athens and Delphos, Bassanes sounds very much like Tecnicus earlier, but there is a crucial difference: Tecnicus recognizes a point at which tragedy becomes inevitable. People are capable of sustaining only so much, and there comes a time when there is no hope that the reason can reassert itself. In contrast, Bassanes continues to proclaim the power of reason. When Penthea goes mad, he speaks hopefully, and to a seventeenth-century audience absurdly, of finding a means of keeping her alive without food. In the final act he seems to delight in tribulations that can test his moral virtue. When Orgilus approaches him to tell him of Penthea's death and win his friendship, he shrewdly appeals to Bassanes' heroic conception of himself by referring to the need for patience, endurance, wisdom, judgment, obedience, and courage. But all of these abstractions take on a hollowness in reference to Bassanes that is totally lacking in Tecnicus' similar philosophizing. While Bassanes has learned that he must depend on reason, he is incapable of getting beyond his preoccupation with his own suffering to achieve an understanding of the tragedies of the others. His vision, like that of the Duke in *Love's Sacrifice,* is sentimental, shallow, and immature. When he thinks of his future, he imagines himself luxuriating in grief:

> Give me some corner of the world to weare out
> The remnant of the minutes I must number,
> Where I may heare no sounds, but sad complaints
> Of Virgins who have lost contracted partners;
> Of husbands howling that their wives were ravisht
> By some untimely fate; of friends divided
> By churlish opposition, or of fathers

Weeping upon their childrens slaughtered carcasses;
Or daughters groaning ore their fathers hearses,
And I can dwell there, and with these keepe consort
As musicall as theirs. (K3; V, iii)

Calantha's appointment of Bassanes as *"Sparta's* Marshall" (K3; V, iii) is a recognition of both his new dedication to virtue and his need for the therapy of an active life. The contrast between the posturing emotionalism of Bassanes and the more restrained dignity of Penthea, Orgilus, and Calantha makes their more profound suffering seem even more tragic. They have a greatness of soul lacking in Bassanes that makes us feel that their tragedies are significant.

The hope for Sparta's future lies in finding leadership that can meet the exacting demands of Tecnicus' concept of honor. Fortunately Nearchus, the *"neighboring Elme"* (H4; IV, iii) of Tecnicus' prophecy, gives every indication of being such a leader. As in *Love's Sacrifice* a new order rises after the excesses of the society have been purged. The basis of that new order is the traditional morality that has been given expression through the precepts of Tecnicus and others and through the emblematic illustrations of heroic behavior in Penthea and Calantha. If Ford has succeeded we should remember not only the magnificient rhetoric and courage of all of the Spartans but also Ford's discriminations of self-deceptions and role-playing. Ford does not deny or deplore the heroic postures of his characters, but he does show the reality beneath the posturing. When we perceive that reality we understand more about how people should and do respond to tragedy. Ford's is no facile proposal for moral rearmament; instead there is the recognition both of the causes of tragedy and of the need for sympathy for the victims who are not always able to respond as they should.

VIII

Perkin Warbeck

Dramatizing the story of Perkin Warbeck's claim to the English throne presented new problems for Ford since history plays were expected to follow the rough outline of historical fact.[1] Custom also dictated a patriotic treatment glorifying the English and condemning any threat of war or rebellion against the throne. Since no history play of note had been written for some time Ford probably would not have needed to follow the older conventions; but he apparently was trying to resurrect the old form, for he emphasizes that the virtues of his play are its truthfulness and its political subject:

> on these two, *rest's the Fate*
> *Of worthy expectation; T[R]UTH and STATE.* (A4ᵛ)

Ford and his contemporaries found the story of Perkin in Bacon's *History of the Reign of King Henry the Seventh* (1622) and in Gainsford's *True and Wonderful History of Perkin Warbeck* (1618). Although Ford follows his sources fairly closely,[2] he makes one significant change. In the sources Perkin confesses before his death that he is not the Duke of York, while in Ford's play Perkin has been bewitched or duped into believing that he is actually the Duke. The effect of Ford's change is to make Perkin a victim rather than a villain—a study in delusion rather than ambition. By allowing Perkin to believe in himself Ford succeeds in making a noble and pathetic tale out of material that might seem more suitable for low intrigue. In all of his appearances Perkin achieves a kind of romantic grandeur that is so obviously sincere that it would inevitably win the sympathetic pity of any audience. The former Perkin no longer exists, and through Katherine's loyalty to him and his own courage, Perkin is able to maintain the integrity of his new personality and rise above the taunts of his detractors. We cannot react with a simple condemnation of the rebel; in fact one feels that Ford's major concern was not the political theme but the question of the nature of individual integrity and the study of how that integrity is either maintained or corrupted.

Ford avoids the opposite danger—that the audience will take Perkin's claim seriously—by having respected observers in both Scotland and England treat his claim with scorn until the final act, when the completeness of his delusion becomes clear. Then pity mixed with a kind of bewildered admiration replaces the scorn, but even then no one questions that political realities require Perkin's execution. Sympathy for Perkin as an individual is never allowed to become respect for his cause.[3]

The image of Perkin that the audience receives before his actual appearance on the stage is unfavorable. Throughout the first act Henry VII and his court are associated with God and justice and Perkin and his supporters with the devil and witchcraft. Henry's opening lines establish the tone:

> STill to be haunted; still to be pursued,
> Still to be frighted with false apparitions
> Of pageant Majestie, and new-coynd greatnesse . . . . (B1; I, i)

Through divine aid Henry has restored peace to England after ninety years of war, but now Margaret of Burgundy "from the unbottom'd myne/ Of Devilish policies, doth vent the Ore/ Of troubles and sedition" (B1ʳ–B2; I, i). In her old age she has given unnatural birth to two full-grown usurpers, Lambert Simnel and Perkin Warbeck, "Idolls of

Yorkish malice" (B2; I, i). The quality of Perkin is to be inferred from the description of Lambert's eager acceptance of a minor position at court in return for giving up his claim to be the Earl of Warwick.

King Henry on the other hand has achieved his ordered reign through dependence on God:

> A guard of Angells, and the holy prayers
> Of loyall Subjects are a sure defence
> Against all force and Counsaile of Intrusion. (B2; I, i)

When Dawbeney outspokenly condemns those nobles at home who must be supporting Perkin, Henry's disdain for the potential rebels reflects the calm moderation and security of his rule. Despite the air of duplicity caused by the presence of the rebel Stanley in a position of influence at the court, Henry's assurance and power remain the dominant impression. Stanley is justifiably terrified when Henry announces after reading Urswick's message that they will move to the Tower. In contrast Henry is confident:

> Come my true, best, fast friends, these clouds will vanish,
> The Sunne will shine at full: the Heavens are clearing. (B3; I, i)

Ford shifts the setting in Scene ii to Scotland and presents a picture of an ordered society which corresponds roughly to the glorification of peaceful England contained in the first scene. The rugged honesty of the proud father Huntley, the dutiful loyalty and virtue of his daughter Katherine, and the aspiring nobility of the suitor Dalyell are images of a stable Scotland. At the very end of the scene, the coming of Perkin to Scotland is mentioned, but the audience is made to feel that if these are typical Scotsmen there is no danger of Scotland's falling under Perkin's spell. Respect exists between father and daughter, between father and suitor, and between all three and the ordered society in which they live. In this atmosphere of stability and reason, the question of the selection of marriage partners seems a suitable subject, and the mutual trust among the three instills confidence in the ability of men to come to reasonable solutions. The threat of Perkin is still remote.

Back in the Tower of London Clifford confesses the treasonous plots of the rebels. By having a conspirator confess before a reasonable king instead of showing the plotting of these rebel nobles, Ford maintains the feeling of stability. Imagery of devilish witchcraft is utilized throughout the scene, and the effect of Clifford's presumably objective analysis of the rebels is to confirm the audience's impression that they are "a confused rabble" (C2ᵛ; I, iii) led by "the *Sorceresse*" (C2; I, iii), Margaret, backed by that "subtill villaine" (C2ᵛ; I, iii) and "Pestilent Adder" (C2ᵛ; I, iii), Stephen Frion. Perkin is described as "This ayrie apparition" (C2ᵛ; I, iii) whose spell over the "superstitious *Irish*" (C2ᵛ; I, iii) is possible only through witchcraft and the ignorance of those who follow him. Several nobles and churchmen and finally Stanley himself are implicated and a revolt by the Cornish is reported, but the king manages to maintain the impression that all he does is supported by God and that rebellion against him will inevitably fail since it is rebellion against God Himself. His final words in the scene repeat the faith of the final words in the first scene:

> When Counsailes faile, and theres in *man* no trust,
> Even then, an arme from *heaven,* fights for the just. (C3ᵛ; I, iii)

At the end of Act I we have still not seen Perkin and can have little expectation of a successful rebellion.

In Act II Ford provides an effective contrast of the monarchs, Henry VII and James IV of Scotland, by including Henry's handling of Stanley to parallel James' treatment of Warbeck. Henry, although deeply troubled by the necessity of convicting his friend Stanley, is aware of the difference between appearance and reality: "But I could see no more into his heart,/ Then what his outward actions did present" (D2; II, ii). Through experience Henry has learned that there is no necessary connection between man's actions and his intentions and that order in the state depends upon basing policy on truth. Even Stanley has now realized that excessive ambition leads to tragedy, and his final words just before he is led off to execution are a repudiation of dependence upon the material fortunes of this world instead of upon true virtue. The *de casibus* implication of his words to the other nobles is unmistakable:

> I was as you are once, great, and stood hopefull
> Of many flourishing yeares, but fate, and time
> Have wheeld about, to turne mee into nothing. (D3; II, ii)

His final message to his brother, Derby, is a plea for accepting one's position in life instead of striving futilely for advancement:

> Tell him, hee must not thinke, the stile of *Darby*,
> Nor being husband to King *Henries* Mother,
> The league with Peeres, the smiles of Fortune, can
> Secure his peace, above the state of man:
> I take my leave, to travaile to my dust,
> "Subjects deserve their deaths whose Kings are just. (D3–D3ʳ; II, ii)

The wisdom of Stanley's parting words can be taken as a norm against which to measure the attitudes of the other characters in the play, for he has learned from experience what the effect of ambition is.

James IV, motivated by his ambition instead of by a rational view of what will bring order to Scotland, receives Perkin as a king. The effects are far-reaching: war for two countries and personal tragedy for many. The ladies of the court, encouraged by James' attitude, are instinctively attracted by the fine appearance and the romantic story of the young English prince. The Countess of Crawford says: "Twere pittie now, if a'should prove a *Counterfeit*" (C4; II, i). She is even impressed by the commoners that Perkin brings with him:

> A'brings
> A goodly troope (they say) of gallants with him;
> . . . they are disguised Princes,
> Brought up it seemes to honest trades. (C4; II, i)

These are the men that Clifford has described as a "confused rabble" (C2ʳ; I, iii) and that we later see are as bad as or worse than Clifford's description. But they are able to win the respect of the Scottish ladies since their outward appearance is noble. When they have actually seen and heard Perkin, the women are even more impressed. The Countess of Crawford praises him once more and notes that even Katherine has become "passionate" (D1ʳ; II, i) as a result of Perkin's appearance. Perkin is undeniably attractive, but much of the fault for the trouble that follows must fall on James for his failure to expose Perkin as a noble impostor. The foolish Scottish ladies accept what they see; the unscrupulous James manipulates appearances; only when wisdom and honesty are combined as they are in Henry can there be good government and an ordered society.

The precise nature of Katherine's relationship to Perkin must be studied closely because of its importance to the interpretation of Perkin's character. Before Perkin appears, she seems to share her father's concern that, if Perkin is a counterfeit, Scotland will be laughed at by the world:

> my father
> Hath a weake stomacke to the businesse (Madam)
> But that the King must not be crost. (C4ʳ; II, i)

After Perkin's appearance she has lost some of her objectivity because of her attraction to Perkin and his cause:

> Beshrew mee, but his words have touchd mee home,
> As if his cause concernd mee; I should pittie him
> If a'should prove another then hee seemes. (D1ᵛ; II, i)

Still present is her deep feeling of duty to her country. Her speech about answering the duke's command is more than a conventional reply; it stresses the same loyalty that we saw in the earlier scene with her father and Dalyell:

> *The Duke*
> Must then be entertain'd, the King obayd:
> It is our dutie. (D1ᵛ; II, i)

This stress on her duty is important for understanding her acceptance of the marriage proposal and indeed her actions in the entire play. When the wedding is suggested, Katherine answers: "Where my obedience is (my Lord) a dutie,/ Love owes true service" (E1ᵛ; II, iii). She is deeply concerned about her father's insistent disapproval, but she realizes that loyalty to her king has to take precedence over other loyalties. Since the king has been a suitor to her for Warbeck, she has no choice but to accept. Dalyell himself makes this clear when he tells Huntley not to blame Katherine for the defection since "it is not fault in her" (F1ʳ; III, ii). There is never any suggestion that she might have re-

fused the king because of her father's objections to Warbeck. Apparently such an option did not exist, probably
because it would have been regarded as an open rebellion
against the king by Huntley himself. I do not mean to imply
that Katherine does not love Perkin. We have seen that she
was strongly attracted to him immediately, and we should
probably conclude that she was willing to be forced into the
marriage. Certainly there is no indication that she wanted to
refuse. But it should be noted that Ford makes Katherine a
girl who places loyalty to duty above her own personal
desires. Throughout the play her behavior corresponds exactly to her noble conception of love and duty. When modern readers are tempted to romanticize her love for Perkin
they should remember that Ford makes the respect for
Christian convention the central facet of Katherine's character.

But Katherine's acceptance of the marriage proposal is
no indication that James has been right in furthering the
marriage. On the contrary the treatment of the scene by
Ford is designed to create the opposite effect, for the scene
is viewed from the perspective of the outraged Lords—
Crawford, Huntley, and Dalyell. In the opening lines of the
scene Crawford stresses once more the themes of witchcraft
and of appearance and reality:

> Tis more then strange, my reason cannot answere
> Such argument of fine Imposture, coucht
> In witch-craft of perswasion, that it fashions
> Impossibilities, as if appearance
> Could cozen *truth it selfe;* this Duk-ling Mushrome
> Hath doubtlesse charm'd the King. (D4; II, iii)

Dalyell, obviously thinking of Katherine, replies by deploring the influence that fine language has on the ladies:

> A'courts the Ladies,
> As if his strength of language, chaynd attention
> By power of prerogative. (D4; II, iii)

Huntley is deeply concerned by the imminent loss of his
daughter. All three of them see that Perkin's followers are
no more than a rabble who are ambitiously striving for
positions of power, and all three argue heatedly with the

king about the folly of enforcing marriage. Huntley had properly allowed his daughter to choose her own wedding partner, but James overthrows this method in a hypocritical attempt to flatter Warbeck. Since James has no interest in Warbeck himself, his forcing Katherine to marry Perkin is a particularly objectionable example of the use of people as tools to achieve one's own ends. Huntley stresses that such action will destroy the basis of order in the Scottish state:

> Let any yeoman of our Nation challenge
> An interest in *the girle:* then the King
> May adde a Joynture of ascent in titles,
> Worthy a free consent; now a'pulls downe
> What olde Desert hath builded. (E1; II, iii)

The approaching disorder that James is bringing will have serious results: "Some of thy Subjects hearts/ *King James* will bleede for this!" (E1; II, iii). James' obstinate refusal to listen to honest criticism recalls King Lear's replies to Cordelia and Kent: "hee is not/ Our friend who contradicts us" (E1; II, iii). Ford forcefully illustrates the injustice and disorder that Huntley describes by juxtaposing the proposal scene with a scene in which the pretentious rabble discuss their concept of law.[4] Astley says: "so no right, but may have claime, no claime but may have possession, any act of *Parlament* to the Contrary notwithstanding" (E2; II, iii). James has brought about the intolerable rise of Perkin and his corrupt associates at the cost of threatening the hierarchical order that has been the basis of stability.

The first three scenes of Act III continue the deliberate contrast of the wisdom and order of Henry VII's rule with the disorder caused by James IV's opportunism. When Henry is faced with the rebellion of the Cornish, he reacts with both firmness and pity. He is filled with wrath for their rebellion against God's representative on earth:

> A bloudie houre will it prove to some,
> Whose disobedience, like the sonnes 'oth earth,
> Throw a defiance 'gainst the face of Heaven. (E3; III, i)

But when the rebels are crushed, he punishes only the leaders who have incited the revolt and releases the rest with an expression of his interest in them:

Oh, Lords,
Here is no victorie, nor shall our people
Conceive that wee can triumph in their falles.
Alas, poore soules! Let such as are escapt
Steale to the Countrey backe without pursuite:
There's not a drop of bloud spilt, but hath drawne
As much of mine. (E4; III, i)

His wisdom in handling the people is in direct contrast to
James' folly in the later scene in which he orders the devas-
tation of Northumberland and thus loses any support that
Perkin might have won. Henry is the image of responsible
kinship, strong when strength is required but sympathetic to
the needs of his people. Even his soldiers are not forgotten
in the moment of triumph; when Henry is reminded of their
loyal service against the Scottish he replies generously:

For it, wee will throwe
A Largesse free amongst them, which shall harten
And cheerish up their Loyalties. (E4ᵛ; III, i)

Contrasted with the order produced by Henry's firm but
kind rule is the disorder seen in James' Scotland. Again the
perspective is that of the suffering lords, Huntley and Dalyell; both are bravely trying to overcome their sorrow but
remain scornful of Perkin, deeply distressed by James, and
grieved for Katherine. Unfortunately the marriage has little chance of a normal development since Perkin's reception
means war with the English. As Huntley says: "Fiddles
must turne to swords, unhappie marriage!" (F2; III, ii).
But despite his many grievances, Huntley expresses disdain
for rebellion in a speech which is an ironic comment on the
other rebellions in the play:

But Kings are earthly gods, there is no medling
With their annoynted bodies, for their actions,
They onely are accountable to Heaven. (F1ᵛ; III, ii)

Although his reasons for rebellion are perhaps more valid
than those of Perkin or the Irish or the Cornish against
Henry, Huntley believes that men must accept their destinies and maintain their faith in the ways of God; rebellion
against God's representative, the king, is never justified.
When we see the wedding participants the celebration is

already over and the preparations for war have begun. For the lovers there is time only for a pathetic farewell scene in which Perkin once again stresses the nobility that will govern his actions and Katherine reaffirms her loyalty even while imploring him to forego his ambitious course. Although Katherine's initial attraction to Perkin might be taken as revealing her susceptibility to noble appearances, her loyalty to him once they are married must be viewed as praiseworthy. Whether Perkin is an impostor becomes irrelevant, since Katherine's duty as a wife is to be completely loving and loyal to her husband. Katherine need not and probably should not concern herself with the political realities that the others must judge.

In contrast to the disorder in Scotland the next scene shows Henry striving to achieve peace through the ministrations of the Spaniard, Peter Hialas. A marriage is proposed between Henry's son and Catherine of Aragon, but this is to be a marriage which, unlike Perkin's, will bring peace rather than war. When Hialas explains that the continued life of Warbeck and of the Duke of Clarence's son, the Earl of Warwick, are hindrances to the peace of the reign and hence to the marriage, we see that Henry's concern for the order of his realm must be translated into effective action against these threats. Only with their deaths can peace throughout Europe be assured.

The scenes that follow permit us to see the reality behind the fine rhetoric and noble intentions expressed by James and Perkin. When James sees the strength of the English opposition, he immediately begins to consider how he can escape without loss of prestige or power. The Bishop of Durham arrives and delivers a long and insulting speech referring to Perkin as "a vagabond, a straggler,/ . . . / An obscure peasant, by the rage of Hell/ Loosd from his chaynes" (G1; III, iv), and to James as the butt of children's laughter for his proclamations and of the country's anger for his slaughters and ravaging; realizing his plight James answers neither charge, and Perkin is forced to come to his own defense. After Durham leaves, the king's wrath breaks out upon Perkin himself, and the newly founded alliance begins to split apart. Perkin, despite many admira-

ble personal qualities, is shown to be a vacillating and hope-
lessly ineffective leader. Although he makes a noble speech
deploring the ravaging of Northumberland, he has no influence with James, and his well-meaning but ineffective plea is
described by Crawford as that of a "passionate" and "Ef-
feminately dolent" (G1ᵛ; III, iv) man. When the report
comes of the approach of the army of the Earl of Surrey
against them Perkin objects pathetically: " 'Tis false! they
come to side with us" (G2; III, iv). When it becomes
apparent that James is going to desert him, Perkin lapses
into the abandonment of reason that characterizes his scene
with Frion. In this revealing scene Ford provides our only
look at Perkin's relationship to his secretary, Frion, and the
picture is not to Perkin's credit. Perkin wavers between
extremes, first lamenting the collapse of his "hopes of glorie" (G3ᵛ; IV, ii) and thinking of his wife's love and then
turning disdainfully on all who have opposed him and vow-
ing defiance until the end. Frion's rebuking words are justified:

> You grow too wilde in passion, if you will
> Appeare a Prince indeede, confine your will
> To moderation. (G4; IV, ii)

Perkin is violently angry at Frion's imputation that he must
be careful to conceal that he is not really a prince, but he
realizes that he would be completely helpless without
Frion's support. In a pathetic revelation of his weakness he
tells Frion:

> Speake what you will; wee are not suncke so low
> But your advise, may peece againe the heart
> Which many cares have broken: you were wont
> In all extremities to talke of comfort:
> Have yee' none left now? Ile not interrupt yee'.
> Good, beare with my distractions! if King *James*
> Denie us dwelling here, next whither must I?
> I preethee' be not angrie. (G4; IV, ii)

When Frion encourages him by mentioning the prospects in
Cornwall, Perkin's attitude, like Richard's in Act III of
Richard II, swings from total despondency to unreasoning
optimism:

> Let me embrace thee, hugge thee! th'ast revivd
> My comforts, if my cosen King will fayle,
> Our cause will never. (G4; IV, ii)

Ford, the admirer of the golden mean, undoubtedly intended that this abrupt transition from pessimism to optimism be interpreted as passionate irrationality.

The Perkin of this scene is not only passionate, sentimental, effeminate, and unreasoning, but he is also cynical in his view of man. He seems to be following earlier wisdom of Frion when he tells him:

> Sir, sir, take heede!
> Golde, and the promise of promotion, rarely
> Fayle in temptation. (G4; IV, ii)

Although Perkin in his worldly innocence seems unsure of the truth of his statement, he seems to realize that his only hope is to trust in its truth. In a later scene with Frion he has more cynical advice:

> "never yet
> "Was any Nation read of, so besotted
> "In reason, as to adore the setting Sunne.
> Flie to the *Arch-Dukes* Court; say to the *Dutchesse,*
> Her *Nephewe,* with fayre *Katherine,* his wife,
> Are on their expectation to beginne
> The raysing of an Empire. If they fayle,
> Yet the report will never. (H3; IV, iii)

Perkin is learning the evil ways of the world and, in attaining this perverted wisdom, is corrupting his own innocence. The cynical and weak Perkin of these scenes can hardly be expected to win the sympathetic support of anyone.

Meanwhile King James has capitulated to the smooth diplomacy of Hialas and Durham, who shrewdly allow James to retain the appearance of nobility even though the disparity between appearance and reality is great. James, eagerly accepting this route of escape, treats the two as ministers of heaven's will and excuses his earlier support of Perkin as the product of the subterfuge of Perkin's noble appearance and the pity of his kingly heart. With a noble gesture he deserts Perkin and vows that James "shall no way interrupt/ A generall peace" (H1ᵛ; IV, iii). But Ford does not allow James to go unexposed before the audience, for his following soliloquy reveals his true motivations:

> A league with *Ferdinand?* a marriage
> With *English Margaret?* a free release
> From restitution for the late affronts?
> Cessation from hostilitie! and all
> For *Warbeck* not delivered, but dismist?
> Wee could not wish it better. (H1ᵛ; IV, iii)

When Perkin reenters, the sham of noble appearances once again assumes control. After revealing his actual motivation to the audience, James tells Perkin:

> But now obedience to the Mother Church,
> A Fathers care upon his Countryes weale,
> The dignitie of State directs our wisedome,
> To seale an oath of peace through Christendome. (H2; IV, iii)

The difference between appearance and reality could not be more striking. Perkin too rises to the occasion and, although well aware that the Scottish king has villainously deserted him, delivers a noble speech in praise of James' munificence. His motivation is complex: he realizes that if he is to win support from others he must maintain the appearance of moderation and dignity; he also is driven by his desire to have all think well of him as a man; and finally he is at least to some extent the innocent dupe who is fooled by James' courtly words into thinking that James' actions may not have been so ignoble after all.

The main theme of the last part of the play is the final downfall of Perkin and the almost incredible loyalty of Katherine to him. In dramatizing this action Ford faced some difficult problems. How was he to explain how a virtuous and beautiful woman could stay loyal to an impostor? How was he to win audience approval for her actions and still have them rejoice in Perkin's downfall? How was he to have Perkin die without making him either a noble and sympathetic claimant to the throne or else a villan who would lower the tone of the play? Ford's solution, implied but not made explicit earlier in the play, was to stress the loyalty and duty of Katherine and the madness of Perkin.[5]

Since Perkin has undeniable nobility in his manner, Katherine's loyalty becomes credible, particularly since she stresses that her loyalty is to Perkin the man and not to Perkin the king. Ford keeps sympathy for Perkin under control by presenting the final noble speeches from the perspective of norm characters who interpret Perkin's claims as an indication of his madness.

The second Cornwall rebellion, which constitutes the major action of the last part of the play, was doomed to failure before it began. We are prepared for the fiasco by the spirit of unreasoning and unrealistic optimism in Perkin along with the cynicism of his followers and by the foresight of King Henry in sending his army to Salisbury before the invasion as "a wise prevention/ Of ills expected" (11; IV, iv). Perkin proclaims the God-given advantages that he possesses because of the "Divinitie/ Of *royall birth*" (11ᵛ; IV, v). But events prove the hollowness of his claim. In putting Perkin's speech in the scene following Henry's inspired foresight in moving his army to Salisbury, Ford seems to be stressing the difference between true and imitation royalty.

When Perkin and Katherine land in Cornwall, Perkin's optimism is balanced by Katherine's profound despondency. Her gloomy submission to fate is both a recognition of the true situation of Perkin in Cornwall and preparation for her expression of loyalty to Perkin just before he dies. Significantly she does not treat her loyalty to Perkin as the product of her love although love is undoubtedly present; rather she feels that the need for continued loyalty is a trial of her moral strength:

> IT is decreede; and wee must yeeld to fate,
> Whose angry Justice though it threaten ruine,
> Comtempt, and povertie, is all but tryall
> Of a weake womans constancie in suffering.
> Here in a strangers, and an enemies Land
> Forsaken, and unfurnisht of all hopes,
> (But such as waite on miserie,) I range
> To meete affliction where so ere I treade. (12; V, i)

When she is informed of Perkin's flight to a monastery, her response is an indication of the motivation of her courage.

> O my sorrowes!
> If *both* our lives had prov'd the sacrifice
> To *Henries* tyrannie, wee had fallen like Princes,
> And rob'd him, of the glory of his pride. (I2ᵛ; V, i)

It is this ideal of personal integrity that impels her to the noble loyalty that she later exhibits in Perkin's death scene. Since man's fate is to a large extent beyond his control, he can only live virtuously and accept whatever befalls him:

> Being driven
> By fate, it were in vaine to strive with Heaven. (I3ᵛ; V, i)

In the death scene itself Katherine affirms the validity of her marriage when the lords taunt her with being faithful to an impostor:

> You abuse us:
> For when the holy *Church-man* joynd our hands,
> Our Vowes were reall then; the Ceremonie
> Was not in apparition, but in act. (K3ᵛ; V, iii)

She pleads to be allowed to join Warbeck in his death, and it is clear that she still believes her earlier claim that by becoming sacrifices, she and Perkin can rise above Henry's justice. Perkin sees this too:

> *Harrie Richmond!*
> A womans faith, hath robd thy fame of triumph. (K3ᵛ; V, iii)

Since Huntley himself expresses admiration for Katherine's loyalty, we are apparently meant to have no reservations about her love. When she gives Perkin a final kiss and vows never to remarry, she becomes the image of perfect loyalty. She elevates duty and love in marriage to an absolute status which takes precedence over all of her personal desires, over father and country, and over the faithful lover Dalyell's logical claim to her, which can never be realized because of her vow. In submitting to her fate she achieves a moral grandeur which was probably intended to win the unreserved praise of Ford's Caroline audience.

The issue of Perkin's sanity is first raised seriously in the scene in which he confronts Henry. When Dawbeney introduces Perkin to Henry as "the Christian worlds strange wonder" (I4; V, ii), Henry's reply stresses the need for the true vision which can see through appearance to the inner reality:

> *Dawbney,* Wee observe no wonder; I behold (tis true)
> An ornament of nature, fine and pollisht,
> *A handsome youth indeede,* but not admire him. (14; V, i)

His questioning of Perkin indicates his calm assurance that there can be no question of the validity of Perkin's claim. When Perkin reiterates his belief in himself, Henry is tolerant but astounded. Perkin's words have been undeniably noble, and Henry can only conclude that he is unbalanced:

> Was ever so much impudence in forgery?
> The custome sure of being stil'd *a King,*
> Hath fastend in his thought that *HE IS SUCH.* (K1ᵛ; V, ii)

Ford never suggests that Perkin's claim may be valid; the only question is whether he is hypocritical or demented. The final scenes leave no doubt that the latter alternative is correct. Simnel says that "a *Bedlum* cannot cure him" (K3; V, iii), but perhaps the most significant speech is from the chaplain, Urswick. After Oxford has told Perkin to "tye up/ The Devill, that raunges in your tongue" (K3ᵛ, V, iii), Urswick continues:

> Thus Witches,
> Possest, even to their deaths deluded, say,
> They have beene wolves, and dogs, and sayld in Eggshells
> Over the Sea, and rid on fierie Dragons;
> Past in the ayre more then a thousand miles,
> All in a night; the enemie of mankinde
> Is powerfull, but false; and falshood confident. (K3ᵛ; V, iii)

Since the imagery throughout the play has stressed the association of Perkin with witchcraft and the devil and of Henry with heaven and the forces of good, it does not seem improper to accept Urswick's analysis of Perkin's madness. A mentally unbalanced character can arouse pity, and Perkin does so in Dawbeney and Huntley, and presumably also in Dalyell and Crawford, but he should not arouse respect for what he has done since he has been merely the tool of ambitious villains. Nevertheless Oxford and Surrey's open contempt for Katherine's loyalty to an impostor is much too merciless. Huntley indicates what is probably closer to a proper view when he forgives Katherine, expresses admiration for the couple's loyalty, and finally gives Perkin "a farewell/ Of manly pittie" (K4^v; V, iii). When Perkin delivers his final death speech we should probably feel a mixture of admiration for his courage along with pity for someone who has been the naive victim of villains taking advantage of his delusion. Wonder, pity, admiration—all are present in the final evaluation of Perkin. But if order is to be guaranteed Perkin must die, and Henry's concluding statement is a just summary:

> that publicke States,
> "As our particular bodyes, taste most good
> "In health, when purged of corrupted bloud. (L1; V, iii)

In the final analysis the order of the state must take precedence over human sympathies.

Ford's summary in the epilogue reinforces his serious political and moral intention:

> *Here ha's appear'd, though in a severall fashion,*
> *The Threats of Majestie; the strength of passion;*
> *Hopes of an Empire; change of fortunes; All*
> *What can to Theater's of Greatnesse fall;*
> *Proving their weake foundations. (L1^v)*[6]

Dependence upon the fickle fortune of this world can lead only to destruction since greatness is based on *"weake foundations."* The wise man puts his trust in God and in God's representative in the world, the king.

IX

Concord in Discord

Anyone attempting to understand the nature of Ford's drama must explain the many elements that at first seem to be contradictory. How can a serious moralist concerned about order in society and in the individual justify presenting sensational stories which appeal to, if not pander to, his audience's interest in murder and illicit love? Why does a Christian humanist who stresses the importance of reason keep coming back to studies of fascinating protagonists who rebel against reason and excuse and even glorify their passionate love affairs as proving their nobility and honor? The usual answer has been a reductive one—that Ford may have been concerned about traditional values but that he was a practical dramatist who was even more concerned about writing successful plays that would exploit the contemporary demand for sensational theater. In fact, it is maintained, what greatness the plays have lies in what the orthodox pattern denies—the assertion of the greatness of the human spirit in a world that is constantly pressing it into submission. Such a formula twists Ford's plays into forms that they do not have.

By close attention to the structure and tone of the works, I have tried to show that the function of the sensational plots and of the elaborate rhetoric of love and honor has been consistently miunderstood. Ford is a shrewd working dramatist who interests his audience through presenting exciting stories dealing with controversial subjects. But, like most Renaissance dramatists, he wants to do more than entertain; and we will understand his plays only if we see that he uses forms that almost invariably have a symbolic moral structure as a framework. Tragicomedies that were at all serious in intention were expected to show how through reason and common sense happy endings are possible, and tragedies were expected to reveal the nobility of heroic virtue and the destructive effect of submission to passion. An audience accustomed to traditional forms would be surprised if plays in these forms did not reinforce traditional religious, political, and social views. When we remember that Ford's Caroline audience was a primarily upper-class, private-theater audience, the significance of these expectations is underlined. Generalizations are impossible since some aristocrats were enough opposed to the spirit of Caroline England so that they joined the Puritans in the Civil War; but nevertheless the audience would tend to represent the more traditional and, as far as institutions are concerned, the more conservative element of the society. In writing plays that would appeal to them, Ford utilizes the full resources of the traditional theater to provide exciting plays dealing with themes that would be of particular interest—the threat of breakdown in society because of rampant individualism and disrespect for traditional values and the perversions of traditional theories of love and individual responsibility in justifying selfish courses of action.

In stressing the audience's conservative presuppositions, we must not exaggerate their moral seriousness. They were genuinely interested in and concerned about the problems of ethics in their changing world, much more so than it is easy for us to realize today with our very different expectations as to what the theater should do; but, if we judge by the plays that they saw, they expected the theater to shock, amuse, titillate, and satirize as well as reassure. Most members of a Caroline audience would probably delight in their broadmindedness and sophistication in considering questions far beyond what the more narrow Puritans thought were

proper subjects. There is something of the deliberately outrageous in some of Ford's plays that must have appealed to
people who were becoming tired of the moralistic preaching
of the Puritans. The title, *'Tis Pity She's a Whore,* is surely
a deliberate assault on tender Puritan moral sensibilities; so
are the dramatist James Shirley's prefatory verses to *Love's
Sacrifice:*

> *Looke here* THOU *that hast* malice *to the Stage,*
> *And* Impudence *enough for the whole Age;*
> Voluminously-Ignorant! *be vext*
> *To read this Tragedy, and thy owne be next.* (*LS,* A4)

We should not expect plays of this type to be at all moralistic, and they are not. But Ford is in his own way a serious
dramatist who is concerned about the course of his society,
and in his own exaggerated, often satiric style he writes
plays that will delight his sophisticated audience by their
very outrageousness and at the same time reassure them
that the values of their Anglican, Christian-humanist society
still have validity.

What permeates all of Ford's work is a genuine concern
for people's essential humanity. Ford's vision of life permits
at once clear-sighted recognition of the forces in man that
are destructive, laughter at and ridicule of the absurdities of
man's behavior, and sympathy for the victims of life's tragedies. To Ford, as to most Anglicans in the tradition of
Hooker, a broad humanistic approach stressing rational
common sense and simple faith is far preferable to narrow
and dogmatic systems of ethics and theology. Never does
Ford get involved in elaborate speculation about anything.
To Ford, man soaring to involved justifications of self is
man corrupted by a deceiving intellect. In *Honor Triumphant* he is already poking fun at the pretense of so much
Platonic theorizing about love. In *Fame's Memorial* he defends a love that he believes is moral in the broadest sense
even though it does not satisfy the rigid dictates of the
conventional moral code. In his prose writing on ethics, he is
always practical, outlining in *The Golden Mean* how a man
can meet misfortune and in *A Line of Life* how he can best
live an honorable life. But Ford does not forget the central

truths of his faith. Like the friar in *'Tis Pity*, Ford is devout as well as practical. In his poem, *Christ's Bloody Sweat*, he accentuates a simple faith that combines his usual moral concern with stress on the efficacy of the sacramental and ritualistic traditions of the Anglican church. Ford is perhaps best seen as a Christian neo-Stoic who conceives of true honor as combining noble thought with heroic action. Man should dedicate his life to carrying out the highest ideals of his Christian society. True honor requires that selfish desires to achieve superficial worldly success and happiness be sacrificed for the deeper spiritual wisdom that comes from following virtue and truth. With the security of this inner wisdom, man can then confidently act in the world because no matter what happens his nobility is secure. If honor is not based upon virtue, however, it is an empty pretense that may fool some men but can never deceive God or the individual himself. He will remain troubled and dissatisfied until he achieves the wisdom that comes from a proper attitude toward the things of this world.

In his plays Ford treats many of the themes of his early works. Modern readers are too apt to read modern values into the plays through failing to realize that the plays are written in a traditional, symbolic mode in which the thematic is much more important than the psychological. If we read the plays as objective or organic treatments of the stories they depict, we are in danger of identifying with the leading characters instead of evaluating them as a part of a larger symbolic structure. The characters are not unique beings different from all others because of their particular heredity and environment. Rather they are representative types facing problems and choices that all men face. The situations are of course often highly unusual, but that heightening serves mainly to clarify or simplify the motivation and the effect of the choices that are made. In the tragicomedies Ford might be said to oversimplify through implying that proper values, wise choices, and restraint will always produce happy endings. The breadth and depth of the studies are thus somewhat limited by the requirements of the genre, but the plays are good illustrations of the views outlined in the early works. In all of the tragicomedies the characters are placed in difficult situations that are potentially disastrous if not handled properly. But in all of the plays virtue and common sense triumph because the characters are led to recognize the importance of working constructively toward solutions instead of falling back on either moralizing judgment or fatalistic excuses. In *The Lover's Melancholy* restraint and the practical advice of Corax and others show that love-melancholy need not be destructive. In *The Fancies* Livio and Romanello are forced to face the immaturity of their early views and become worthy of marriage to the fancies. In *The Queen* Alphonso is cured of his misogyny and Velasco of his excessive adulation through patience, understanding, and some shrewd maneuvering that forces them to recognize their foolishness. In *The Lady's Trial* Auria carefully plots out and carries through a plan that enables him to solve his problem and still retain his honor. The attitudes in the tragicomedies toward Platonic and fatalistic defenses of passions are particularly significant in light of the controversy about Ford's attitude toward these matters in the tragedies. In *The Lover's Melancholy* the virtuous victims of melancholy avoid Platonic posturing and endure in silence while Thamasta's fatalism and her rhetoric defending love are ridiculed. The characters in the other tragicomedies who use Platonic or fatalistic defenses of lust are also severely criticized by Ford. When Octavio in *The Fancies* and Adurni and Malfato in *The Lady's Trial* use such arguments with Castamela and Spinella, Ford makes clear that the lady's proper response is shocked indignation. Both Castamela and Spinella exemplify the rational position that Annabella in *'Tis Pity* and Bianca in *Love's Sacrifice* abandon with disastrous results. In fact it might be said that the difference between Fordian tragicomedy and tragedy is the difference between following reason and following passion.

But any serious examination of the tragedies must begin with the recognition that they are much more than the dramatization of conventional ethical formulas. That claim might be made for the tragicomedies, where following virtue leads to happiness, but in the tragedies Ford places his characters in such difficult situations that any criticism of them for failing to follow reason would be oversimplified. There is nothing in the tragedies that opposes the moral doctrine of Ford's other work, but Ford's is no easy message of rational morality as a sure means of overcoming all problems. Implicit in his choice of themes is his recognition that living a virtuous life is difficult because of the temptations that face man. Ford does not pick situations in which a character is faced with a clear moral choice and brings about his own destruction by choosing wrongly. Instead he picks protagonists who represent the highest ideals of their society and places them in perilous situations not entirely of their own making.

In each of his three tragedies, there is an obstacle separating noble and at the beginning virtuous lovers. In each case the mutual admiration that exists is a natural and proper expression of respect for virtue and nobility. The members of each of the three couples—Giovanni and Annabella, Fernando and Bianca, and Orgilus and Penthea—would be ideally suited for marriage if barriers to their love did not exist. Ford seems to have been fascinated by the theme of misalliance, for in each play there are pressures on the virtuous heroine to marry someone unworthy of her love. Thus Bianca and Penthea are both forced into obviously unwise marriages because of the selfishness of others. Although in Giovanni and Annabella's case no one can be blamed that they are brother and sister, Annabella's attraction to Giovanni is more understandable because of the pressure on her to marry someone unworthy of her. Her father's choice of suitors for her is determined by money and prestige, and we cannot imagine that Annabella would have been able to hold out very long against his indirect but powerful maneuverings. In each of the plays circumstances beyond the lovers' control contribute to their problems and make facile moral judgment unwise. In a world in which ambition, cynicism, and materialism lead to corruption, forced marriages, and hypocrisy, it is difficult for the individual to remain virtuous. Even if one succeeds in avoiding sins of commission, what one does not do can bring tragedy. Penthea and Calantha die of broken hearts that only the most severe moralist can suggest they should have avoided.

Undoubtedly they should have followed the mean in their reactions to tragedy, but they can hardly be blamed for breaking under the strain of the series of tragedies forced on them.

But what must be made clear is that Ford, although he sympathizes, does not excuse or romanticize his lovers. Even though there are countless mitigating circumstances, the failure of individuals to control their passions is the direct cause of the tragedies in each play. Ford shows that love outside the moral code results in the moral deterioration of the individuals involved. A love which cannot develop naturally into marriage inevitably becomes destructive, and justifiable Platonic admiration of beauty and virtue inevitably becomes twisted into diseased, heroical love unless reason exercises control. Although the characters try to excuse themselves through elaborate Platonic and fatalistic arguments, Ford suggests that these are only rationalizations of minds made illogical by passion and that there is nothing attractive or ennobling about illicit love. We can explain and understand and pity these unfortunate lovers, but we should not romanticize them. They are products of a society in which an absolute, idealized morality is applied to human beings no matter what their situation, but Ford believes in those standards.

Even though Ford shows the difficulty of following high codes in a society whose institutions have been corrupted by human weaknesses, he does not question the moral order. Instead he indicates that a difficult situation requires correspondingly greater effort on the part of the individual. It is a measure of Ford's Christian neo-Stoicism that his highest praise is reserved for those who recognize their plight honestly and overcome it through humility, restraint, and common sense. The most obvious examples are Annabella in *'Tis Pity* and Katherine in *Perkin Warbeck*. Annabella becomes in the last part of the play the symbol of heroic values through recognition of her own fault, sympathy toward Giovanni even though he has helped bring about her downfall, and acceptance of her death with courage and humility. In her approach to death she is made to represent the spiritual values that both she and Giovanni had been corrupting earlier. Katherine too is ready to live out her life in heroic dedication to the values that she believes are right. She could have deserted Perkin when his cause was hopeless or she could have married Dalyell after Perkin's death, but instead she makes the meaningfulness of her marriage vows to Perkin the absolute of her life and determines to live out her life in devotion to that ideal. Both Annabella and Katherine become symbols of the same virtue exemplified by Castamela and Spinella in the tragicomedies and, with the reservations noted above, by Penthea and Calantha in *The Broken Heart.*

If this description of Ford's intention is essentially correct, a charge that is sure to be raised is that his work is lacking in variety. The answer must be a qualified admission that the charge is justified. Ford does concern himself in play after play with the same themes—the nature of love, honor, resolution, justice, order, etc.—and he uses the same techniques—a symbolic structure in which representative figures are faced with difficult choices that test their ability to find honorable solutions to sometimes almost insoluble problems. A defender of Ford's variety cannot claim that each play adds something new to our interpretation of Ford's thought, as one can argue that there is development in Shakespeare, for example. There is no such development in Ford's plays; in fact the dating of them proves to be of little consequence since the point of view in all of the plays is so similar. Once acquainted with his overall position, one can predict quite accurately what his attitude toward a given situation will be. Ford is no Shakespeare, but studies of Jacobean drama have suffered too long from attempts to find Shakespearean breadth and depth. We must be satisfied with a dramatist whose vision is circumscribed by his seventeenth-century context and not try to force him into a more universal, by which we usually mean a more modern, context. But Ford deserves recognition, of a different kind than he has received, for the diverse ways in which he illustrates his vision of life.

There is still too strong a tendency to dismiss works that operate within a Christian humanist framework as simple-minded illustrations of a few now-outmoded truisms. Instead we should recognize in Jacobean drama what has

long been recognized in studies of seventeenth-century poetry—that we are dealing with a sophisticated philosophy of
life that has become complex and rich through centuries of
artistic and intellectual development. Ford is well acquainted with that tradition, and in his analysis of the structure of society and the nature of the individual, he reflects
the most advanced and articulate thinking of his time. His
studies of individual psychology are solidly grounded in the
work of the highly respected Burton, and his philosophical
position is close to that of the liberal Anglican thinkers of
the time. He is alert to the changing contemporary situation: his studies of the perversions of Platonic and Stoic
thinking reflect both his awareness of fashionable topics and
his ability to place these controversies in the context of a
larger philosophical position.

Most important, of course, is his skillful use of the various techniques of the drama of his time. Ford does not
simply rewrite the same play over and over again as so many
of his contemporaries did. In each of the plays he attempts
something a little different—a fact that is made clear when
we remember the variety of types of plays that he writes. In
his collaborative works, *The Witch of Edmonton* and *The
Sun's Darling,* he works within the forms of domestic tragedy and the masque. In *The Lover's Melancholy* and *The
Queen* he writes romantic tragicomedy. In *The Lady's Trial*
he is much closer to the Cavalier drama. In *The Fancies* he
tries his hand, albeit none too successfully, at bawdy, almost
farcical low comedy. Among his tragedies, *'Tis Pity* and
Love's Sacrifice are satirical and ironical while *The Broken
Heart* is a much more sober and elevated attempt at high
tragedy.[1] He even attempts with some success to resurrect
the history play in *Perkin Warbeck.* Despite this variety,
however, he manipulates the form in which he is working so
that it can become the vehicle for his own characteristic
themes.

Similarly a study of Ford's dramatic style reveals consistency despite the widely different forms that he uses. There is
in all of Ford's plays a simplicity and economy of language
that is somewhat surprising when we remember the elaborate patterns of his early poetry and the involved rhetoric
of much of his prose, particularly the prefatory letters to

the plays themselves. It is probable that in this variety Ford reveals a sense of decorum that dictates one manner for long religious poems, another for prose treatises, another for prefatory letters, and still another for plays. It is also likely that Ford's dramatic style owes something to the Fletcherian manner that dominates the period. But I am convinced that the simplicity of expression in the plays is also closely related to the philosophy that Ford expresses throughout his work. H. J. Oliver has, I think, found the right explanation for the long-noted absence of involved patterns of imagery, diction, and rhetoric in Ford's plays: "Ford uses extensive imagery only when characters are speaking, as it were, artificially. . . . When Ford's characters speak from the heart, with no need to camouflage or conceal their feelings, they always do so with a remarkable directness. There is a scarcity of imagery, even of adjectives; and a high proportion of the words become, as in the great poetry of Vaughan, monosyllabic." [2] My examination of the speeches in the plays indicates the general accuracy of Oliver's observation. Those who speak directly are not always virtuous, but those who speak in a highly rhetorical way are usually deluding someone, often themselves. I would go beyond Oliver to suggest that this style reflects Ford's insistence on honesty, rationality, naturalness, and simplicity as the values on which a meaningful life can be based.

Like the musician Parthenophil in *The Lover's Melancholy,* Ford tries to make his art the expression of the harmony of "Concord in discord" (*LM,* B3^r; I, i). The unity and coherence of his plays can be taken as another reflection of the principle of order that Ford thought should govern man in all that he does. Variety is not lacking in Ford, but it comes neither from a changing or ambiguous treatment of themes nor from a thickly textured poetical style, but rather from the richness and complexity of his traditional vision and the diversity of forms through which he expresses that vision. My final impression of Ford is of a skilled professional dramatist with a shrewd sense of what his audiences wanted, a clear idea of what he wanted to give them, and a sense of dramatic form that is much more highly developed than has been realized.

REFERENCE MATTER

NOTES

Short titles are used throughout for works listed in bibliography.

INTRODUCTION

1 For more detailed studies of what we know about Ford's life, see Sargeaunt, *John Ford,* pp. 1–31; Davril, *Le Drame de John Ford,* pp. 45–63; and Bentley, *The Jacobean and Caroline Stage,* III, 433–38.

2 For a systematic account of the facts about the plays in which Ford may have had a hand, see Bentley, *The Jacobean and Caroline Stage,* III, 433–64.

3 See William Hazlitt, "Lectures on the Dramatic Literature of the Age of Elizabeth," *The Miscellaneous Works of William Hazlitt* (New York, 1859), III, 107–14; Charles Lamb, "Specimens of English Dramatic Poets," *The Works of Charles and Mary Lamb,* ed. E. V. Lucas (New York, 1904), IV, 195–218.

4 William Gifford, Introduction to *The Works of John Ford* (London, 1869), pp. xxxi, xxxiv–xxxv; Hartley Coleridge, Introduction to *The Dramatic Works of Massinger and Ford* (London, 1840), p. lviii; George Saintsbury, *A History of Elizabethan Literature* (London, 1887), pp. 401–9; Adolphus William Ward, *A History of English Dramatic Literature to the Death of Queen Anne,* rev. ed. (London, 1899), III, 77–83; James Russell Lowell, *Works,* Vol. XI, *The Old English Dramatists* (Boston and New York, 1891), pp. 312–14; Felix E. Schelling, *Elizabethan Drama, 1558 1642* (New York, 1908), II, 330–36; Ashley H. Thorndike, *Tragedy* (Boston and New York, 1908), pp. 226–29; W. A. Neilson, "Ford and Shirley," *The Cambridge History of English Literature* (New York, 1910), VI, 212–21; C. F.

Tucker Brooke, *The Tudor Drama* (Cambridge, Mass., 1911), pp. 445–46. For a discussion of pre-Hazlitt opposition to the morality of Ford, see Sargeaunt, *John Ford,* pp. 174–78. T. S. Eliot's reaction to *'Tis Pity* also parallels Hazlitt's criticism in certain respects (*Selected Essays,* pp. 193–204).

5 Algernon Charles Swinburne, "John Ford," *The Complete Works of Algernon Charles Swinburne* (London, 1926), II, 369–406; Havelock Ellis, Introduction to *John Ford* (The Mermaid Series; London, [1888]), pp. vii–xvii.

6 Introduction to *John Ford,* p. xvii.

7 Introduction to *'Tis Pity She's a Whore and The Broken Heart,* pp. ix–lv.

8 A typical response is that of Miss Sargeaunt. She argues that Sherman's thesis cannot be right because Ford's non-dramatic works and his tragicomedies are conventionally moral; but when she turns to the tragedies she readily grants Ford's romantic idealism and his sympathy for the passionate lovers (*John Ford,* pp. 132–41). The Sherman position has been widely influential among American scholars, especially in Sensabaugh's *The Tragic Muse of John Ford.* The summaries of Ford scholarship by John Wilcox ("On Reading John Ford," *SAB,* XXI [1946], 66–75) and by Wallace Bacon ("The Literary Reputation of John Ford," *HLQ,* XI [1947–48], 181–99) are both sympathetic to Sherman's position.

9 Sargeaunt, *John Ford,* p. 154.

10 Bradbrook, *Themes and Conventions of Elizabethan Tragedy,* pp. 250–61; Ellis-Fermor, *The Jacobean Drama* (4th ed., revised), pp. 227–46; Oliver, *The Problem of John Ford;* Leech, *John Ford and the Drama of his Time.* See also Leech, *John Ford.*

11 Bradbrook, *Themes and Conventions of Elizabethan Tragedy,* p. 250.

12 Ellis-Fermor, *The Jacobean Drama* (4th ed., revised), p. 244.

13 Oliver, *The Problem of John Ford,* pp. 2–4.

14 *Ibid.,* pp. 68–70, 84–85.

15 Leech, *John Ford and the Drama of his Time,* p. 62.

16 *Ibid.,* pp. 96–97.

17 *Texas Studies in Literature and Language,* I (1960), 522–37.

18 Sargeaunt, *John Ford,* p. 67.

19 Cochnower, "John Ford," in *Seventeenth Century Studies,* pp. 121–275; Lawrence Babb, "John Ford and Seventeenth Century Psychology" (Unpublished Dissertation, Yale, 1934), and *The Elizabethan Malady;* Ewing, *Burtonian Melancholy in the Plays of John Ford;* Sensabaugh, *The Tragic Muse of John Ford;* Davril, *Le Drame de John Ford.*

20 In a recent article ("John Ford Revisited," *SEL,* IV [1964], 195–216), Sensabaugh is less insistent on these earlier views; but Ford is still seen as a pessimistic analyst who portrays the tragic

dilemmas of his lovers as a means of indicating the impossibility of meaningful moral decision in an increasingly absurd world.

21 Ornstein, *The Moral Vision of Jacobean Tragedy;* Ribner, *Jacobean Tragedy.*

22 Bowers, *Elizabethan Revenge Tragedy,* pp. 206–16.

23 Critical interest in Ford continues to run high. In addition to the published studies there have been several recent unpublished dissertations. They include Theodore Tucker Orbison, "The Tragic Vision of John Ford" (Boston University Graduate School, 1963); Howard Lee Ford, "John Ford: The Temple and the Stage" (Louisiana State University, 1963); Benjamin John Lucow, "The Function of Satire in the Plays of John Ford" (University of Washington, 1964); and Wayne Howe Phelps, "John Ford's *Perkin Warbeck* and the Pretender Plays: 1634–1746" (Princeton University, 1965).

CHAPTER I

1 *Fame's Memorial* must have been written after the death of the Earl of Devonshire on April 3, 1606. Whether it precedes or follows *Honor Triumphant* cannot be finally determined, but in his dedicatory letter Ford implies that *Fame's Memorial* was first when he notes that his work has been "hitherto confined to the Innes of Courte studyes much differente" (*FM,* sig. A3). Subsequent references to Ford's works will appear in the text. Full details of the editions used may be found in the bibliography.

2 See Sherman, Introduction to *'Tis Pity She's a Whore and The Broken Heart,* pp. ix–x; Sargeaunt, *John Ford,* p. 6; Sensabaugh, *The Tragic Muse of John Ford,* p. 151; Davril, *Le Drame de John Ford,* p. 178. Leech is more restrained but remarks that "it is not surprising that the man who was to write *The Broken Heart* found the subject of his elegy attractive and gave a special stress to his love-theme" (*John Ford and the Drama of his Time,* p. 19). Oliver argues in opposition that Ford had to be sympathetic since the poem was dedicated to Penelope and that we are not justified in giving the poem much biographical significance (*The Problem of John Ford,* p. 11).

3 My account of their lives is based on two recent studies: Cyril Falls, *Mountjoy: Elizabethan General* (London, 1955); and William A. Ringler, Jr., *The Poems of Sir Philip Sidney* (Oxford, 1962), pp. 434–47.

4 The tract is reprinted in Maud Stepney Rawson's *Penelope Rich and her Circle* (London, 1911), pp. 320–42.

5 Falls, *Mountjoy,* p. 227.

6 *Ibid.,* p. 227.

7 *Ibid.,* p. 227.

8 *Ibid.,* p. 238.

9 *Ibid.,* p. 227.

10 Introduction to *'Tis Pity She's a Whore and the Broken Heart*, p. xiv.

11 Leech, Oliver, and Ornstein see that parts of the pamphlet are humorous, but they do not question Ford's support of the arguments for love (*John Ford and the Drama of his Time*, pp. 20–22; *The Problem of John Ford*, pp. 11–12; *The Moral Vision of Jacobean Tragedy*, p. 292). Miss Cochnower thinks that Ford "was *wishing* to believe rather than believing what he wrote there." She sees that in *Honor Triumphant* "Plato's idealism appears to be marshalled into the service of worldly love." But her conclusion is that Ford's ideal of love is a worldly one (*John Ford*, pp. 137–38). Davril follows the Sherman interpretation (*Le Drame de John Ford*, p. 81).

12 See *Calendar of State Papers: Domestic, James I*, XXII, June 1, 1606.

13 I quote from the copy of the letter in John Nichols, *The Progresses, Processions, and Magnificent Festivities, of King James the First* (London, 1828), II, 49–50.

14 A second letter, dated "Greenwich June 28" and preserved by Drummond, records a reply: "To the Errant Knights of the *Fortunate Islands*, Servant-men to the Destinies, awaking our ever-awake courages with their *Mavortial* greetings:
"Most tonitruous astonishing Chevaliers; Re-know ye, that we of hereditary and fee-simple blood, and undegenerating valour to *Doucel del Phoebus, Amadis de Gaul, Palmerin de Oliva*, and *Ascuper le Huge*, rather by the bonds of your challenge than by the show of your meanings, have echoed in the vault of our understanding the volley of your desires; and do allow you this for answer. We confidently entertain your challenge with your circumstance proposed already, seeing the event in the cause; for old defended virtue of women is expired; and men, overcome with women, are made less than themselves, and far inferior to the valour of uneffiminate Knights. We are sorry that any in the shape or apparel of valour, should either be so short of experience, or so unable to bring to their wills their knowledges, as to undertake the long forsaken cause of a sex, that have spent all their virtue, which is sullied by falsehood, to the abuse of their own defenders; at the first their minds drew wrath and judgment, and now their bodies draw passion into a blind adventure. Wherefore we deny your assertions, being assured of these truths which tread down your fancies; and these ours, in peace and pity, we offer to your second considerations; which, otherwise, if you believe not, will prove themselves masters of you and yours. 1. That a man at the years of discretion hath his love in his own hand. 2. That Beauty melteth Valour, and maketh the tongue far readier than the sword. 3. That fairest Ladies are falsest, having fairest occasions. 4. That to love and to be wise, were ever two men's parts. Against you, armed with the truth of these, we shall come with sharp argu-

ments, not doubting to beat falsehood into her darkness, unable to endure the beams of the *Lucent Pillar;* The mystery whereof, &c. vaunt we honour. Expect us therefore, if your rash heat consume not before performance."

The letter continues: "The King, not without laughter, can see, read the Challenge, and put the Noblemen Defenders in expectation to be answered. But the Answerers have not appeared." (Nichols, *Progresses . . . of King James the First,* II, 51–52.) A tournament resembling the one described actually took place on Tuesday, August 5, 1606 (*ibid.,* II, 80). Whether the challenge theme was carried through is not clear.

15 *A Transcript of the Registers of The Company of Stationers of London, 1554–1640,* ed. E. Arber (London, 1876), III, 327 (fol. 142).

16 Two interpretations of the Mars-Venus relationship persisted into the Renaissance. The more familiar one was based on the Homeric story and treated Mars' submission to Venus as submission to lust. Erwin Panofsky, in discussing this view, mentions the "furtive passion of the Homeric lovers" (*Studies in Iconology* [New York, 1939], p. 164). Panofsky also points out that the relationship of Mars and Venus was sometimes interpreted as the virtuous union of beauty and valor (*Studies in Iconology,* pp. 163–64). From the context it is clear that Ford is referring to the Venus of the Homeric tradition.

17 For a discussion of the association of the blind Cupid with lust, see Panofsky, "Blind Cupid," in *Studies in Iconology,* pp. 95–128.

18 For a discussion of the Elizabethan attitude toward Paris, see Hallett D. Smith, *Elizabethan Poetry* (Cambridge, Mass., 1952), pp. 4–8. Even Ford's persona is critical of Helen in position three (*HT,* sig. D2ᵛ). For the Elizabethan attitude toward Troilus, see Dickey, *Not Wisely But Too Well,* pp. 118–32, and O. J. Campbell, *Comicall Satyre and Shakespeare's Troilus and Cressida* (San Marino, 1938), pp. 188–89. The traditional story of Pelops and Hippodamia would have been familiar. See, for example: Matthew Grove, *The Most Famous and Tragicall Historie of Pelops and Hippodamia* (London, 1587). Ironic mythological allusions are utilized in the other positions as well. Ford is fond of referring to such inappropriate stories as Paris' choice of Venus over Pallas, Hercules' disastrous love for Deianeira, the refusals of Achilles and Ulysses to fight in the Trojan War because of love, and Jason's unhappy life after winning the fleece. The obvious reference to the Earl of Devonshire and Penelope Rich in the praise of Ulysses, Hector, Penelope, and Opia is curious in this context, since Ford praises them in *Fame's Memorial.* Unless we postulate a sudden change in attitude toward Devonshire and Penelope, we must take the praise seriously; but it is hard to see how anyone could be flattered by praise from the persona of *Honor Triumphant.*

19 For a discussion of the controversy, see Louis B. Wright, *Middle-Class Culture in Elizabethan England* (Ithaca, 1958), pp. 465–507. For all questions relating to women in the Renaissance, see Carroll Camden, *The Elizabethan Woman,* and Ruth Kelso, *Doctrine for the Lady of the Renaissance* (Urbana, 1956).

20 In *The Golden Mean* Ford takes a position directly opposing that of the persona: "Since when mention is made of the unworthinesse of bodie, it is not any defect in Nature, or naturall proportion, but in manners outwardly acted. For many times it is commonly seene, that where Nature hath fail'd in some parts of the outward man, she hath oftentimes supplied those wants with a pregnancy of minde" (*GM,* sig. D4^v).

CHAPTER II

1 I have used the editions listed in my bibliography. *Christ's Bloody Sweat* is included in *The Poems of Joseph Fletcher,* ed. Rev. Alexander B. Grosart (The Fuller Worthies' Library, X; Blackburn, Lancashire, 1869). *A Line of Life* is included in the Gifford-Dyce edition, *The Works of John Ford* (London, 1869), III, 381–419, and in *Honour Triumphant; and A Line of Life* (The Shakespeare Society, XIX; London, 1843). There is no modern edition of *The Golden Mean.*

   Mention should also be made of Ford's other extant nondramatic writing, all of which is fairly inconsequential occasional poetry. For a list of these writings, see Leech, *John Ford and the Drama of his Time,* pp. 124–26. Frederick M. Burelbach, Jr., in his unpublished Harvard dissertation, "The Nondramatic Works of John Ford" (1965), discusses the traditionally Christian moral thought in all of these poems. See particularly, pp. 7–8.

2 See M. Joan Sargeaunt, "Writings Ascribed to John Ford by Joseph Hunter in *Chorus Vatum,*" *RES,* X (1934), 165–76; for more recent support of the attributions, see Davril, *Le Drame de John Ford,* pp. 83–84, 87–88; Oliver, *The Problem of John Ford,* pp. 12–14; Leech, *John Ford and the Drama of his Time* p. 22. Sensabaugh (*The Tragic Muse of John Ford,* p. 174.) supports Ford's authorship of *Christ's Bloody Sweat* but does not mention *The Golden Mean.*

3 Sargeaunt, "Writings Ascribed to John Ford by Joseph Hunter in *Chorus Vatum,*" pp. 173–74.

4 *The Problem of John Ford,* p. 13. Oliver questions the evidence of the dedications and of the parallel passages on the torments of hell. I agree that the dedications, although strikingly similar, are not conclusive evidence because of the conventional element in all dedications. The evidence of the parallel passages, however, seems to me stronger than Oliver believes. The description of hell in *Christ's Bloody Sweat* seems to be based upon Nashe's description in *Pierce Penilesse.* Ford must have borrowed from both earlier

versions for the friar's speech in *'Tis Pity*. (See *TP*, sig. F3ʳ; Thomas Nashe, *Pierce Penilesse His Supplication to the Divell, Works of Thomas Nashe*, ed. R. B. McKerrow [London, 1904], I, 218; *CBS*, sigs. E1ʳ–E2.) Racks of burning steel are mentioned in both *'Tis Pity* and *Christ's Bloody Sweat* but not in *Pierce Penilesse*. In some other details the *'Tis Pity* passage is closer to *Pierce Penilesse*. In both the gluttons eat toads. They eat "worse meat then toads" in *Christ's Bloody Sweat*. The term "Usurer" is used in *'Tis Pity* and *Pierce Penilesse*, but *"Miser"* is substituted in *Christ's Bloody Sweat*. If Ford wrote *Christ's Bloody Sweat*, it would have been natural for him to use both it and his earlier source, *Pierce Penilesse*, for the passage in *'Tis Pity*. If he did not write it, it seems unlikely that in writing *'Tis Pity* he would utilize both the *Pierce Penilesse* passage and an imitation of it made some twenty years before *'Tis Pity* in what was most likely not a widely read poem. This evidence is not conclusive, but I think it is stronger than Oliver believes. Taken together with the other evidence that Miss Sargeaunt presents, I find it impossible to avoid the conclusion that Ford wrote *Christ's Bloody Sweat*.

5 Sargeaunt, "Writings Ascribed to John Ford by Joseph Hunter in *Chorus Vatum*," p. 175. Miss Sargeaunt also points out that *The Golden Mean* was dedicated to the Earl of Northumberland, who was in prison for his alleged conspiracy in the gunpowder plot, while a manuscript of *A Line of Life*, now in the British Museum, is dedicated to Northumberland's son-in-law, Viscount Doncaster (*John Ford*, pp. 11–12, 16).

6 Ford's prose works fit most closely with what has come to be called the neo-Stoic tradition. The most detailed work on the subject has been done by Rudolf Kirk, who includes lengthy introductions in his editions of three of the more important neo-Stoic works for Rutgers Studies in English. They include: Justus Lipsius, *Two Bookes of Constancie*, tr. Sir John Stradling (New Brunswick, 1939); Joseph Hall, *Heaven upon Earth and Characters of Vertues and Vices* (New Brunswick, 1948); and Guillaume Du Vair, *The Moral Philosophie of the Stoicks*, tr. Thomas James (New Brunswick, 1951). For a discussion of these works and similar writings in relation to Hooker, Montaigne, and Renaissance thought generally, see Robert Hoopes, *Right Reason in the English Renaissance* (Cambridge, Mass., 1962), pp. 123–45; see also Caputi, *John Marston, Satirist*, pp. 52–79.

7 The Anglican explanation of the nature of law and of the authority for different kinds of law—divine law, the law of reason, the law of nature, etc.—is discussed in detail in Richard Hooker's *Of the Laws of Ecclesiastical Polity*, Book I. For a concise summary of the attitudes toward reason and faith in the early seventeenth century, see Herschel Baker, *The Wars of Truth* (Cambridge, Mass., 1952), pp. 90–134; see also Hoopes, *Right Reason in the English Renaissance*.

8 Sargeaunt, "Writings Ascribed to John Ford by Joseph Hunter in *Chorus Vatum,*" p. 166.
9 Research on the subject has been carried out by Lily B. Campbell and others. See Campbell, *Shakespeare's Tragic Heroes;* Hoopes, *Right Reason in the English Renaissance;* Anderson, *Elizabethan Psychology and Shakespeare's Plays;* Babb, *The Elizabethan Mallady.* For a discussion of the link between the humours and the passions see Campbell, *Shakespeare's Tragic Heroes,* pp. 51–78.
10 Campbell, *Shakespeare's Tragic Heroes,* p. 93.
11 Since reason is emphasized repeatedly, it seems wrong to argue, as Miss Sargeaunt does (*John Ford,* pp. 9–11), that stress on the redemptive power of Christ's blood is an indication of revivalistic enthusiasm.
12 For a discussion of the allegorical interpretation of the Song of Songs in the early seventeenth century, see Stanley Stewart, *The Enclosed Garden: The Tradition and the Image in Seventeenth-Century Poetry* (Madison, 1966), pp. 3–30.
13 For a discussion of the place of Fortune in Renaissance thought, see Campbell, *Shakespeare's Tragic Heroes,* pp. 5–15, and the chapter on Fortune in Russell A. Fraser, *Shakespeare's Poetics in Relation to King Lear* (London, 1962), pp. 46–60.
14 Pierre Charron, *Of Wisdom,* tr. George Stanhope (London, 1697), sig. N2^r.
15 For a discussion of this tradition, see Eugene M. Waith, *The Herculean Hero* (London, 1962), pp. 11–59.
16 Ford's references to Byron and Barnevelt are of particular interest because of Chapman's tragedy on Byron (1608) and Fletcher's (?) tragedy on Barnevelt (1619). Ford's view of Byron and Barnevelt (and Essex) fits the older *de casibus* tradition of the tragic protagonist and is relevant to Chapman and Fletcher scholarship as an indication of the presuppositions of one Jacobean playgoer and to Ford scholarship as early evidence of Ford's own view of tragedy.
17 Ford's ideas on death are, of course, commonplaces. For a discussion of changing attitudes toward death in the period, see Theodore Spencer, *Death and Elizabethan Tragedy* (Cambridge, Mass., 1936). An extended treatment of many of the same themes is found in Jeremy Taylor's *The Rule and Exercises of Holy Dying* (London, 1651).

Chapter III

1 For the French backgrounds see Alfred Horatio Upham, *The French Influence in English Literature* (New York, 1908), pp. 308–19; for the English phase of the cult see Upham, pp. 319–64, and Jefferson Butler Fletcher, "Précieuses at the Court of Charles I," *The Religion of Beauty in Woman and Other Essays on*

Platonic Love in Poetry and Society (New York, 1911), pp. 166–205.

2 James Howell, *Epistolae Ho-Elianae: The Familiar Letters of James Howell,* ed. Joseph Jacobs (London, 1892), I, 319–20. Jacobs points out that the dates of the letters are uncertain (Introduction, pp. lxxi–lxxvii). This letter is dated June 3, 1634, but should not be used as evidence for dating the love cult.

3 Alfred Harbage, *Cavalier Drama* (New York, 1936), p. 13.

4 Discussions of the history of Christian love are to be found in Anders Nygren, *Agape and Eros,* tr. Philip S. Watson (London, 1953); and M. C. D'Arcy, *The Mind and Heart of Love* (New York, 1947).

5 See Sears Jayne, "Ficino and the Platonism of the English Renaissance," *CL,* IV (1952), 214–38.

6 *Marsilio Ficino's Commentary on Plato's Symposium, The Text and a Translation,* with an Introduction, by Sears Reynolds Jayne (The University of Missouri Studies, XIX, 1 [Columbia, Mo., 1944]), p. 143.

7 Sensabaugh discusses the period's Mariolatry in *The Tragic Muse of John Ford,* pp. 96–100; for a discussion of Protestant attitudes toward love, see William and Malleville Haller, "The Puritan Art of Love," *HLQ,* V (1941–42), 235–72; see also Dickey, *Not Wisely But Too Well,* p. 21.

8 The non-dramatic works attacking the cult are examined by Sensabaugh in *The Tragic Muse of John Ford,* pp. 140–51; see also Sensabaugh, "Platonic Love and the Puritan Rebellion," *SP,* XXXVII (1940), 457–81.

9 Harbage, *Cavalier Drama,* p. 36.

10 Harbage, *Cavalier Drama,* p. 162. On the Cavalier plays Harbage concludes: "The term decadence usually carries with it a sense of moral obliquity, and from such a charge Cavalier plays can be triumphantly acquitted. They are astonishingly innocent productions. . . . The Cavalier hero never has a wayward impulse; torrents of precept rain upon him if he so much as wavers into jealousy or fickleness. These plays were one of the most wholesome interests at the court of King Charles . . ." (*Cavalier Drama,* p. 45).

11 Dates given in parentheses are the dates of first production suggested by Bentley in *The Jacobean and Caroline Stage.*

12 Lodowick Carlell, *The Passionate Lovers* (London, 1655), sig. C1ᵛ; I, ii.

13 Carlell, *The Deserving Favourite* (London, 1629), sig. E2; II, iv.

14 *Ibid.*

15 Thomas Marc Parrott and Robert Hamilton Ball, *A Short View of Elizabethan Drama* (New York, 1958), p. 254. For a similar judgment, see Henry W. Wells, *Elizabethan and Jacobean Playwrights* (New York, 1939), p. 253. Lawrence Stone, in *The Crisis of the Aristocracy, 1558–1641* (Oxford, 1965), pp. 662–68,

argues that, despite some immorality, the court of Charles was "a far more respectable place" (p. 667) than the extremely corrupt court of James. The relationship of the professional playwrights to the court is discussed in detail in Harbage, *Cavalier Drama,* particularly pp. 149–72. Harbage reveals among other things that it is difficult to draw a sharp line between the court drama and the professional drama since the plays of the Cavalier playwrights were frequently presented at the private theaters while plays of the professionals were often put on at court. My comments on Brome, Massinger, Shirley, and Davenant are based mainly on the following detailed studies: R. J. Kaufmann, *Richard Brome, Caroline Playwright* (New York, 1961); T. A. Dunn, *Philip Massinger, The Man and the Playwright* (Edinburgh, 1957); Robert Stanley Forsythe, *The Relations of Shirley's Plays to the Elizabethan Drama* (New York, 1914); and Alfred Harbage, *Sir William Davenant, Poet Venturer, 1606–1668* (Philadelphia, 1935). Of particular relevance to this study is Kaufmann's excellent analysis of Brome's *The Love-sick Court* as a satiric commentary on the Platonic love cult (*Richard Brome,* pp. 109–30). The nature of the influence of Fletcher on the Caroline drama is still disputed, partly because the intention of Fletcher's own plays is still controversial. The most common view is that Fletcher is more concerned with exciting theater than with making any kind of serious point about the nature of man and society (see Eugene M. Waith, *The Pattern of Tragicomedy in Beaumont and Fletcher* [New Haven, 1952]). Clifford Leech, however, sees the lack of resolution in the Fletcher plays as reflecting a lack of assurance in any values (*The John Fletcher Plays* [London, 1962], pp. 24–47). But even Leech grants that only the manner, not the "mode of vision," was passed on to his "less thoughtful successors" (p. 47). See also Leech's discussion of Fletcher's influence in *John Ford,* pp. 7–9.

16 See Ewing, *Burtonian Melancholy in the Plays of John Ford,* pp. 24–91.

17 For a discussion of the audience at the private theaters, see Harbage, *Cavalier Drama,* pp. 149–55; and Clifford Leech, "The Caroline Audience," *MLR,* XXXVI (1941), 304–19. Leech, in *The John Fletcher Plays,* pp. 8–10, argues plausibly that some merchant class families would be present. The prologue to Davenant's *The Platonic Lovers* includes a discussion of the problems of presenting a play on court fashions before a private-theater audience.

18 See Bentley, *The Jacobean and Caroline Stage,* III, 244, 247–48, 249–50, 252–56, 269–72, and 459–61. There is some evidence of Ford's authorship of four other lost plays, *Beauty in a Trance, An Ill Beginning Has a Good End, The London Merchant,* and *The Royal Combat.* See Bentley, III, 438–39, 444–46, 447–48, and 458.

19 Cases have been made for Ford's at least partial authorship of *The Spanish Gypsy, The Welsh Ambassador, The Fair Maid of the Inn,* and the lost source of the Restoration play, *The Duke of Lerma.* On *The Spanish Gypsy,* see H. Dugdale Sykes, "John Ford the Author of 'The Spanish Gipsy,' " *Sidelights on Elizabethan Drama* (London, 1924), pp. 183–99, and Sargeaunt, *John Ford,* pp. 41–57. Bentley comments: "I have seen no persuasive evidence to contradict the normal assumption that the play was an ordinary collaboration between Middleton and Rowley" (*The Jacobean and Caroline Stage,* IV, 895). On *The Welsh Ambassador,* see Bertram Lloyd, "The Authorship of *The Welsh Embassador,*" *RES,* XXI (1945), 192–201. On *The Fair Maid of the Inn,* see F. L. Lucas, *The Complete Works of John Webster* (London, 1927), IV, 148–52. On various conjectures as to authorship of this play, Bentley comments: "The best of the evidence cited seems to me only faintly suggestive" (*The Jacobean and Caroline Stage,* III, 338). On *The Duke of Lerma,* see Alfred Harbage, "Elizabethan-Restoration Palimpsest," *MLR,* XXXV (1940), 297–304. Bentley thinks that Harbage "has made a good case that Howard's *The Great Favourite, or The Duke of Lerma* is a Jacobean or Caroline play slightly revised. His further contention that the old play which Howard revised was not written by Henry Shirley but by John Ford is much less convincing" (*The Jacobean and Caroline Stage,* V, 1064). Oliver is also skeptical: see *The Problem of John Ford,* pp. 131–39.

20 See among others: Davril, *Le Drame de John Ford,* pp. 115–20; Leech, *John Ford and the Drama of his Time,* pp. 27–28; Oliver, *The Problem of John Ford,* pp. 23–25. Although Oliver agrees with the usual view that Ford wrote much of the Frank-Winnifred plot, he thinks that the extent of Ford's part "has been exaggerated" (p. 23).

21 See Bentley, *The Jacobean and Caroline Stage,* III, 460–61.

22 *The Sun's Darling, The Dramatic Works of Thomas Dekker,* III, 21. Subsequent references will be found in the text.

23 For discussion of the moral aim of Renaissance drama in theory, see Madeleine Doran, *Endeavors of Art: A Study of Form in Elizabethan Drama* (Madison, 1954), pp. 85–93; Dickey, *Not Wisely But Too Well,* pp. 11–18; Campbell, *Shakespeare's Tragic Heroes,* pp. 25–38.

24 See Campbell, *Shakespeare's Tragic Heroes,* pp. 25–27. Among those who argued for the moral purpose of dramatic literature is Thomas Heywood: "If we present a Tragedy, we include the fatall and abortive ends of such as commit notorious murders, which is aggravated and acted with all the Art that may be, to terrifie men from the like abhorred practises" (*An Apology for Actors* [London, 1612], sig. F3ᵛ).

25 The charge of moral decadence is most often found in older studies such as Felix E. Schelling's *Elizabethan Drama, 1558–1642*

(New York, 1908; reprinted 1959); see particularly Vol. II, pp. 333–35. But the same tendency can be found in the recent study by T. B. Tomlinson, *A Study of Elizabethan and Jacobean Tragedy* (Cambridge, 1964); see particularly the discussion of Ford, pp. 265–76.

26 Ribner in his *Jacobean Tragedy* utilizes this latter approach.

27 *The Moral Vision of Jacobean Tragedy,* p. 9.

28 Fourth ed. revised, p. 18.

29 Ellis-Fermor, *The Jacobean Drama* (4th ed. revised), p. 19.

30 *Jacobean Tragedy,* p. 21.

31 See Ornstein, *The Moral Vision of Jacobean Tragedy,* pp. 3–46, particularly pp. 23–24.

32 *Elizabethan and Jacobean* (Oxford, 1945), p. 18.

33 Possible exceptions to this generalization are some of Middleton's comedies and some Fletcher plays.

34 "The Shackling of Accidents: A Study of Elizabethan Tragedy," *PQ,* XIX (1940), 1–19.

35 Craig, "The Shackling of Accidents," p. 12.

36 Studies which have helped restore a balance include: Ennis Rees, *The Tragedies of George Chapman: Renaissance Ethics in Action* (Cambridge, Mass., 1954); Douglas Cole, *Suffering and Evil in the Plays of Christopher Marlowe* (Princeton, 1962); and Peter B. Murray, *A Study of Cyril Tourneur* (Philadelphia, 1964).

37 See Doran, *Endeavors of Art,* particularly pp. 353–62.

38 In this insistence on interpretation, I attempt to follow the example of H. D. F. Kitto in his excellent book, *Form and Meaning in Drama* (London, 1956). See especially his introductory comments on pp. v–vii. On the distinction between criticism and interpretation, see also G. Wilson Knight, "On the Principles of Shakespeare Interpretation," *The Wheel of Fire* (London, 1956), pp. 1–16.

CHAPTER IV

1 I agree with G. E. Bentley that Ford's Blackfriars plays, *The Lover's Melancholy* and *The Broken Heart,* were probably produced earlier than the Phoenix plays (*The Jacobean and Caroline Stage,* III, 439). Publication dates might suggest that *Perkin Warbeck* (1634), *The Fancies, Chaste and Noble* (1638), and *The Lady's Trial* (1639) were produced after the three tragedies, all published in 1633, but no certain chronology can be established. Since *The Broken Heart* is more complex in theme and characterization, I have thought it best to defer discussion of it until after I have considered the other two tragedies even though it may have been produced earlier.

2 *The Queen, or The Excellency of Her Sex* was published anonymously by Alexander Goughe in 1653. Since W. Bang first suggested that Ford was the author of the play, scholars have ac-

cepted it as a part of the Ford canon (see Bang's Introduction to his edition of *The Queene, or The Excellency of Her Sex,* pp. vii–ix). As G. E. Bentley summarizes: "All subsequent Ford students of any standing have agreed with Bang's attribution, though none has been able to find any external evidence of authorship. Ford's interests, methods, and style are so clear in the play, however, that it may be accepted as his until evidence of its composition by a very clever imitator is forthcoming" (*The Jacobean and Caroline Stage,* III, 457). References in this chapter are to Bang's facsimile edition of *The Queen.*

3 See Ewing, *Burtonian Melancholy in the Plays of John Ford,* pp. 24–91; and Sensabaugh, *The Tragic Muse of John Ford,* pp. 13–93; see also Robert Rentoul Reed, Jr., *Bedlam on the Jacobean Stage* (Cambridge, Mass., 1952), pp. 130–60.

4 *Sanity in Bedlam: A Study of Robert Burton's Anatomy of Melancholy* (East Lansing, Mich., 1959), p. 79.

5 Babb, *Sanity in Bedlam,* p. 77.

6 Harrison's study of Platonism in Renaissance poetry comes to a similar conclusion: "Platonic love, then, meant either a love devoid of all sensual desire, an innocent or hopeless passion, or it was a form of gallantry used to cloak immorality" (John Smith Harrison, *Platonism in English Poetry of the Sixteenth and Seventeenth Centuries* [New York, 1915], pp. 160–61).

7 Ford also used Athens as a symbol of wisdom in *The Broken Heart* (*BH,* B1–B2; I, i and I3–I3^v; V, i).

8 T. S. Eliot comments on Ford's "prurient flirting with impropriety" (*Selected Essays,* p. 196). Miss Sargeaunt thinks that the main plot is "silly and rather indecent" (*John Ford,* p. 76). Miss Bradbrook writes that Ford's "licentiousness has an air of frigid calculation that is worse even than the skilful lubricities of Fletcher" (*Themes and Conventions of Elizabethan Tragedy,* p. 259). H. J. Oliver notes that the play "seems more than any other of Ford's plays to have been written down to popular taste" (*The Problem of John Ford,* p. 109).

9 For a good discussion of Romanello's disease, see Ewing, *Burtonian Melancholy in the Plays of John Ford,* pp. 50–54.

10 See Oliver, *The Problem of John Ford,* p. 121.

11 For a discussion of the belief that man must have sovereignty over woman, see Dickey, *Not Wisely But Too Well,* pp. 38–40; and Camden, *The Elizabethan Woman,* pp. 112–13, 121–23.

12 Burton comments that "The husband rules her [the wife] as head, but she again commands his heart, he is her servant, she his only joy and content" (*AM,* III, 58; 3, 2, 1, 2). Ford does not seriously consider the question of whether a woman ought to rule, but he implies that the Queen's decision to allow Alphonso to rule is wise because men are more suitable rulers. In *Love's Sacrifice,* Roseilli quickly assumes the power even though his right comes only through his marriage to Fiormonda. In *The Broken Heart,*

Calantha questions woman's ability to rule and asks for advice in choosing a husband who can rule for her.

CHAPTER V

1 This view is summarized by Leech, *John Ford and the Drama of his Time*, p. 61. For similar views, see Babb, *The Elizabethan Malady*, pp. 152–53; Ornstein, *The Moral Vision of Jacobean Tragedy*, pp. 202–13; Ribner, *Jacobean Tragedy*, pp. 163–74; Kaufmann, "Ford's Tragic Perspective," pp. 532–37. Christian interpretations have been presented by H. H. Adams, who tries to link *'Tis Pity* to the moral tradition of domestic tragedy (*English Domestic Or, Homiletic Tragedy, 1575 to 1642* [New York, 1943], pp. 177–83), and by Cyrus Hoy in an important article which treats *'Tis Pity* and *Dr. Faustus* as Christian tragedies ("'Ignorance in Knowledge': Marlowe's Faustus and Ford's Giovanni," *MP*, LVII [1960], 145–54). Hoy does not discuss the subplots and our interpretations of the main plot differ considerably, but my discussion of Giovanni parallels his in many ways. Alan Brissenden in a recent article ("Impediments to Love: A Theme in John Ford," *Renaissance Drama*, VII [1964], 95–102) discusses Giovanni's moral degradation. See also N. W. Bawcutt's sensible introduction to *'Tis Pity She's a Whore* in the Regents Renaissance Drama Series (Lincoln, Neb., 1966), pp. xi–xxii.

2 Ornstein, *The Moral Vision of Jacobean Tragedy*, pp. 203–7.

3 The charges against the friar mentioned in this paragraph are summarized by Ornstein in *The Moral Vision of Jacobean Tragedy*, pp. 207–9.

4 For a discussion of the importance of this distinction in Renaissance England, see Campbell, *Shakespeare's Tragic Heroes*, pp. 99–101. Similar advice from a voice of morality is found in *The Atheist's Tragedy*. The chaste Castabella tells D'Amville:

> If it be your lust; O quench it
> On their prostituted flesh, whose trade
> Of sinne can please desire with more delight,
> And less offense. (*The Works of Cyril Tourneur*, ed. Allardyce Nicoll [New York, 1963], p. 233; IV, iii)

5 For a discussion of the importance of disciplined meditation in the period, see Louis L. Martz, *The Poetry of Meditation* (New Haven and London, 1962).

6 Another objection to fatalistic interpretations is that the predominantly non-Puritan Caroline audience would have been immediately suspicious of any questioning of man's free will. Anglican theology of the period emphasized the importance of belief in man's free will and was severely critical of Calvinistic determinism. See the section on predestination in *Anglicanism: The*

*Thought and Practice of the Church of England, Illustrated from
the Religious Literature of the Seventeenth Century,* ed. P. E.
More and F. L. Cross (Milwaukee, 1935), pp. 307–16. Giovanni's fatalism is not of the Calvinistic kind, but any determinism
would have been suspect.

7 In *Christ's Bloody Sweat,* Ford takes the moral view:

> Love is no god, as some of wicked times
> (Led with the dreaming dotage of their folly)
> Have set him foorth in their lascivious rimes,
> Bewitch'd with errors, and conceits unholy:
> It is a raging blood[,] affection's blind,
> Which boiles both in the body and the mind.
>   (*CBS*, sig. F3)

8 Sensabaugh, *The Tragic Muse of John Ford,* pp. 109–26.
9 See, for example, Ornstein, *The Moral Vision of Jacobean Tragedy,* p. 209; and Ribner, *Jacobean Tragedy,* p. 168.
10 Ornstein, *The Moral Vision of Jacobean Tragedy,* p. 208.
11 The passage from *Christ's Bloody Sweat* is as follows:

> Here shall the *wantons* for a downy bed,
> Be rackt on pallets of stil-burning steele:
> Here shall the *glutton,* that hath dayly fed,
> On choice of daintie diet, hourely feele
>   Worse meat then toads, & beyond time be drencht
>   In flames of fire, that never shal be quencht.
>
> Each moment shall the *killer,* be tormented
> With stabbes, that shall not so procure his death:
> The *drunkard* that would never be contented
> With drinking up whole flagons at a breath,
>   Shal be deni'd (as he with thirst is stung)
>   A drop of water for to coole his tongue.
>
> The *mony-hoording Miser* in his throat
> Shall swallow molten lead: the *spruce perfum'd*
> Shall smell most loathsome brimstome: he who wrote
> *Soule-killing* rimes, shall living be consum'd
>   By such a gnawing worme, that never dies,
>   And heare in stead of musicke hellish cries. (*CBS,*
>   sigs. E1ᵛ–E2; Cf. *TP,* sig. F3ᵛ; III, vi)

12 "What death more sweet than to die for love?"
13 "To die in grace is to die without sorrow."
14 Bowers, *Elizabethan Revenge Tragedy,* p. 186.
15 Annabella's words to the friar imply that the letter has a repentant tone: "bid him read it and repent" (sig. I1; V, i).
16 Donald K. Anderson, Jr., in "The Heart and the Banquet:
Imagery in Ford's *'Tis Pity* and *The Broken Heart,*" *SEL,* II
(1962), 209–17, notes the many references to hearts and to

feasting in the play. Ford makes the heart represent the source of deep feeling and often describes love in imagery of food and feasting. The two strains are linked in this banquet scene when Giovanni refers to Annabella's heart as his food:

> You came to feast *My Lords* with dainty fare,
> I came to feast too, but I dig'd for food
> In a much richer Myne then Gold or Stone. (sig. K2; V, vi)

It should be apparent that none of Giovanni's feasting on Annabella has provided proper sustenance.

In addition to this imagery of hearts and feasting, Ford makes his customary frequent use of images of blood, tears, flames, and disease. Such language relates in fairly obvious ways to Ford's preoccupation with guilt, suffering, and spiritual corruption.

17 Ford uses the same symbolic device in *The Broken Heart* when he has Tecnicus leave Sparta just before the final act after a warning of impending tragedy.

Chapter VI

1 S. P. Sherman, Introduction to *'Tis Pity She's a Whore and The Broken Heart*, p. xxxiii.

2 See Oliver, *The Problem of John Ford*, pp. 76–85; Ornstein, *The Moral Vision of Jacobean Tragedy*, pp. 216–21; Sargeaunt, *John Ford*, pp. 134–39; Ribner, *Jacobean Tragedy*, pp. 162–63.

3 An interpretation of the play in Platonic terms has been made by Peter Ure ("Cult and Initiates in Ford's *Love's Sacrifice*," *MLQ*, XI [1950], 298–306). Ure rejects Sensabaugh's view that the play is sympathetic to a libertine Platonic philosophy and argues instead that it has a moral structure with Fernando depicted as a virtuous Platonist and Bianca as an imperfect initiate in the love cult. My study of the play's Platonism and of Bianca's deterioration parallels Ure's in some respects, but our readings of Fernando differ widely.

4 For a discussion of Fortune, see Campbell, *Shakespeare's Tragic Heroes*, pp. 5–15; Ewing (*Burtonian Melancholy in the Plays of John Ford*, pp. 65–70) notes that the Duke is a victim of jealous melancholy and gives four reasons: 1) his naturally melancholic temperament; 2) D'Avolos' plot; 3) the Duke's ugliness; 4) his unwise marriage to a woman of different age and lower standing.

5 Bianca's reaction parallels Spinella's reaction to Adurni in *The Lady's Trial* and Penthea's reaction to Orgilus in *The Broken Heart*.

6 See Matt. 5:27–28: "Ye have heard that it was said by them of old time, Thou shalt not commit adultery: But I say unto you, That whosoever looketh on a woman to lust after her hath committed adultery with her already in his heart." Burton is specific in condemning dalliance of the kind that Fernando and

Bianca justify: "To kiss and to be kissed, which amongst other lascivious provocations, is as a burden in a song, and a most forcible battery, as infectious, *Xenophon* thinks, as the poison of a spider; a great allurement, a fire itself, *prooemium aut antecenium,* the prologue of burning lust (as *Apuleius* adds), lust itself" (*AM,* III, 126; 3, 2, 2, 4).

7 Burton's description of heroical lovers is applicable: "all their speeches, amorous glances, actions, lascivious gestures, will bewray them, they cannot contain themselves, but that they will be still kissing" (*AM,* III, 157; 3, 2, 3).

8 Burton includes a long section on despair and explicitly links it to suicide and sin (*AM,* III, 449–67; 3, 4, 2, 2–5).

CHAPTER VII

1 The quotations from Una Ellis-Fermor (*The Jacobean Drama* [4th ed. revised], pp. 229, 235) refer to all of Ford's work but are applied particularly to *The Broken Heart.* The recent studies by Charles O. McDonald ("The Design of John Ford's *The Broken Heart:* A Study in the Development of Caroline Sensibility," *SP,* LIX [1962], 141–61, reprinted with some changes in his *The Rhetoric of Tragedy: Form in Stuart Drama* [Amherst, 1966], pp. 314–33) and Brian Morris (Introduction to John Ford, *The Broken Heart,* The New Mermaids [London, 1965], pp. ix–xxx) discuss Ford's symbolic theatrical techniques. Although high claims have been made for *The Broken Heart,* a tone of uneasy dissatisfaction is present in much of the criticism. Oliver discusses the "air of melodrama" (*The Problem of John Ford,* p. 70) in the play; Leech thinks that "an effort of the historical imagination" (*John Ford and the Drama of his Time,* p. 91) is needed to understand the play's attitudes; and Ribner writes of the play's artificiality and suggests a debt to Beaumont and Fletcher (*Jacobean Tragedy,* p. 156). The studies by Ornstein (*The Moral Vision of Jacobean Tragedy,* pp. 213–16), McDonald, and Morris are more sympathetic and more satisfactory. My analysis of the play parallels each of these three studies in certain respects.

2 There has been some question as to how binding the betrothal of Penthea and Orgilus was. (See particularly Peter Ure, "Marriage and the Domestic Drama in Heywood and Ford," *English Studies,* XXXII [1951], 200–216; and Glenn H. Blayney, "Convention, Plot, and Structure in *The Broken Heart,*" *MP,* LVI [1958], 1–9.) Since the setting is ancient Sparta, Ford does not describe the contract in seventeenth-century terms. Thus it is unclear whether their contract is intended to be taken as *de futuro* and therefore no more or not much more binding than a modern engagement, or *de praesenti* and therefore a legal marriage lacking only the blessing of the church. (The two types of espousals are

described by Carroll Camden in *The Elizabethan Woman,* pp. 86–91.) If we judge by the views expressed in the play, their case falls somewhere between the two types. Penthea and Orgilus have become committed to each other so fully that loving someone else is impossible even though marriage to someone else is not technically immoral or illegal. Ithocles is morally but not legally at fault for forcing the marriage.

3 For travel as a cure, see Burton, *AM*, III, 229; 3, 2, 5, 2. For the association of Athens with wisdom, see Paul Olson's discussion of the contemporary attitude toward Athens in "A Midsummer Night's Dream and The Meaning of Court Marriage," *ELH,* XXIV (1957), 104–7. In *The Lover's Melancholy* Menaphon is sent to Athens as a cure for love-melancholy, and Eroclea praises Athens as a city of wisdom (*LM,* sig. M2; V, i).

4 It would be natural to associate Sparta with martial ambition and excessive interest in worldly honor. For example, Milton in *Areopagitica* states "how museless and unbookish they were, minding nought but the feats of war" (John Milton, *Prose Selections,* ed. Merritt Y. Hughes [New York, 1947], p. 209).

5 The thematic importance of this image is suggested by its similar use by Euphranea to Orgilus (sig. B2ᵛ; I,i), Tecnicus to Orgilus (sig. E2; III, i), and Armostes to Ithocles (sig. G2ᵛ; IV, i).

6 "Convention, Plot, and Structure in *The Broken Heart,*" pp. 1–9.

7 The confused synthesis of fatalism and free will is reminiscent of Giovanni.

8 Burton treats ambition as a disease (*AM,* I, 324–27; 1, 2, 3, 11).

9 Ford uses a variation of the same image in *The Golden Mean,* where he warns that he who seeks the favor of the multitude "doth with the dogge in *Aesope, Amittere carnes, captare umbres;* imbrace clouds, and beget Centaures" (*GM,* sig. E6).

10 Burton includes a long study of jealousy (*AM,* III, 295–357; 3, 3).

11 See Burton, *AM,* III, 467; 3, 4, 2, 5. Penthea's case is a study in excessive melancholy and can be footnoted in *AM,* III, 214–17; 3, 2, 4.

12 Ford's use of "opinion" in this sense is paralleled in many neo-Stoic writings of the time and can be traced to various classical and Christian sources. See Peter Ure, "A Note on 'Opinion' in Daniel, Greville, and Chapman," *MLR,* XLVI (July, 1951), 331–38. See also Caputi, *John Marston, Satirist,* pp. 63–65. These traditional views of Tecnicus are reinforced by statements by Prophilus and Penthea. Prophilus praises the contemplative life of Tecnicus' scholars (sig. C3; I, iii), and at one point states that "He cannot feare / Who builds on noble grounds: sicknesse or paine / Is the deservers exercise" (sig. E2; II, iii). Penthea makes the same point: "let us care / To live so that our reckonings may fall even / When w'are to make account" (sig. E2; II, iii). In the quarto this speech is attributed, probably wrongly, to Bassanes.

13 For a discussion of English attitudes toward revenge, see Bowers, *Elizabethan Revenge Tragedy,* particularly pp. 3–61.
14 Lamb's comment is conveniently quoted in the Mermaid *Ford,* ed. Havelock Ellis, p. vi. The contrast between shallow and profound grief goes back to Seneca and is alluded to in many English plays. F. L. Lucas, in his edition of Webster's *The White Devil* (New York, 1959), p. 161, mentions several references. See also *The Misfortunes of Arthur* (London, 1587), sig. E1ᵛ; IV, ii, 14.
15 See Anderson, *Elizabethan Psychology and Shakespeare's Plays,* p. 13; and Cochnower, "John Ford," p. 143.

CHAPTER VIII

1 For a brief summary of English views of the history play, see Irving Ribner, *The English History Play in the Age of Shakespeare* (Princeton, 1957), pp. 3–32. A sensible summary of the political themes in *Perkin Warbeck* is found in Donald K. Anderson, Jr.'s article, "Kingship in Ford's *Perkin Warbeck,*" *ELH,* XXVII (1960), 177–93. I have assumed Ford's authorship of the entire play. For a contrary view see Alfred Harbage, "The Mystery of Perkin Warbeck," *Studies in The English Renaissance Drama, in Memory of Karl Julius Holzknecht,* ed. J. W. Bennett, O. Cargill, and V. Hall (New York, 1959), pp. 125–41.
2 See J. Le Gay Brereton, "The Sources of *Perkin Warbeck,*" *Anglia,* XXXIV (1911), 194–234; Mildred C. Struble, "The Indebtedness of Ford's 'Perkin Warbeck' to Gainsford," *Anglia,* XLIX (1925–26), 80–91.
3 For a perceptive but highly subjective reading of the relationships of the play's characters in terms of modern psychology, see Winston Weathers, "*Perkin Warbeck:* A Seventeenth-Century Psychological Play," *SEL,* IV (1964), 217–26.
4 Although criticism of the masses is present in *Fame's Memorial* and in various prefaces and prologues, perhaps the most forceful statement is in *The Golden Mean.* Speaking of the common people Ford says, "for as they are wonne in an houre, so are they lost in a minute; & whosoever coveteth popular applause, or depends upon the praises of the vulgar, doth with the dogge in *Aesope, Amittere carnes, captare umbres;* imbrace clouds, and beget Centaures; and doth justly deserve no commendations at all for so seeking to be commended" (*GM,* sig. E6).
5 Lawrence Babb was the first to emphasize Perkin's madness. See "Abnormal Psychology in John Ford's *Perkin Warbeck,*" *MLN,* LI (1936), 234–37.
6 Since the epilogue is not included in the quarto copy reproduced on microcard, I have quoted from the facsimile edition. (See *John Ford's Dramatic Works.* Reprinted from the Original Quartos, ed. Henry De Vocht. Materials for the Study of the Old English Drama. New Series, I [Louvain, 1927].)

CHAPTER IX

1 The charge made by one of Ford's first critics, the poet Richard
Crashaw, that "Thou cheat'st us *Ford,* mak'st one seeme two by
Art. / What is *Loves Sacrifice,* but *the broken Heart?"* (*The
Poems English, Latin and Greek of Richard Crashaw,* ed. L. C.
Martin [Oxford, 1927], p. 181), is somewhat unfair. We may
grant that the vision of life in the two works is the same: there is
the same submission to passion that leads to tragedy, the same
concern with the psychology of frustrated love, the same exposure
of the characters' self-deceptions, the same purgation of corruption
and restoration of order at the end of the play. But such a charge
fails to acknowledge sufficiently the radical difference in tone in
the two plays. Incidentally it is hard to imagine how the religious
poet, Crashaw, would get interested enough to comment on the
Ford that so many modern critics describe; it is of course evident
why he would be interested in the Ford described in this study.
Miss Sargeaunt also notes that *The Broken Heart* is radically
different in tone from *'Tis Pity* and *Love's Sacrifice* (*John Ford,*
pp. 143–48).

2 Oliver, *The Problem of John Ford,* p. 128. For specific discussions of Ford's style, see Sargeaunt, *John Ford,* pp. 155–66, and
Davril, *Le Drame de John Ford,* pp. 425–71; see also the references to stylistic matters in the studies of Ford by Eliot, Miss Ellis-
Fermor, and Leech.

Selected Bibliography

Anderson, Ruth Leila. *Elizabethan Psychology and Shakespeare's Plays.* (University of Iowa, Humanistic Studies, Vol. III, No. 4.) Iowa City, 1927.

Babb, Lawrence. *The Elizabethan Malady: A Study of Melancholia in English Literature from 1580 to 1642.* (Michigan State College, Studies in Language and Literature.) East Lansing, Michigan, 1951.

Bentley, Gerald Eades. *The Jacobean and Caroline Stage.* 5 vols. Oxford, 1941–56.

Bowers, Fredson Thayer. *Elizabethan Revenge Tragedy, 1587–1642.* Princeton, 1940.

Bradbrook, M. C. *Themes and Conventions of Elizabethan Tragedy.* Cambridge, 1935.

Burton, Robert. *The Anatomy of Melancholy,* ed. A. R. Shilleto, with an Introduction by A. H. Bullen. 3 vols. London, 1893.

Camden, Carroll. *The Elizabethan Woman.* Houston, New York, and London, 1952.

Campbell, Lily B. *Shakespeare's Tragic Heroes, Slaves of Passion.* With Appendices on Bradley's Interpretation of Shakespearean Tragedy. New York, 1952.

Caputi, Anthony. *John Marston, Satirist.* Ithaca, 1961.

Christes Bloodie Sweat, or the Sonne Of God in his Agonie. By I. F. London, 1613.

Cochnower, Mary Edith. "John Ford," in *Seventeenth Century Studies* by Members of the Graduate School, University of Cincinnati, ed. Robert Shafer. Princeton, 1933, pp. 121–275.

Davril, Robert. *Le Drame de John Ford.* Paris, 1954.

Dekker, Thomas. *The Dramatic Works of Thomas Dekker,* ed. Fredson Bowers. 4 vols. Cambridge, 1953–61.

Dickey, Franklin M. *Not Wisely But Too Well: Shakespeare's Love Tragedies.* (Huntington Library Publications.) San Marino, 1957.

Eliot, T. S. "John Ford," *Selected Essays.* London, 1951, pp. 193–204.

Ellis-Fermor, Una. *The Jacobean Drama: An Interpretation,* 4th ed. revised. London, 1958; 1st ed. 1936.

Ewing, S. Blaine. *Burtonian Melancholy in the Plays of John Ford.* (Princeton Studies in English, ed. G. H. Gerould, XIX.) Princeton, 1940.

Ford, John. *The Broken Heart.* A Tragedy. Acted By the King's Majesties Servants at the private House in the Black-Friers. Fide Honor. London, 1633.

———. *The Chronicle Historie Of Perkin Warbeck.* A Strange Truth. Acted (some-times) by the Queenes Majesties Servants at the Phoenix in Drurie lane. Fide Honor. London, 1634.

———. *Fames Memoriall, Or The Earle of Devonshire Deceased: With his honourable life, peacefull end, and solemne Funerall.* London, 1606.

———. *The Fancies, Chast and Noble:* Presented By The Queenes Majesties Servants, At the Phoenix in Drury-lane. Fide Honor. London, 1638.

———. *Honor Triumphant. Or The Peeres Challenge, by Armes defensible, at Tilt, Turney, and Barriers.* . . . London, 1606.

———. *John Ford,* ed. Havelock Ellis, with an Introduction and Notes. (The Mermaid Series.) London, [1888].

———. *The Ladies Triall.* Acted By both their Majesties Servants at the private house in Drury Lane. Fide Honor. London, 1639.

———. *A Line of Life. Pointing at the Immortalitie of a Vertuous Name.* London, 1620.

———. *Loves Sacrifice.* A Tragedie Received Generally Well. Acted by the Queenes Majesties Servants at the Phoenix in Drury-lane. London, 1633.

———. *The Lovers Melancholy.* Acted At The Private House In The Blacke Friers, and publikely at the Globe by the Kings Majesties Servants. London, 1629.

———. *'Tis Pitty Shee's a Whore.* Acted by the Queenes Majesties Servants, at The Phoenix in Drury-Lane. London, 1633.

———. *'Tis Pity She's a Whore and The Broken Heart,* ed. S. P. Sherman, with an Introduction. (The Belles-Lettres Series. Section III, The English Drama from its Beginning to the Present Day.) Boston and London, 1915.

The Golden Meane. Enlarged by the first Authour. As it was formerly written to the Earle of Northumberland. Discoursing The Noblenesse of perfect Vertue in extreames. The second Edition. London, 1614.

Kaufmann, R. J. "Ford's Tragic Perspective," *Texas Studies in Literature and Language,* I (1960), 522–37.

Leech, Clifford. *John Ford and the Drama of his Time.* London, 1957.

————. *John Ford.* (Writers and Their Work: No. 170.) London, 1964.

Oliver, H. J. *The Problem of John Ford.* Melbourne, 1955.

Ornstein, Robert. *The Moral Vision of Jacobean Tragedy.* Madison, 1960.

The Queen, or The Excellency of Her Sex. Nach der Quarto 1653 in Neudruck Herausgegeben von W. Bang. (*Materialien zur Kunde des älteren Englischen Dramas,* XIII.) Louvain, 1906.

Ribner, Irving. *Jacobean Tragedy: The Quest for Moral Order.* London, 1962.

Sargeaunt, M. Joan. *John Ford.* Oxford, 1935.

Sensabaugh, G. F. *The Tragic Muse of John Ford.* Stanford University, 1944.

Index

Achilles, 18, 201n

Adam, 11

Ambition: in Ford's early works, 6, 30–32; in *The Broken Heart,* 149–57; in *Perkin Warbeck,* 169, 171–72, 183; mentioned, 190

Anderson, Donald K., Jr., vii

Aristotle, xviii, 15, 16, 21, 61

Arundel, Earl of, 8–9

Augustine, St., 37, 70

Babb, Lawrence, xviii, 69–70

Bacon, Francis, *History of the Reign of King Henry the Seventh,* 168

Ball, Robert, 44

Bang, W., 208–9n

Barnevelt, Sir John van Olden, 34, 151

Bawcutt, N. W., vii

Beaumont and Fletcher, 145. *See also* Fletcher, John

Beauty: in *Honor Triumphant,* 10, 11, 13–16, 17; in *Christ's Bloody Sweat,* 28; in *'Tis Pity,* 98–99, 102, 104, 107, 115; in *Love's Sacrifice,* 123–24, 125, 127, 128, 137; in *The Broken Heart,* 148, 165; mentioned, 37, 38, 71, 191

Beeston, Christopher: dramatic companies of, xiv

Berkeley, Sir William, *The Lost Lady,* 41

Bible, references to the, 11, 27, 212n

Blackfriars theater, the, xiv, 45

Blayney, Glenn H., 148

Blount, Charles (Lord Mountjoy, later Earl of Devonshire), 3–7, 201n

Bowers, Fredson, xix, 114

Bradbrook, M. C., xvi

Briseis, 18

Brome, Richard: *The Love-sick Court,* 206n; mentioned, xiv, 44

Brooke, C. F. Tucker, xv

Buckingham, Duke of, 37

Burelbach, Frederick M., Jr., vii

Burton, Robert, xviii, 45, 68–72, 78, 92, 99, 100, 101, 109, 158, 165, 193, 209n, 212–13n, 213n, 214n

Byron, Charles, Duke of, 34, 151

221

DATE DUE

APR 16			
JUL 1 8 1988			
GAYLORD			PRINTED IN U.S.A.